Susan Visvanathan brings a critical eye and a rich, poetic imagination to bear on crucial issues relating to concepts of freedom in the contemporary making of community and citizenship. Her command over the work of a range of thinkers from Gandhi to Virginia Woolf and the care with which she has uncovered hidden treasures in the archives make this book a stunning contribution to the way we conceive the notions of tradition, community, freedom and fidelity. Reading this book is a very enriching experience and the innovations in thinking continue to provoke and educate long after.

—Veena Das

FBA, Johns Hopkins University

For four decades, I have enjoyed reading Susan Visvanathan's essays covering various topics—from Christianity in India to Gandhi and indigo workers. I am happy to see them put together in her new book, *Wisdom of Community: Essays on History, Social Transformation and Culture.*

—Triloki Nath Pandey

Professor Emeritus, University of California, Santa Cruz, USA

Susan Visvanathan, the author of *Wisdom of Community*, was our Research Excellence Award Fellow at Central European University, Budapest, Hungary, in 2018, and has been—for twenty-four years—a Professor of Sociology at Jawaharlal Nehru University in New Delhi. She is a very important public intellectual representing liberal, leftist and feminist thought, and also a wonderful fiction writer.

—István Perczel

Professor of Religion, Ancient Epigraphy for Aramaic Texts and Mediterranean Studies

Susan Visvanathan's *Wisdom of Community* is a multipronged and simultaneous probe into the workings of sociology in India—implications of history on people and social and political change on the ground. She paints a vast intellectual textual mural, tempered by both detailed ethnography and nuanced reflection; it is informative, thoughtful, empathic as well as being a reservoir of hope and anxiety, urging to be heard.

—Sasanka Perera

Professor of Sociology, South Asian University, New Delhi

Wisdom of Community is a long-awaited book on Mission histories, language use and colonialism.

—Catherine Clementin-Ojha

Professor, École des Hautes en Sciences Sociales Études

Despite the tendency of the sociological imagination towards predictability and determinism, Susan Visvanathan sees life as unpredictable, surprising, even formless.

—Bruce King

Writer, editor, literary critic and the author of *Rewriting India: Eight Writers*

Wisdom of Community

Wisdom of Community

Essays on
History, Social Transformation and
Culture

Susan Visvanathan

BLOOMSBURY
NEW DELHI • LONDON • OXFORD • NEW YORK • SYDNEY

BLOOMSBURY INDIA
Bloomsbury Publishing India Pvt. Ltd
Second Floor, LSC Building No. 4, DDA Complex, Pocket C – 6 & 7,
Vasant Kunj, New Delhi, 110070

BLOOMSBURY, BLOOMSBURY ACADEMIC INDIA and the Diana logo are trademarks of Bloomsbury Publishing Plc

First published in India 2022
This edition published 2022

Bloomsbury Academic
An imprint of Bloomsbury Publishing Plc

ISBN: HB: 978-93-54350-58-0; eBook: 978-93-54350-74-0
ePdf: 978-93-54355-18-9

2 4 6 8 10 9 7 5 3 1

Typeset in Manipal Technologies Limited
Printed and bound in India by Replika Press Pvt. Ltd.

For Shiv … as ever

Contents

Acknowledgements

I would like to thank my colleagues and teachers at Delhi University and Jawaharlal Nehru University (JNU), as this book could not have been made possible without their support and encouragement for research. The compilation of these essays has taken many years, and I am grateful to the Maison des sciences de l'homme, Paris, and especially Gilles Tarabout, for giving me a Visiting Professorship in 2004, so that I could compile my work. I am deeply grateful to Prof. T.K. Oommen and Prof. Yogendra Singh, as well as all my friends at JNU, who supported me in the writing of a book over literally two decades, and the support of the UGC capacity Build Up Fund, which permitted the purchase of books, and generous fieldwork grants. Ratna Raman, S.R. Iyer, Chitra Harshvardhan, Jayati Ghosh, Avijit Sen, Neeladri Bhattacharya, Chitra Joshi, Praveen Jha and Smita Gupta have my thanks for their many kindnesses to me during the early years at JNU as I needed support due to the severity of illness in 2001.

Geetha Ganapathy Dore and Nicholas Porret Blanc were generous hosts to me at Universite Paris 13, in 2011, which allowed me the opportunity to put together the later published essays. I am extremely grateful to Bruce King for the friendship and support that Adele and he gave me during my visits to Paris. Their kindness and hospitality helped me understand the city better. It is not easy to bring the work of a lifetime together, as the first essay, on St Thomas the Apostle, was integrated into my background reading in 1981, before leaving for the field. Prof. Veena Das, Prof. J.P.S. Uberoi and Fr George Gispert-Sauch (SJ) were critics helping me very early on questions of clarity when I was a young woman. To Christoph Wulf and Michael Sontag, I am deeply grateful for the careful way in which they helped me to collage an essay that I had written in fragments over 30 years!

Shiv Visvanathan was companion and friend, father of my three daughters, and also continually purchased books for my personal use, which would be necessary for my research in the forty-five years of our association. Many of these years have been spent apart in the pursuit of learning, in different cities where we carried out our obligations as teachers. I am grateful to our daughters, Meera, Sandhya and Mallika, now all grown-up with intellectual lives of their own, for giving me the freedom to be a writer, making no demands on my time, but so much generosity on their part for my mistakes and caustic humour.

Let me acknowledge the help of Peter Thayil and his friends and family in Ponnappra, Allapuzha district for sharing their lives with me, during the sporadic field visits I made between 1994 and 2006. My mother Mariam Paul, who died at ninety-five years of age, was a catalyst in many ways, and her home in Allapuzha town, a refuge for me for twenty years, from 1981 to 2000, every summer, where I could read and write and collate my notes. My mother-in-law Rajam Viswanathan similarly provided me with the space in which I could visit the libraries in Chennai in the 1980s and 1990s. Much of my mission history work was done from her home with visits to Connemara Library. Although this was 40 years ago, I would say that the incentive to work on the Dialogue of Religions, which has informed my life, came from her own ritual discipline, while being completely syncretistic and having a hospitable attitude to people born in other religious faiths. I am the richer for that long association.

Abraham Varghese, South of Stone Bridge, Allapuzha was an invaluable host in the long years that I continued to visit my hometown as a Delhi-based academic, and I am grateful to Zubin Varghese and his family for their continued involvement in providing me with a safe space from which to work. My father's brother K. Kuruvilla and his wife Asha Kuruvilla have always supported my work and continue to bring new insights over the years to my field data. The memory of my father remains a beacon intellectually even today, as I followed many of his ideas on trusteeship and responsibility.

A book is written by the kindness of so many! To my editors and friends in many places, late Ishwar Modi, Manas Ray, Ashok Sharma, Peter DeSouza, Harsh Sethi, Vimala Ramachandran, Harish Trivedi, Bharat Kumar, Taisha Abraham, Stephanos Stephanides, Edie Saberwal, Tejbir Singh, Geeti Sen, Jon Sayles, Istvan Perczel,

Shankar Baruah, Ajit Pandey, Saagar Tewari, Tashi Lundup, Suresh Kumar, Sarita Bassi, Vineetha Menon, Gitika De, Ravindra Karnena, Renny Thomas, Radhika Singha, Sucheta Mahajan, Anil Nauriya, Jaya Ravindran, Nandini Sundar, K.V. Subrahmonyan, Jyoti Sahi, Fr Denzil Fernandes (SJ), Shabeen Ara, Arun Venkatraman and all his family in Tiruvannamalai and finally to my editor at Bloomsbury Chandra Sekhar—may we continue to share common interests. Thanks to Shreya Chakraborti, Nilanjana Dey, Amit Srivastava and Jaishree Ram Mohan for their kindness and eye for detail. I would also like to thank Rajshri, K.N. Lakshmi Narayan, Colonel Venugopal and Girija Venugopal. My thanks to Sriram Panchu, K.V. Krishnan and Dayan Krishnan. Shobha and Suresh Pillai, by their support for my work, have made my stay in South India always exciting. I am deeply grateful to Ramanasramam for providing me with a safe house, whenever I wanted a place to rest and recover. Much of my library work was done at Nehru Memorial Museum and Library (NMML), New Delhi, and I remain in the debt of the librarians and archivists at National Archives, New Delhi as well. Thanks to Spitting Image Design Workshop, Bengaluru, for help with collating photographs.

These essays have been previously published as:

'The Fishing Struggle in Kerala'. *Seminar*, November 1994.
'The Legends of St Thomas'. *IIC Quarterly*, 1995 and in *Exploring Alteriety in a Globalized World*, edited by Christoph Wulf. Delhi: Routledge, 2015.

'Women and Work—From Housewifization to Androgyny'. Nehru Memorial Museum and Library, Occasional Papers, 1993 and in *Economic and Political Weekly*, xxxi (45, 46), 9–16 November 1996.

'Workers of the Sea'. *Seminar,* January 2000.

'Vast Sargasso Sea'. *Seminar*, March 2003.

'India and Fiction'. *Seminar*, January 2004.

'On Writing Fiction'. In *Desert in Bloom: Contemporary Indian Women's Fiction in English*, edited by Meenakshi Bharat. Delhi: Pencraft, 2004.

'The Past Is Always Alive'. In *Usha Prabha*, edited by Pratima and N.V. Shastri. Nagpur: Jayshree Prakashan, 2004.

'Ringeltaube in the Midst of the Natives: 1813 and the Narratives of Distress'. In *Halle and the Beginning of Protestant Christianity in India, Volume 2 Christian Mission in the Indian Context*, edited by Andreas Gross. Halle: Frankesche Stiftungen, 2006.

'An Empty Sea and a Silver Beach'. *The Hindu*, 13 May 2007.

'Foresters and New Orientations to Survival'. *Indian Journal of Human Development*, 3 (1), January–June 2009; also published in Vineetha Menon, ed. *Environment and Tribes in India*. Bhopal and New Delhi: Concept Publishing House and Indira Gandhi Rashtriya Manav Sanghralaya.

'Forestation and New Educational Practices in Living Together'. Symposium on intercultural dialogue, problem posed by Ramin Jahanbegloo, published in *Seminar*, 6 (10), June 2010.

'Fishers, Farmers and Industrial Workers in India: An Analysis of Narendra Dev's Contributions'. In BHU *Journal of Social Science*, 2009.

'Writing for the Fisher People: Intellectuals and the Intelligentsia', *Think India*, 9 (2): 55–62.

'Romain Rolland and Gandhi', *Think India*, 10 (2), April–June 2007: 35 (translated into French in the *ICCR Journal*, 2007).

'Weavers and the Fashion Industry', *Think India Quarterly*, 11, 2008.

'Shakespeare and Music', *Think India Quarterly*, 2009.

'Summer Hill: The Building of Vice Regal Lodge'. In *Humanities and Social Sciences*, xvii (1, 2) edited by Manas Ray, Shimla:. Indian Institute of Advanced Study.

'Detachment and Faith'. In *Religion and Society: A Tribute to Sister Nivedita*, edited by Samit Kar, Kolkata: Monoshakti, 2017 (also translated into French and published by Dr Shanta Ramakrishna in the *ICCR Journal Recontre aved L'Inde,* 2017).

'Time, Space and Memory: The Politics of Being Home in Virginia Woolf's Orlando', *The JMC Review*, 2017, 56–72.

'Representing Joan of Arc', *India International Centre Quarterly*, 24 (4), Winter 1997: 22–32.

'Gandhi and the Indigo Workers', *Social Action*, October to December 2019, 69 (4): 387–397.

Introduction

The essays in this collection span 30 years, and were earlier published in popular journals, magazines and newspapers and also include some scholarly articles. They are divided into essays on travel, feminism as well as activist, literary and analytical essays. The reader will find in them the insights of three decades spanning the years of teaching and writing while living in Delhi. The link connecting these essays is time and memory as well as the belief that we can learn from the past. The 'circulation of ideas' appears as a dominant theme in all the essays along with emphases on agency and the celebration of the right to choose and the articulation of human will since the themes of democracy and freedom are common to all.

When we think of the past, we presume that tradition is always hierarchical in its forms of organisation and that everywhere the world is represented in terms of varieties of patronage, or power in the unbridled sense of 'haves' and 'have-nots'. It is also presumed that there is a consensus over this, or what is thought in Weberian terms to be the consent to be governed or implicated in what is the truth as a given. One has only to remember the functionalist perspectives of the early 20th century in Britain, or the village studies of the 1960s in India, where the analyses of conflict were represented in terms of the ever-present configuration of a sacrosanct sense of order. Nevertheless, the sociologies of the late 20th century were overwhelmed by the significance of multiple layers of readings and events. There are some well-known strands of social theory we could consider in terms of the rereading of structures and events, such as Mikhail Bakhtin's preoccupation with the life of the people and heteroglossia in *Rabelais and His World* (1980), Roland Barthes' analyses of the conventions of writing and desire in *Image, Music, Text* (1977), Claude Levi Strauss's preoccupation with deep structure and mythemes in *Structural Anthropology* (1977), Paul Ricoeur's *History and Truth* (1977) with its honoured interventions of time as interpretative discourse or Pierre Bourdieu's *Outline of a Theory of Practice* (1977) with its preoccupation with habitus, strategy and the 'white lie' as modes of social reconnaissance. This corpus of work led many of us to work with narratives as the key domain of sociological analyses.

The essays are derived from a corpus of work which I did in the 1990s, and which was published as Occasional Papers by the Nehru Memorial Museum and Library (1993), further elaborated and compounded as Mission History texts by the Indian Institute of Advanced Study, Shimla (Visvanathan [1998] 2007). I was preoccupied with how local communities took on the questions of freedom. What sense did they make of their rights? As a result, the continuing interrogation of colonialism in whatever form it occurred became extremely important to me. I was not persuaded of the passive subjugation of local communities but believed that their identity rested on a basic notion of civilisation, which represented their work as free subjects in an overarching culture of superordination. This book, then, is a result of separate exercises in understanding the history of colonialism, missionary imperatives hundreds of years ago, which highlighted collation of archival materials, the use of archives in understanding urban projects in building a hillside town that would, in time, allow easy access to the historical city of Delhi, and of course Gandhi's contribution to our understanding of slavery and freedom. Each of the essays thus became aspects of the same preoccupation: how can we, as Indians, understand why we have a memory of the things that happened before Independence? Even if they are forgotten, what are the pedagogic reasons for distilling these lost chords of the past of others for our own purposes of surviving present-day crises?

I always had an interest in historical materials which informed our present-day consciousness. So, the essays written in the 1990s and the first decade of the 21st century could be located in contemporary contexts. They continue to provide curious answers to questions such as 'How did we arrive here?' and 'What are the repercussions of being free to ask questions?'

Max Weber presumed that bias was evident in the choice of problems for analyses. This sheds some light on the relationship between biography and the search for a field of study. This obvious aspect of relating the questions we ask and the contexts in which we find ourselves is the existential framework in which these essays must be located. Each essay has a biographical location, and I will try to explain the reason behind writing it.

The analysis of Colonialisms remains a vantage point for understanding the nature of reflection among subject populations, and the production of discourses. The first essay in this collection, 'The Legends of St Thomas', makes the reader aware of the varieties of 'great traditions' (associated with the ecclesiastical Syrian, Portuguese and British traditions) that went into the formation of what we know as the Syrian Christian history in Kerala. New elements are added into the frame, which is a result of the dramatic inflexions that new data bring into the reading of the past. Istvan Perczel, a scholar from the Central European University Hungary, digitalised a collection of medieval documents from both obscure and well-known monasteries of the St Thomas Christians in Kerala. This was a revelation to many scholars, who came to hear about this achievement from a story on him in *The Hindu* (online edition, 14 September 2008). The interesting human-interest aspect was that Prof. Perczel was as an epigraphist interested in Aramaic language usage and the St Thomas Christians in Kerala, and was able to persuade the monks of the various libraries in monasteries all over the state to allow him to have access to the materials. They opened their vaults to him for digitalisation and translation from Aramaic to Malayalam and English. While doing so, Istvan Perczel rewrote some of the strands of the history of the Christians of Kerala, which had said that the Portuguese had destroyed all the documents of the Nestorian Christians (Brown 1956; Visvanathan 1986). From Perczel's educated hunch, it seems that the medieval monks had hidden some of these away in vaults. The first essay in this book, therefore, looks at some of the elements of the pre-Portuguese period, as they appear in popular culture, particularly the life and work of one Kadmattath Cattanar, who is thought to be a sorcerer priest, and around whom a cult is still predominant in the precincts of a 6th-century-church in the village called Kadmattath near Kochi.

Many of the questions of colonialism have been well posed by the St Thomas Christians of Kerala since, over the centuries, they were always clear that they would decide their destiny even though this has resulted in fission and multiple denominations. Many of the problems of foreign domination, by the Portuguese or by the British, were well posed by them in terms of ecclesiastical jurisdiction, which they might or might not accept. In *The Christians of Kerala*, first published in 1993 (Oxford University Press, Madras) and which was a doctoral dissertation submitted to Delhi University in 1987, I sought to show that Indian Christianity was essentially Eastern in disposition, drawing from the ancient Eastern churches of the Middle East with Aramaic as its liturgical language according to a legend from 52 CE. Therefore, the conversations or confrontations with the Western interpretations were not static.

Much of this book is concerned with how ideas influence the framework of actions. The essential assumption is that networks of influence work substantially in the direction of change. The impetus for this comes from shifting away from the concept of 'subalternism' to the idea of agency, where power and authority combine in certain historical moments.

I first wrote this essay in order to communicate to my research supervisor Prof. Veena Das at the Department of Sociology in the Delhi School of Economics what my doctoral interests were. It was an elaboration of the materials culled from books written about the St Thomas Christians. I spent a year in 1981 at the Vidya Jyoti Library, New Delhi, having been introduced to the Jesuit librarian Fr Gispert by my teacher Prof. J.P.S Uberoi before I went to the field to learn about who these Christians were. Gilles Tarabout and Catherine Clement Ojha invited me to spend three months as a Visiting Professor to Maison des sciences de l'homme to compile my collection of previously published essays. I was able to collate the present book as it grew in essays in 2011 in the company of Cultural Studies scholars like Geetha Ganapathy Dore and Nicolas Porret Blanc of Universite Paris 13 as they were actively interested in me as a fiction writer and my analyses of English as a *bhasha* language. I had always been interested in the Annales School as represented in the writings of Marcel Mauss and Marc Bloch. While the essays had been written in India on the invitation of scholars who required contributions to conferences, nevertheless,

Paris was a hospitable space in terms of having people to talk to, who thought my work was very much in their area of expertise and interest. As writers, we are able to bring certain materials to light only when the intellectual climate permits us to do so. Till then, we remain protected in a specialist radius, always respectful of our survival strategies and the circumstances which allow us to hope for academic futures for a new generation.

In Chapter 2, 'Work, Gender and Parallel Politics', my essays on the fisher people of Kerala have been amalgamated and thus may be seen as culturally specific moments of this elaboration where, against the hegemony of the Syrian Christians (implicit in their acceptance of their high-caste status attributed to them by legend), we now witness the struggle of the Latin Christians in Kerala. Often this is posed in terms of the artisanal communities and their struggle for survival. Praxis has always been important to sociologists, for unless ideas are elaborated in terms of the contexts of survival and adaptation, how can we apply the techniques of veracity and cross-checking one another's data? No community can be understood in isolation, in terms of time and space, for the concept of the 'ethnographic present' has come under criticism. Whatever is stated at one time in one text will well be disproved by the passage of time and circumstance, particularly given that globalisation transcends postmodernity, by framing tradition in juxtaposition with technological advancement. Traditional communities represent either through migration, education or technical skills that they are well able to adapt to the time of the present. I started conducting interviews among the fisher people in 1994, using local representatives to help me to construct the story of their struggle. Consequently, I came to understand that studying movements over several years meant that the canvas of materials constantly changed. History was being made by the moment, and activists were able to communicate how significant their own knowledge base was. By the year 2000, however, artisanal fishing was under pressure from the lobby of trawler fishers, and soon after the tsunami affected their livelihood more substantially.

The fisher people have always shown that the contexts of liberation theology or the forces of communalisation may well be maps by which we understand the changes in the social structure over thirty years.

Further, we must accept that the tsunami of 2004 changed the very nature of ecology and environment, with the emptying of the sea of fish, by changes in the sea and the morphology of coasts and seabeds. This last aspect is discussed by me in the context of disaster management. The very substantial contribution of the 'intelligentsia of the people' converges as Paulo Freire describes it. The dialogue set up between scientists and the intelligentsia among the fishers represents the fact that if the poor are educated, they can be valuable bridge builders in the process of development by articulating what it is that they want. The 'listening' to people's voices is what is most significant in this dialogue. Roland Barthes in the *Responsibility of Forms* (1985) makes a distinction between 'hearing' and 'listening', and the consequences of this would be in the true spirit of democracy and the vision of politics as good government. The fisher people entered the domain of seeking legal rights with regard to occupational endeavour, and in that process communicated how important women activists were to the cause.

Chapter 3, 'The Vast Sargasso Sea of Indian English', is an extensive argument for looking at English not merely as a commercial language but to accept it as a way by which we understand its adaptation in India as a link language, as a *bhasha* language giving it a certain legitimation across the different states. The core of the homogenising debates in the politicisation of common-language usage is to think of English as a predatory language, which indeed it is. I attend to this problem essentially by foregrounding the contexts of colonialism and language use, slavery and liberation, by asking who has access to the use-value of any language. I am keenly interested in power, hierarchy and colonialism, thereby raising problems about English education, which is sometimes sharply debated over in the discussions on the continuing impact of colonialism in postmodern India. Interestingly, the Dalits have given themselves an English goddess. The paper was read first in 2003 for the retirement seminar of Prof. T.K. Oommen and subsequently published in *Seminar*. As an ongoing debate about the writing and teaching of English fiction and other types of literary production, the questions about what is acceptable or manageable in the acceptance of texts is central to the essay.

Chapter 4 is a literary essay titled 'Joan of Arc', whose contribution as a warrior is understood in many of the iconic ways she appears in modernity. The paper written in 1994 and published by the *IIC Quarterly* in 2007 attempts to locate the varieties of ways in which fiction, drama, historical materials and court cases provide us with a window into the reading of biography. This essay too is about colonialism and how Joan has the ability to integrate the aristocracy, the peasants and the soldiers into an army, and to take on the role of the heroic virgin liberating France. The details of the story are well known, and by using the contributions of historians such as Georges Duby and artists like Vita Sackville West and the French sculptor Rodin, I look at the images that early medievalism construct in understanding pageantry, war and the inquisitions against those who see their responsibility as leaders very clearly. Betrayal and trust have been key motifs of much of the work that I have done in the last thirty years, and in each of the forays into texts, ethnographic or historical materials (the study of tradition being central to my focus), it seems to me that the perspectives depend on who the protagonist is. The common theme following Hannah Arendt's work *The Human Condition* (1958) is that the enslaved (women, slaves, the colonised, those treated like beasts of burden) emerge as agents and representatives of self-aware populations, regardless of caste, class, gender, race or ethnicity, and they indeed become the inheritors of the earth, which they hold so dear, as Jesus's Sermon on the Mount prophesied.

Chapter 5 tries to understand the catalytic nature of the sole missionary taking on the force of social and organisational institutions in order to convey the power of personal faith to native peoples and is called 'Ringeltaube in the Midst of the Natives: The Politics of Mission, Colonialism and Language'. Here, in an essay which was written for the 500-year celebration of the Halle mission on the invitation of Andreas Gross, I show how the emergence of Protestantism in India with the establishment of the Tranquebar Mission set up an entirely new vocabulary of adaptation, where the questions of survival and adaptation are not read from the converts' point of view, as is common practice (Visvanathan 1998, 2007), but the costs that missionaries paid when the internal hierarchies of their organisation came to the fore.

The assumption here, as in all my work, is that there is much internal differentiation within structures and organisations, and it would be an error to compound reality into convenient generalities. The nuances of difference are integral for our analyses as sociologists, a point well established by those who follow the debates on langue and parole, grammar and speech, or structure and event. In this relation between the grassroots movements, activist organisations and the sociologist as document writer or archivist, the political authority of state and bureaucracy becomes flecked with an entirely different set of assumptions and questions. Between structure and normative behaviour lies my preoccupation with biography. I am, in this book, interested in the question of freedom and rights, where citizenship is guarded not just by those who are conventionally represented as powerless, but by those who offer the idea of freedom as an end. This is intermeshed with the ideas of Marcel Mauss that structures and institutions are peopled by individuals, who have distinct persona and modes of conduct. Mauss' central problematic was to extend the Durkheimian principle to ask what the role is, the mask and the persona (Mauss 1979).

In Chapter 6, 'Summer Hill: The Building of the Viceregal Lodge', I offer insights drawn from materials that are archival in nature, showing how the British planned their summer capital and the many arrangements that were necessary for making it ready for its use. From finding suitable land to the employment of local labour to the configuration of electricity and the debates that went into its final establishment, colonialism was a tapestry of hierarchical social placements and concomitant desires, often including women and lower classes. This novelistic aspect of social relations conjured through letters and biographies is further extended by a short story, propelling the idea that the humanities confer upon a variety of narratives social legitimation, just like mirrors held up to reality. Science and the humanities have always been closely related, as we know from the work of Gaston Bachelard, where poetry and abstraction are metalanguages to the laboratory. Ethnographers, too, realise that when narratives become history, after the passage of decades, there is no way that we can lose sight of the variables that still make them valid. Why do we read 'The Nuer' to explicate ideas about the diffusion of light and segmentary structures? The data for the 1930s collected by a colonial anthropologist is still necessary for the classroom, although Sudan in the 21st century, with its rivalries and decimations, and battles over oil may not bear any resemblance. 'The Building of Summer Palace or the Vice Regal Lodge in Shimla' brings us back to questions of urbanism, where the problem of colonialism and its contemporary motifs, and of how familiar these frameworks of analyses remain, when we look at costs, labour and our own implication in the modern contexts of building up sites of carnival, work or religious effervescence. Are we so different from the overlords of previous years? Each of the viceroys engaged in extensive correspondence with powerful administrators in Britain often received discouraging responses. Bureaucracy, therefore, represents itself with a human face, and the conspicuous consumption of the social elite is in stark contrast to the enslavement of workers and missionaries like C.F. Andrews. Following many visits to the library of the Indian Institute of Advanced Study (Shimla) as I had been part of the Religion and Culture Network as an Honorary Fellow from 1990 to 1995, my interest in Shimla continued to grow. I inserted a fictional fragment into the text, as 'probable histories', as Natalie Zemon Davis called it, are replete with narratives that take on some of the expressive aspects of history writing, however leaving us in doubt whether we will ever actually know what happened in the past. As Zemon Davis so forcefully argues, history and fiction writing conjecture in similar ways.

In Chapter 7, 'Romain Rolland and Gandhi', I follow up the correspondence between Romain Rolland and Madeleine Slade (Mirabehn) to engage with questions about weaving and the freedom movement, where friendships and solidarities are the stuff of dreams. Yet, the court case that put Gandhi in jail culminates in interesting soliloquies about the celebration of rights and duties, about citizenship, and moral questions of authority in colonialism. This essay asks the reader to understand why khadi became an important motif in the freedom movement, and calls contemporary designers to reinvent handloom into new vocabularies for the survival of traditional skills and local communities. This link between theoretical interests, litigation webs, and activist and practical concerns is a kind of narrative map that is very important today. The loss of skills in the pursuit of smart cities impoverishes the countryside, forcing people to leave traditional occupations of farming and weaving. Gandhi in his 1945 messages demanded that there should be an integration of capabilities, so that rural people would be able to survive. More than ever, we need to understand that the coexistence of rural and urban landscapes cannot result in forced labour. The will to live and the right to life and the freedom to choose one's occupation have made many enter traditional occupations such as farming and weaving with newly learnt skills. The sociologist should look at diversity as the key to life. We are concerned as much with the survival of the earth in the sense of ecological rhythms and patterns. While the essay on 'Romain Rolland and Gandhi', as I argue, deals with the substance of a friendship, it is also concerned with several layers of the consequences of this friendship. The paper analyses law court cases pertaining to Gandhi's role in documentation, witnessing and writing as key catalysts in the telling of a story. While the study of movements takes decades in crystallising or analysing, we have to be very clear that reading the past has its creative essence in research. The researcher plays a key role in the questions that he or she asks, and also learns from others who work with the same palette of materials. Curiously, the essay on Romain Rolland and Gandhi prefigures the intellectual assumption that the question of khadi is not just about Madeleine Slade (Mirabehn) appearing on the horizons of the ashram at Sevagram, introduced to Gandhi by Romain Rolland, but that the conversations about texture, fabric and rights of workers would continue right up to the present times, with startling vividness. Designers, and the fashion industry specifically, are concerned with how this debate is taken on by those concerned with linking several segments of the industry around cloth, whether it is handicrafts or mill cloth, and they, as designers, certainly devise new arguments for adaptation. Gandhi, as we know, in 1942, and previously in essays published in *Young India* in the 1920s and 1930s, centrally argued that cotton farmers must also be simultaneously trained as carders, spinners, weavers and sellers of cotton fabrics. The essay began with the preoccupation of trying to understand how intellectuals reading Gandhi coped with the Second World War. Just as the years between the two world wars were immensely interesting for me as a writer of literary fiction, I was concurrently working on concepts of labour and intellectual freedom. Gandhi was a central thinker for me in these terms, but laterally working with European writers for the same period led me to interesting resources. Simultaneously, the Fashion Council, based in Gurgaon, asked me to present a talk to them and I became interested in the practical questions of understanding handlooms and the debate around the use of power looms in textile production for fashion use. A consultancy with the National Institute of Fashion Design, New Delhi, at the same time allowed me to meet students and teachers and work further in this direction. My close association with Uzramma of Dastkar, Hyderabad from 1992 onwards was certainly a catalyst, as I then had access to her lectures, reports and conversations.

Yet, Chapter 8 in this collection of essays, 'Fishers, Farmers and Industrial Workers in India: An Analysis of Narendra Dev's Contributions', shows, modern forms of slavery are disguised as wage labour. Concepts we have long worked with may be transformed by time or reiterated in terms of their constancy despite social change. Peasant movements, during the national movement, specifically prescribe the formation of associations. Narendra Dev brought in interesting socialist dilemmas into the Congress, and this paper chronicles some of his thoughts, as he attempted to galvanise farmers into stating their needs. The essay was written on the invitation of Ajit Kumar Pandey for a keynote address in Banaras Hindu University, and published consequently by him in the BHU *Journal of Social Science* in 2009.

The ability to transform is a political moment, and when we use metaphors to galvanise the present as cultural anthropologists, we often learn from history. Myth, history and legend offer us startling revelations on how politics often depend on traditional vocabularies where the sacred appears as manifestation. Our task is to document and analyse. The secular frame of the Independence movement, encapsulating the differences between Nehru, Ambedkar and Gandhi, so frequently collated and analysed by social scientists has been a useful matrix for 20th- and 21st-century conceptualisations of freedom and rights to livelihood. Battlegrounds between contesting ideologies have been frequent, and the stuff of both identity politics and electoral contestation.

As we saw, loss of livelihood leads to the tragic space of personal nullification, but when the fisher people form guilds or expect state-sponsored support for the survival of their people, then new grammars begin to emerge. If the state defines their helplessness as beyond their purview, then clearly the church or other religious organisations do step in and provide advice and material support and form of education and the possibilities of mobility.

Much of the preoccupations of this collection of essays is not just about varieties of colonialism but also about how the freedom movement set up many of the parameters of how to think about communities and the survival of local peoples and their crafts. Language, hybridity, syncretism and conflict are some of the key questions which inform the debate around freedom and citizenship today. Much of what happens in India today can only be understood in terms of categories that are translatable from one group to another, as recompense for monolingualism, cultural homogeneity and closure.

As I showed in Chapter 3, the essays which organise themselves around the political debates around the validity of English as Use Language look at novels and political contexts in the 1990s. During that decade, the aspect of homogenisation as much as survival of communities in the framework of equality, community and freedom was larger than we could ever imagine. I strongly believe that for sociologists, political domains of homogenisation are tremendously dangerous, whether in terms of religious monolithism or terms of development models. Chapter 8, 'Fishers, Farmers and Industrial Workers in India: An Analysis of Narendra Dev's Contributions', also returns to the question of the freedom movement by focusing on the writing of Narendra Dev, and how all the problems of modern India might be located around the negligence of peasant economies. Food, clothing and shelter remain the preoccupation of those who are concerned with the fate and lifestyle of 80 per cent of India's people. Why the 'push pull' type migration theory and the existence of cheap labour are two sides of the same record is what I am centrally concerned with here, for sociologists have always been concerned with the dramatic poverty and the rich cultures of India.

By interviewing farmers with small landholdings and labourers in the rice fields of small towns with hinterland agriculture, I try to communicate the immediacy of the problem where there is no interlinkage between costs of production and the farmers' ability to receive repayments or the locus of survival chances for agricultural labour. The labour associations and supportive activities of the National Movement provided a clear map of how we think of the farm and industrial labour in terms of a theory of charismatic leadership and action. Defeated sections of people's movements are never entirely forgotten as the role of the archivist is to safeguard these for future generations. The Farmers' Movement spearheaded by the Punjab farmers in the winter of 2020–2021 braving the wrath of the state as it takes on the vicissitudes of the imposition of farm laws has brought the judiciary, journalists, concerned citizens and free people in juxtaposition with the police and political participants, who have submitted to the capitalist hegemony of farm produce.

In Chapter 9, 'Foresters and New Orientations to Survival', I show how the line between peasant and foresters diminishes with the new greening debates and the multicultural and globalised contexts of these in local contexts. By highlighting legal cases which define the autonomy of sacred space and the contestation by fractured small-town communities, I attempt to show how significantly activist organisations have drawn in varieties of actors.

Chapter 10, 'Medieval Music and Shakespeare's Sonnets', extends the language and civilisation debates made familiar to us by Norbert Elias (1978) to the problem of Macaulayism and India in the new questions of digital education, and the interlocking of various questions of time and narrative and the questions we ask with regard to the division of labour and social production. I am concerned with the way in which the question of time and pedagogy is referenced in digital archives and jump centuries to help us in our understanding of relevant materials for classroom teaching. I refer to the debates not just on medievalism as represented in digital debates on technology and the immediacy of the past as it appears to us but return the reader to feminist debates on work, gender, parallel politics and varieties of colonialism. The essay was written for a conference in Sattal, arranged by Shankar Barua in 2009 to call together what he referred to as agents of e-creativity. As internet aficionados, mainly artists and musicians gathered, I needed to contribute to the conference by locating digital archives suitable for the conference, as pedagogic tools were expected by the conference organisers.

Chapter 11, 'Time, Space and Memory: The Politics of Being at Home in Virginia Woolf's *Orlando*', looks at the complexity of narratives that emerge in the telling of fictionalised biography. I am keen to understand Victorianism through a prism and use several biographical cameos to look at how Virginia Woolf constructs a grand and timeless text. I aim to show that the text transcends time and place to show how reincarnational histories are woven into the matrix of the continuity of ideas. The house creates a homology between body and cosmos, and its ordering metaphors are then used by Virginia Woolf to explain both continuity and cultural transitions into new vocabularies.

In Chapter 12, 'Gandhi and the Indigo Workers', I work with certain ethnographical materials which are drawn from historical studies. Jacques Pouchepadass, Shahid Amin and others bring to us the complex story of indigo as a trading pivot for the colonists. Champaran and earlier Chauri Chaura become sites of working-class rebellion. The prized commodity which usurped the rights of local people to growing food became the way by which agitations, struggles for rights and consequently the development of the people's orientation to Gandhi during the 1920s and 1930s are analysed. Following the previous essays on the national movement, I show that Gandhi's preoccupation with freedom and equality are hard won. It involves long years in prison by him and his confederates.

References

Arendt, Hannah. 1958. *The Human Condition*. Chicago: University of Chicago Press.

Bakhtin, Mikhail. 1980. *Rabelais and His World*. Boston: MIT Press.

———. 1985. *The Responsibility of Forms: Critical Essays on Music, Art, and Representation*. New York: Hill and Wang.

Barthes, Roland. 1977. *Image, Music, Text*. London: Fontana.

Bourdieu, Pierre. 1970. *Outline of a Theory of Practice*. Cambridge: Cambridge University Press.

Brown, L.W. 1956. *The Indian Christians of St Thomas*. Cambridge: Cambridge University Press.

Elias, Norbert. 1978. *The Civilising Process: The History of Manners*. Oxford: Basil Blackwell.

———. 1997. *The History of Manners*. New Jersey: Blackwell.

Freire, Paolo. 2014. *Pedagogy of Hope*. London: Bloomsbury.

Levi Strauss, Claude. 1977. *Structural Anthropology*, 1. Hammondsworth: Penguin.

Mauss, Marcel. 1979. *Sociology and Psychology*. London: Routledge and Kegan Paul.

Ricoeur, Paul. 1977. *History and Truth*. Evanston: North Western University Press.

Visvanathan, Susan. 1986. 'Reconstructions of the Past among the Syrian Christians of Kerala', *Contributions to Indian Sociology (n.s.)* 20 (2).

———. 1993. *The Christians of Kerala: History, Belief and Ritual Among the Yakoba*. Madras: Oxford University Press.

———. 1998. *An Ethnography of Mysticism*. Shimla: Indian Institute of Advanced Study.

———. 2007. *Friendship, Interiority and Mysticism*. Delhi: Orient Blackswan.

1

The Legends of St Thomas

Niranam Marthoma Church conveys its interest in familiarizing tourists with the actual sites of the legendary visit of St Thomas to Niranam; August 2019.
© Author.

The river Pamba in August 2018, next to the Niranam Marthoma Church, the sacred place where St Thomas is thought to have converted people to Christianity; August 2019.
© Author.

This essay is concerned with the aspects of magic in Syrian Christian Society as a narrative around the everyday pursuits of the recognition of the unfamiliar. I use data from various sources to understand why the theme of magic appears in the life of the St Thomas Christians of Kerala. They are divided into many segments by the nature of historical schisms but their customs are often marked by the dramatic, as stories are passed down from generation to generation.

The possibility of St Thomas visiting India from the West is affirmed by the strong commercial links that existed whereby gold and pepper changed hands. This trade, which included precious stones, pearls, spices, perfumes and peacocks was mostly in the hands of Egyptians and Syrians (Zaleski 1912: 22). By 47 CE, the West was making use of knowledge about the monsoon winds and a Roman could accomplish in a year the voyage to India and back (Moraes 1964: 37).

About 5 CE, Strabo wrote 'I was with Gallus at the time he was prefect of Egypt and accompanied him as far as Syene and the frontiers of Ethiopia and I found that about one hundred and twenty ships sail from Myos Hormos to India' (Perumalil and Hambye 1972: 22).

Perumalil also writes that Hippalus 'observed the periodic change of the Indian monsoon and boldly set sail at the proper time in A.D. 47'. The pepper trade, as Pliny noted, was the central focus of activity for these ships. Muziris, the other name for Kodungallur in ancient times, was so important to the Romans that 'a temple of Augustus was erected in that city' (ibid.: 32).

The oral traditions of Kerala where Thomas is supposed to have arrived around 52 CE, is a living tradition unlike the apocryphal Acts of Thomas.

The local legends describing St Thomas' visit to Kerala are extremely colourful and evocative, and a few of the sources of this oral tradition include written and unwritten songs and stories.

The most famous of these are the ceremonial songs performed at marriages and on feast days. The Thomas Ramban Pattu is claimed to have been originally composed by the first disciple of the Apostle in Malabar. In the design it stands now, it is possibly a 16th-century reinterpretation by one Thomas Ramban Mallikal, the 48th in a hereditary line of priests. Today they are available as the Mar Thoma Geetham. According to the songs, Thomas came to Kodungaloor in 50 CE, and founded seven churches in Kerala. It gives a very explicit list of the many miracles that Thomas wrought in Malabar.

Another song that describes St Thomas' visit to Kerala is the 'Margam Kalli Pattu', which means 'The Song of the Way'. It describes the introduction of the *Marga* or the Christian way of worship in Kerala. The cross of Thomas (who was known to have been a carpenter, like Jesus), is often represented in the shape of a carpenter's hand-rule, as may be seen even today in the churches of Kerala. The legends say that Thomas went to South India because of the invasion of the 'Northern kingdoms' (where he had gone as a craftsman for King Gudnaphares) by the Kushans. Farquhar has a hypothesis that Habban who brought Thomas to India was a *rajavaidehaka* or royal merchant. 'We suppose, then, that

Habban, King Gudnapher's Trade commissioner, arrives in Alexandria on one of his frequent visits to the West, to sell Indian exports and to buy western goods for sale in India' (Farquhar in Menacherry 1998: 315). He persuades Thomas to come with him to India to Taxila, which is the Athens of India.

> In the Punjab, within a short distance of the upper Indus, they have a famous capital city, named Taxila, where Greek is spoken as well as the tongues of India and Iran. There he may preach to Scythians, Parthians and Greeks as well as to Indians; in the University he may meet learned Hindu, Buddhist and Jain scholars; while in the streets of the city and in the country around, he may talk with the famous ascetic philosophers of India, men of every type and every belief, naked and clothed, theists, aethists and pantheists. (Menacherry 1998: 316)

King Gudnaphar (Vindopharna or Gundopharos) was ruling the Scytho-Parthian empire till some date between 50 and 55 CE (ibid.: 317). Farquhar believes that

> Within a few years of the arrival of Thomas in Taxila, the whole empire of Gudnaphar was overthrown by the Kushans. The destruction was so complete that the very memory of the great dynasty was utterly obliterated. In no ancient history, Indian, Persian or Greek is there the slightest reference to Gudnaphar or the earlier kings of the dynasty. Until the spade brought their coins and inscriptions to light, nothing was known about this mighty line of monarchs, except the mention of Gudnaphar and Gad in the Acts of Judas Thomas and that was believed to be mythical. (ibid.: 318)

It is said by the people that Thomas landed at Kodungaloor in 52 CE. It was an important commercial town and he lived in the Jewish quarter and preached in the Synagogue, according to *Apostolate and Martyrdom of St Thomas* (George 1964). In the Acts it only says that Thomas went to 'another kingdom' but it chronicles his work and death in Mylapore. But V.C. George argues that Cranganore (Kodungallur) was known as a royal city. It was known as Chandrok, which later became Muziris. Most of this (legendary) history is written in the form of 'perhaps' and 'probably'. V.C. George quotes Vincent Smith from *Early History of India*, 1924:

> It must be admitted that a personal visit of the Apostle to Southern India was easily feasible in the conditions of the time, and that there is nothing incredible in the traditional belief that he came by way of Socotra, where an ancient Christian settlement undoubtedly existed. (18)

Thomas is said to have come to Kapaleeswarar where he spent a year, and according to the Ramban Song initiated 1,200 people. He planted a cross near the Kapaleeswarar temple, which according to the legends, angered the Hindus. They pulled out the cross and threw it in the river. It came to rest on the other side of the river. The Christians went in search of St Thomas and found him in Chayal (Nilakal). Thomas found the cross and established it at Niranam on the southern side of the river. He spent two months at Niranam and baptised 200 people (George 1964: 61). The writer provides details of the legend of Thomas as delineated in the Rambhan Pattu where Chavakatt or Chapakatt, the cursed forest is referred to. According to him, orthodox Nambudhiris still think the place to be cursed. George describes the case of a single Brahmin family unwilling to leave their ancestral home. This is the Orumanayoor family—'a village consisting of one Brahmin house'. He also describes ancient ruins in Palayur where 'even after the lapse of nineteen centuries the compound where the shrine had stood is known as Bharadevatha Parambu' or the compound of the family deity. The Christian congregation of Palayur still visits the sea as a survival of an old Brahmin custom of ritual procession to the sea (ibid.: 71). In Kuruvilangad, an ancient village, there is a 4th-century well, which is associated with Mary the Mother of Christ; there is also presented in the church compound, as a narrative in contemporary life-size Diorama, the consecration of Brahmins, as a consequence of their belief in Thomas Sleeha's unusual miracles shown to the priests bathing in the pond. The question of magic and miracle, and the distinction between them is a frequent symbolic space for the St Thomas churches, as they present themselves to devout parishioners. The stories around Kadamattath Kattanar (a magician priest) are equally well known to all and often reproduced in film, play, graphic novels, newspapers, cartoons and TV serial shows.

This essay was begun as a prefatory paper for fieldwork in 1980 and has been expanded for various reasons. I preface the paper with a letter from the eminent historian and linguist, Prof. Istvan Perczel, written to me in the course of our correspondence on the story of Kadamattath Kattanar, a legendary figure I had first encountered through stories, as a child visiting relatives in Kerala, and later as part of my fieldwork.

Istvan Perczel, Professor of History and Ancient Languages at Budapest, wrote to me on 17 July 2008, regarding my query about a text on the ritually decorated coffin at Kadamattam:

> Dear Susan,
>
> Thank you for this! Here is the translation of the Syriac text:
>
> 'The holy bones of Priest Manisha (?) of Kadamattam, which were found here on the first of the month Adar (March), in the year 1990 of Our Lord, were placed here.'
>
> Do I understand Malayalam correctly when I read something like this?
>
> 'In 1990, on the 1st of March, there were found the holy remnants of a Father?'
>
> Now I have several questions:
>
> Do I misunderstand the Malayalam, when I read kandedukkappetta as 'were found'? Then, the name would be missing from Malayalam, simply speaking about 'a Father'.
>
> In the Syriac, I read the name of the buried person as Priest Manisha of Kadamattam, but the Kadamattath Kattanar's name was Paulos.
>
> Do I understand well that in 1990 people found the bones of an unidentified person at the location where this commemorative inscription is placed and that now they think these are the remnants of the Kadamatthath Kattanar?
>
> Now the question is where these bones were found. Was it in the southern wall of the church? Because if it is so, then, we may safely identify the bones with those of Mar Denkha, which, according to the Malayalam Church history, the Kadamatthath Kattanar placed in the southern wall. Mar Aprem would be very happy to learn about this because the burial places of the Nestorian bishops are usually unidentified (Mar Gabriel, who died in 1732, if I am not wrong, is buried in the Cheriyappally in Kottayam, but—as the church belongs to the Orthodox—he is not commemorated at all).

This is really exciting! I am awaiting your answers.[1]
Istvan.

One of the significant aspects of the changes sought by the synod of Diamper of 1599 was the repudiation of the belief in astral signs and witchcraft. However, in the early 1980s, when my data was collected for the purposes of writing my doctoral thesis, the Christians believed in the stories told to them about one Kadamattath Kattanar. His exploits, similar to Mandrake the Magician, were still recounted in the form of stories, cartoon scripts, plays, and then, in the 21st century, as a TV film.

We must remember that Thomas the Apostle himself was associated with rites that veered between magic and miracle. It is said that the first disciple of Thomas the Apostle in Kerala was a young Brahmin boy from the village of Niranam. He was returning home in the early morning, having worshipped at the temple, when he met the Apostle Thomas, who asked him if the gods ever heard his prayers. The boy replied that they were carved out of stone but he worshipped them because his father did so, and his grandfather before him. He is reported to have told Thomas that it was the custom, and if he did not observe the ritual, every morning, his mother would not feed him.

Thomas instructed him in the ways of the Christian faith and the boy returned to him often. When he was baptised by Thomas, his father drove him out of his house. The boy was ordained as a priest and named Thomas, after the Apostle.

According to legend, the majority of the conversions made by the Apostle were of Brahmins. Were there Brahmins in Kerala during the 1st century CE? K.P. Padmanabha Menon says that this is a disputed question, but he is inclined to believe that Brahmin colonisation took place very early, perhaps earlier than the 1st century (24). The debate still goes on vociferously, but the St Thomas Christians are impervious to the idea that conversions among them to Christianity were historically probable from the 9th century, as some historians assert. According to the Thomas Christians, the Raja of Kodungaloor permitted Thomas to

1 Cp. www.hindu.com/mag/2008/09/14/stories/2008091450170500.htm website link for an interview with Istvan Perczel (accessed on 21 October 2013).

preach the gospel and gave him gifts of money. The Apostle is said to have built seven churches—at Kodungaloor, Quilon, Chayal, Niranam, Kokamanglam, Parur and Palayur. The Raja also became a Christian. The legends say that the Brahmins were infuriated at seeing their Raja becoming a Christian. But Thomas performed many miracles and the conversions continued. Here is a version of a legend recorded by Zaleski. This version is still a very popular narrative in terms of its form, since an MPhil student, Ashok Kumar, produced a verbatim account in a classroom discussion in my course on *Historical Method in Sociology* in JNU in 2006, saying that his grandmother had told him this story (in Malayalam of course, when he was a young boy). Zaleski writes:

> Then in July, on the day of the full moon, he went to the Brahmin quarter. He was passing by a pond which was sacred and many Brahmins were bathing. They took water in their hands and threw it into the air. Thomas asked them why they did so and the Brahmin replied 'We are offering it to the Gods.'
>
> Thomas said 'Do not the Gods reject your offering? See the waters fall back into the pond?'
>
> The Brahmins said 'Such is the nature of the water, it was made so, that it falls always down.'
>
> The Apostle then took some water into his hand, and threw it into the air. And the drops remained suspended shining like so many gems, then fell at Thomas' feet in a shower of beautiful flowers whose fragrance filled the whole place. Many of the Brahmins then followed the Apostle who instructed and baptised them. (1912: 132)

This happened according to tradition at Palayur. Those Brahmins who remained attached to their traditional faith left the place, cursing it and swearing that they would never return or eat or drink from that place—it was cursed. Fr. Hambye S.J. writes that a Brahmin family called Kalathu Mana keeps a document, *nagargarandhavaryola*, where it is written, in 'Kali Year 3153 (A.D. 52) the foreigner Thomas Sanyasi came to our village (gramam) and preached there, causing pollution. We, therefore, came away from that village' (Perumalil and Hambye 1972: 370f).

Another legend describes a procession in Parur—a multitude following an elephant with an idol carried ceremoniously on its back and accompanied by drummers and musicians. Several in the procession recognised Thomas as 'the magician who corrupted the people of Palayur' and they crowded around him threateningly. But then the sky darkened, according to the legends, thunder came from the clouds and the people were frightened.

When the time came for St Thomas to leave for Mylapore, where the legends say he died, the people went and could not reconcile themselves to the fact that their Muttapen (old father) was leaving them. His departure is described by these legends in very ceremonial terms. The people followed him as he rode in a cart driven by two white bullocks. They were disconsolate because the apostle had foretold his martyrdom and they knew he would never return to them again (Zaleski 1912: 139f). He would 'return', however, in memory and ritual, in the miracle healings and the liturgies, and sometimes people would even 'see' him (Visvanathan 1993: 72).

One of the central problems the story of Thomas raises is that of the stranger. Nowhere does Thomas the renouncer really stay, nowhere does he belong. The commands he obeys are never temporal, but always purely of the Spirit—'and he who does not take his cross and follow me is not worthy of me' (Matthew 10:38). The Gospel of Luke records 'And he said to them, Take nothing for your journey, no staff, nor bag, nor bread, nor money and do not have two tunics. And whatever house you enter, stay there and from there depart' (9:3).

The stranger, as Simmel argued, is the potential wanderer who is tied down for a time with a particular group in a specifically bounded space. The stranger—and the sanyasi is precisely that—is essentially quasi-social for he can never overcome the demand to move on, he will never be settling. This threshold identity gives him a certain freedom of action, speech and thought. It is his difference from the group that makes him powerful, that creates tension, which allows him to leave for his wandering.

Some of the legends express the ambiguity of Thomas' identity. Hostility, curiosity, respect, awe and love are some of the emotions recorded in the legends. Perhaps these can be understood in terms of the relationship and the distinction between magic and religion, sorcerer and priest.

The appellation 'sorcerer' sounds hostile when looked at from the perspective of a stable association of believers centring around a transcendent god. Was Thomas seen as a magician?

The legends emphasise the use made of discourse and instruction, of teaching the ethic of peace, gentleness and humility, which embodied Christ's life. Thomas was directly in the tradition of Christ, and as with Jesus, miracles were part of the spiritual mission rather than proof of it. According to the legends, the people loved Thomas, they crowded to hear him and followed him wherever he went, for he worked great miracles (Zaleski 1912: 130).

But the legends of Kerala also describe certain acts of Thomas which do not seem merciful or beneficent or expressive of Christian humility.

When a Brahmin gave him a cruel blow, St Thomas predicted, 'Thou will soon lose the hand that has struck me.' A few days later a mad dog (in some versions a tiger) bit off the hand of the Brahmin. When the latter repented the hand healed, showing not even a scar. Not surprisingly, in A.J. Klijn's edition of the legends, the Raja of Mylapore locks up his wife in order to keep her safe from the magical rituals of St Thomas, who was thought to 'bewitch' with oil, wine and water (Klijn 1962: 146).

The legends represent the fact that Thomas' acts are considered by some to be god's authentic works. Therefore the multitudes who follow him believe in his teachings and treat him as a priest. To describe him as magician or priest thus seems to be offered in the legends as value judgements.

Furthermore, Thomas as the renouncer threatens the conceptual order of Hinduism, and it is not surprising that the legends continually emphasise the roles of kings and Brahmins. Both J.P.S. Uberoi and Veena Das have shown this to be central to the issue of Hinduism in its relationship to the formation of sects. Susan Bayly (1989) in her classic work *Saints, Goddesses and Kings* attempts to understand the relationship between Hindu kings and Christian subjects.

Even if we accept the oral traditions and the legends of Thomas' visit to Kerala as a curiosity, there is evidence, according to the St Thomas Christians, of Christian presence here as early as 345 CE. This refers to the coming of immigrant Christians of Middle-Eastern origins. According to the oral tradition, they were led by one Thomas of Cana, who brought with him seventy families from Jerusalem, Baghdad and Nineveh. These immigrant Syrians according to the Kerala Christian legends did not intermarry with the indigenous St Thomas Christians but merely supported them in their religious life. The King gave, it is said, to Thomas of Cana an area of jungle land and built there for him church and houses; also,

> seven kinds of musical instruments and all the honours, and to travel in a palanquin and that at weddings the women should whistle with the finger in the mouth as do the women of kings, and he conferred the privilege of spreading carpets on the ground and to use sandals and to erect a pandal and to ride on elephants. (Brown 1982: 74)

These copper-plate injunctions are now strongly disputed to have existed by many Kerala scholars. Many of these were seen to be high-caste privileges. This link with the immigrant Christians was reinforced by the arrival of Syrian prelates through the centuries and had a variety of ecclesiastical consequences. The Indian Church of St Thomas was drawn by this association into a number of controversies, not of its own making which were to affect its existence and identity. Every schism affecting the Persian church was to have its effect upon the Syrian Christian church in Kerala. As the Church of Persia also claimed to have been founded by Thomas the Apostle, this led to an allegiance between the Indian and Persian churches. By the 9th century, India was under the control of the See of Seleucia Ctesiphon, and the most important prelates who visited Kerala (Quilon) were Mar Sapor and Mar Prodh. Tradition states that the Christians of Kerala were reinforced once again by immigrants from Persia at this time (Podipara 1970). Copper plates record the privileges given by the King (Ayyan of Venat) to the Christians (Brown 1982: 74).

There were other travellers, too, who came to Kerala in search of ancient Christians and spices. Marco Polo, who came probably in 1293 CE to Quilon, was one of them, and he found both Christians and Jews. John of Monte Corvino had been another such traveller. Then there was Jordanus, who in 1328 was consecrated by the Pope as Bishop of Quilon and sent to the Nascarene. (The St Thomas Christians were called Nazranis, followers of Jesus of Nazareth.) In 1328, Odoric of

Undine came to Quilon and Mylapore. John de Marignolli came in 1348. Leslie Brown cites him:

> On Palm Sunday 1348 we arrived at a very noble city of India called Quilon where the whole world's pepper is produced. Now this pepper is grown on a kind of vines which are planted just as in our vineyards ... nor does it grow in forests but in regular gardens, nor are the Saracens the proprietors but the St. Thomas Christians. And these latter are the masters of the public weighing office .... (1982: 83)

Kathleen Morrison, in her paper 'Environmental History, the Spice Trade, and the State in South India', published in *Ecological Nationalisms*, suggests that prior to the cultivation of pepper in gardens it had been wild pepper that was collected by foresters and brought to the seaside towns for purchase and trade (Morrison in Cederlof and Sivaramakrishnan 2005: 46–48).

The 'discovery' of a sea route to India with the coming of Vasco da Gama (Subrahmanyam 1997) to Kerala marks the beginning of the Portuguese period in Syrian Christian history (Panikkar 1959: 30; Visvanathan 1993: 14). From this moment onwards, the identity of the St Thomas Christians would undergo a change. In the meeting of orthodox Christianity with imperialism, commerce and the Latin rites of Portuguese Christianity, its autonomy would be continually threatened (Menacherry 1973). There would be allegations of heresy against it, attempts to ritual unification, then bifurcation and schism. It would encounter the Protestant interpretations of Christianity through the British colonists, and more splits would occur. One of the greatest ironies would be the questioning of the authenticity of the legend of St Thomas in Kerala (Visvanathan 1993).

As long as the Christians in Kerala remained in their local enclaves, participating in a plural culture, which was both ranked and separate, visited by peripatetic Middle-Eastern bishops, they remained autonomous. They were part of the fabulous imagery of what it was to be Oriental. They were sought out because they were 'Other'. This notion of 'otherness' allowed them their unique ceremonies, liturgical language and cultural self-definition. It was an autonomy that came from maintaining separation, difference, reciprocity and dialogue. But when they, as Orthodox Christians, were assimilated into the ritual colonisation of both Catholicism and Protestantism, they began to lose confidence. The last 400 years have been a period of staying alive as a unique cultural expression of India's idea of pluralism and difference. We must not lose it to the new metaphors of homogeneity or alienation.

Legends tell us to listen. In the listening, we discover voices, words, tones, nuances, cadences, timers, patterns and reasons. When we listen to the 'Other' in the dialogical sense that Martin Buber offered, we hear stories that are strange but not alien—because every listener is capable of both empathy and diagnosis, is both subjective and distanced. Every legend thus calls out. This is why Roland Barthes says that hearing is physiological, but listening is psychological—and of course social because it involves the deciphering of signs and symbols (Barthes 1985: 245). Interestingly, Barthes says that 'listening is intimacy, the heart's secret. Sin. This curious linkage is a consequence of his intuitive understanding of the religious attitude. He argues, 'A history and a phenomenology of interiority (which we perhaps lack) should here form a history and a phenomenology of listening for at the very heart of a civilization of sin interiority has developed steadily' (ibid.: 250).

Can we understand what Barthes calls transgression as engendered by god's gaze? Sociology of religion must attempt both of these: understanding the voice of the 'other' and diagnosing the sources of religious anger. This means looking at the fusion of language, space and time in a new way. The work of Istvan Perczel has been extremely important to the writing of history in Kerala, since Perczel, out of love for the subject, set about digitalising the archives of the St Thomas Christians on the hunch that not all the records of the Christians might have been burnt by the Portuguese, who had accused the St Thomas Christians of being heretics. Perczel communicated this intuition to the monasteries by offering to help them archive their ancient documents, and he was allowed access to even those materials which had been hidden away for 400 years. He found the evidence of the 4th-century documents giving noble privileges to the migrant traders called Vadakkambaghar or Southists in the literature in the documents left by the Portuguese (KCHR YouTube lecture July 2020)

Independently of his project, supported by the Central European University, Budapest, one of the most interesting documents that have appeared in print are the notes of one traveller, Dutch in origin, who kept a chronicle of the early 1600s while travelling in Malabar and Ceylon. His work is published as *A Description of the East India Coast of Malabar and Coromandel* (Baldaeus 1996). The work that I quote here at length is extremely interesting with regard to the question of the interpolation of narratives and the manner of dissemination of sacred histories, whether canonical or legendary. Baldaeus writes:

> The Malabars write upon the leaves of the wild palm trees with iron pencils; their letters are very ancient, and distinguished into short or running letters long ones, vowels, consonants, diphthongs, letters used only in the beginning of a work, such as are used only in the middles, and such as are used only in the end, as will more clearly appear out of the annexed cuts. And feeling that the Malabar letters have hitherto not appeared in public print, in Holland or Germany, it will not be amiss to allege the reasons thereof, and to show that this language is no less worth our care nowadays than the Hebrews, Chaldean, Arabian, Persian, Samaritan and other languages.
>
> The main reason why the Malabar language has remained so long unknown to us, is because that country was not conquered by the Dutch country till in the years 1661, 1662, 1663, from the Portuguese; and it is not their custom to send any ministers into those places, where they are not sovereign masters. (ibid.: 663)

Baldaeus then writes that he got a good interpreter who was skilled in both Malabar and Portuguese languages and served him well for eight years. The reason for Baldaeus' interest in learning Malayalam was for purposes of establishing commercial interests through religious intervention. He not only found the Malabar language difficult to learn because of the vast number of letters but the language expressed that 'the Indians are not so unpolished as some Europeans represent them, and that they treat one another (especially persons of quality) with singular civility and respect' (ibid.: 665).

Baldaeus describes the ability of the Portuguese to contribute to language shifts and debates in mission history:

> Thus 1622, a Syriac Dictionary was published at Rome, by John Baptist Ferarius, a Native of Siena; and the Syriac grammar of Georgius Ameira,

> a famous divine and philosopher of the college of the Maronites, born near the Mount Labanus. And 1628, Abrahamus Ecchelensis obliged the World with his Introduction to the Fundamentals to the Christian Faith, in the same Language. Whence it is evident that the Roman clergy exceed ours, in their zeal of propagating the Roman Religion; though on the other hand it must be allowed that their Plenty furnishes them with sufficient opportunities of performing those things which the Reformed ministers for want of means are forced to let alone. I have seen diverse Books printed with the Portuguese characters, in the Malabar language, for the instruction of the Paruas, one whereof I keep by me to this day; though at the same time I must confess that in case we should follow the same method, in printing with our characters, though in their Language, it would not have the same effect, they being much more bigoted both to the Roman Clergy and the Portuguese Language, for that I have met with some of the Paruas who spoke as good Portuguese as they do at Lisbon. For the rest, the Products of Cranganor are the same as in the other parts of Malabar, except that now and then they meet with some Gold Dust, but in no great quantity. (Baldaeus 1996: 631)

The Synod of Udeyemperoor or Diamper took place in 1599 and is popularly associated with the destruction of the Nestorian heresies and archives of the Christians by the Portuguese. But just as Istvan Perczel wishes to argue, the records of the pre-Diamper obliterations did exist, for Baldaeus had seen them. The latter provides a succinct and clear narrative of the history that would become familiar to all specialist readers of this ancient tradition of orthodox Christianity before the coming of the Portuguese and the British as colonial powers invested in converting the Indians. Baldaeus wrote:

> The Christians of St. Thomas teach their children in their very infancy these following heads concerning St. Thomas. St. Thomas was the Man who first abolished idolatry; it was he that baptiz'd them, and taught them the true Faith, and to profess God the Father, the Son and Holy Ghost. They also tell you, that he converted the three kings of the East (one of whom, call'd Perumal, they say was King of Ceylon) and that St. Thomas' body was transferred from Maliapour to Edessa in Mesopotamia. (ibid.: 638)

Baldaeus also states:

> Setting aside all these uncertain relations, the most secure way (founded upon no small probabilities) is that St. Thomas was actually in these parts and converted a great number of people to the Christian faith which contradicts that bold assertion of the Roman Catholics that all nations have received the Christian Faith from Rome it being beyond all question, that at the time of the arrival of the Portuguese in those parts under de Gama, the Inhabitants declar'd themselves to be Christians from most ancient times, desiring the Protection of the King of Portugal against the Pagans, and in token of their Obedience presented him with a Silver Scepter gilt. Nay, the Church of Rome can't boast of that Honour, even of all parts of Europe itself, since the Kings of England and Scotland, Lucius and Donaldus embraced the Christian Faith 124 years after our Saviour's Nativity, without having the least communication with the church of Rome. The Christians of St. Thomas remained many years in the Primitive Purity of the Christian Religion, till in time, for want of good Pastors, they began to be infected with some Pagan Superstitions, and were in most imminent danger of losing the Remnants of the Truths of the Gospel, had not Martome a native of Syria, taken care of the decayed fate of Christianity in these parts, and being seconded in his endeavours by divers other Teachers out of Syria, Babylonia, Chaldaea and Egypt, the Syriac Language was introduced, and the former purity of religion restored among them, till in time the Nestorian heresy got a footing in Syria, and was from thence transplanted hither, as is sufficiently evident from the Records of the Malabars.
>
> This Martome (signifying in their Language as much as Lord Thomas) being respected by the Kings of Cranganor (Kodungaloor) and Coulang, (Kollam) and by the Christians of St. Thomas in general, was declared by them their Head: and the bishops of Cochin, Coulang and Cranganor, being afterwards sent for out of Syria, there introduced the Syriac language, and acknowledged the Patriarch of Alexandria or Babylon for their Metropolitan, till at last, they submitted to the Pope of Rome. For the Supreme Ecclesiastical Head of the Indians (at the persuasion of the Portuguese) did in 1562 acknowledge the Supremacy of the Pope of Rome, provided they might continue in the former free exercise of their religion, which was confirmed in the Synod of Goa, where they would not content to

> the least alteration of any of their Church Ceremonies. But after the Decease of this Bishop, his successor 1599, embraced with the rest of his clergy in another synod the Roman Faith. (Baldaeus 1996: 638)

Baldaeus was writing in 1622, published the work in Dutch in 1672 and English in 1703. His work is available in the reproduction of antique book form in a 1996 Indian edition.

The refusal of the Christians of Kerala to lose all their customs to Rome is the obvious reason for the Koonen Kurishu episode of 1653, and the shifting away from the pomp and ceremony of Rome. This event was marked by tying a rope to the cross in Muttencherry in Kochi; crowds collected to touch the rope to affirm that they rebelled against Roman Catholic customs (Visvanathan 1993). As social anthropologists and historians know, there is also much which is not talked about. Traces, as Marc Bloch would write, is all we have to follow the clues of the past and tradition. The following lines are from my fieldwork log, penned in August 1982.

> 12 August 1982
>
> Although most families when asked of their heritage will hark back to 52 AD, to Thomas the Apostle and the Brahmins, evidently assimilation across caste lines did occur, and there are instances when lower castes were absorbed within the higher-status Christians. But in such cases, their past was remembered, and alliances with better-placed families were not possible unless they suddenly came into a lot of wealth or when one of them acquired education of a very superior kind.
>
> One of the most eligible families known for their unusual prosperity were some generations ago extremely poor. In fact, one of the residents of the Angadi (the street of Christian households) while speaking of their own difficult times said that some generations ago, they would give what excess vegetables they had to this particular family, who would give in return a coconut or some other item from their own yard. Their wealth today is attributed to the marriage of one of their people with a family that was blessed by Parimalla Tirumeni. As the Tirumeni was travelling by boat one night, he asked the boatman to row the boat to shore as he wished to visit the family that lived there. It was midnight and the boatman said hesitantly, 'Tirumeni, let us return in the morning, they must

be sleeping now.' But Parimalla Tirumeni was insistent and when they went to the house and waited outside they heard the family at prayer—at the *padrathri namaskaram* (midnight worship). Tirumeni blessed the startled family and said that they would be prosperous in the coming generations. A daughter of this family was married into the Puthengadi family because the man she was married to had a BA degree, a rare achievement in those times. With her marriage into the Angadi family, they shot from obscurity to positions of great economic power.

The mysticism of Parimalla Tirumeni and the shakti that even now is associated with his personality is attributed to the love God had for him and for the fasting and abstinence that characterised his life. He sacrificed all pleasures of the flesh and indeed was given to creating periods of Lent of his own, which he followed assiduously living on pepper water for long periods at a time. The miracles attributed to him are many, and easily and often remembered. He is a living saint, and every house carries a framed picture of the ascetic gentle face with its long beard and Semitic nose; in one hand, he carries a hand-cross and in the other, a shepherd's crook.

Kadamattath Kattanar, on the other hand, is a much more ambiguous figure, when compared to St Thomas the Apostle or Parimalla Tirumeni. He is believed to have lived in the 15th century when Malabar was still visited by itinerant bishops from the Middle East. Hidden manuscripts are the subtext of survival of customs thought to be unacceptable to those in power, and we will find this evident in the following material.

Kadamattath Kattanar is remembered by old women who tell small children about him as entertaining stories. He is the trickster figure, one who fooled the devil, and the stories about him are amusing, a little foolish, but often remembered. He fooled, for instance, one of the most famous robbers of his time, Kayamkollam Kochunny, a type of Robin Hood figure. As the robber baron was sailing on the river one day, he saw a boat approaching and made for it intending to rob its passengers. In that boat sat Kadamattath Kattanar. His boatman told the Kattanar (priest) that he recognised the thief, and they should try to get away. But the priest insisted that they do not change course, and instead went forward to meet the robber. As their boats came close to each other, Kadamattath Kattanar hypnotised Kayamkollam Kachunny, and said, 'I have no clothes, no money, no food!' and before the robber knew what was happening he found that instead of robbing the passenger of the other boat, he had willingly given him everything that he had in his possession, that he had been swept clean of all that was in his boat except the clothes he stood in.

Another story tells how Kattanar while on his travels met a Namboothiri who had heard of his magical powers. So, he tied up the boat in which the priest was to travel in the higher branches of a tree, and when the priest requested that he bring it down, the Namboothiri refused saying that he wished the priest to exhibit his prowess. After some gentle persuasion, the priest discovered that the Namboothiri had no intention of listening; so, when next, the Brahmin looked toward the tree, he found that the Brahmin ladies of his house had come out of seclusion and were climbing up the tree. He was utterly ashamed and begged that the Kattanar should not cause him and his family this loss of face and dignity and that the ladies should be sent back to the privacy of their house. The Kattanar did so and the boat was restored to him, and the ladies returned to the inner rooms of their house.

A third incident describes how a Tirumeni visited the Kattanar in the wilds of the North of Malabar far away from the comforts of urban civilisation and suddenly said, 'How nice it would be if we could get some grapes.' At this, the Kadamattath Kattanar produced a bunch of grapes, most perfect and luscious from nowhere at all. The Tirumeni asked for an explanation and then said, 'These things are not for us, for we are Christians, and you must never play with these forces again. What you have learnt from the devil you must eschew.' He desired that Kadamattath Kattanar should bring to him all the books that he had got of black magic and that these should be burnt. The Kattanar brought all to be burnt, except two which he hid in the shoes that he was wearing. When Tirumeni asked whether he had brought all before him, the Kattanar said 'All of them are in front of the Tirumeni', which was a true statement concealing however the fact that two of the manuscripts were hidden in his shoes.

Interestingly, witchcraft is seen to be a view of the world acceptable to the Izhavas or Tiyyas in Kerala. Gilles Tarabout's path-breaking essay looks at how witchcraft is part of modern traditions among alcohol merchants, where seva or service to *kutti chatthan* (little demons) is not at all derogatory. Tarabout (2003) is very clear that what is the devil to some is God to another, and, like Veena Das (1977), is critical of the Durkheimian preoccupation with the hierarchy of the sacred and profane, the good sacred and the malevolent. In the case of Kadamattath Kattanar, the story goes, the priest served the devil in order to trick him and learn the craft so that he could utilise it for his own purposes, which were not malefic. In the analyses of the blurring of terms, Gilles Tarabout writes:

> Let us consider the example of Cattan, a god already mentioned and called often also Kutticattan ('small baby' Cattan). He may be worshipped either as a lone figure, or as a pair or yet as hordes of Kutticattans (10, 12, 336, 390, 400, or more still), in which case he is the leader of the horde and represents simultaneously its totality. This child of Siva, brought up by a Parayan woman (or according to some claims, a tribal woman in the mountains), has a dubious reputation throughout Kerala. He may routinely display his power by polluting food with hairs or bits of fingernails, by transforming water into urine, by polluting statues of gods, by provoking spontaneous combustions of clothes or haystacks, and by various other mischievous acts in bad taste. (Tarabout in Vidal et al. 2003: 229)

Tarabout further provides eleven reasons why the occult may be a part of everyday events, requiring consultation with specialists. These are, specifically, the wrath of the gods, the family deity, serpents, one's forbears or ancestors, one's master, Brahmins; the influence of planets in a malevolent fashion; the wrath of unsatisfied deads, *preta* or ghosts; the evil eye; poison administered through mantras; and the act of an enemy through a sorcerer (ibid.: 226). Do Christians continue to share the customs and beliefs of their neighbours? The data from Kadamattam seems to suggest they do. In *Christians of Kerala: History Belief and Ritual among the Yakoba* (1993), I discuss how Ezhavas or toddy tappers, working as household servants, use witchcraft as a means for controlling the excesses of the Syrian Christian landlords who often ill-treated them. Satan is unleashed for the *chathan* appears in a fearsome form; the Ezhavas are paid to 'tie up the devil' through possession and ritual actions. An Ezhava woman recounted the story to me in 1981:

> At night, my father's father and his brothers all gathered in Chakko's house to perform the magic. The pounding of the herbs and the preparation of the medicines began. They saw there was just one villaku (lamp) and the men started singing and beating the drum. Just then there were loud shouts at the gate. Chakko Saar had returned without warning. His wife started shivering and trembling; after all, she had wanted this done behind his back. She had wanted Satan to be tied up before her husband returned. Chakko Saar came in with his big stick and said, 'Eddo aa ra?' (Hey, who is that?), and began to swing the stick around. Everyone left in a hurry except my grandfather's brother who was beginning to leap, having become possessed by the devil; as Chakko Saar descended on him with the stick, my relative said, 'Have you recognised me?' in a very menacing tone. For the first time, Chakko Saar felt fear, for the question kept being repeated. 'Have you understood me, do you know who I am?' He said, 'I will give whatever you ask: but go away.' So the devil said, 'Ask my pardon.' Chakko Saar did so, and after that, the curse was removed, and life returned to normal. Since it had been my grandfather's brother who had been responsible for tying up the devil, we were given a privilege for two generations—our family's needs for rice were met by them. (Visvanathan 1993: 89)

In the following section, I will show how the presence of witchcraft is recorded in the Mannanam document (provided by Istvan Perczel and believed to be written after 1816 and before 1830), where it is written:

> With the order of Mar Hirihānātthios (Ignatius) in Antioch, a man called Thomas, a merchant from abroad, came here and brought here bishops, priests, men, women and children and, with all of them, he came to Kodungalloor and met the mahāraja Cheruman Perumal and bought, by agreement, land for churches and a city. The foreigners and the local people together built there a church and the city named Mahōdēvarupattanam (the City of the Great God). While they were residing there, the foreign bishops gave the ranks of bishops (vispumar) and priests (pathiri) to many persons in Malankara. After that, they also established churches at other places. In these times, when Christianity (the religion of baptism) was flourishing, in the year 825 of Jesus, a merchant called Iōh (that is, Job) brought, from a foreign country, two bishops whose names were Mar ... (here a place is left blank, apparently the scribe or author did not know the name of

the bishop and wanted to supply it later—one would expect here the name Sapor or Shahpur) and Mar Aprōt (Aphraat). They ruled over the Christians (*māmōdisākarar or those baptised*) for some time.

A few years later, two or four persons, who studied in depth the books of the devils, came from abroad to Malankara. Their names were known as Mārābhanmār [Mar Abba's]. One of these, who were called, Mar Dehanā (that is, Mar Denhā), a sorcerer (kšudraka<ra>n), taught sorcery to a priest from the Pozhiyedutthu family (tharavad) in Kadamattam (here: Kat,amuṙṙam). The two of them, by the help of the devils, wrought many miracles. At that time the sorcerer called Mar Dehanā died. His disciple, the Kadamattam priest (Kat,amaṙṙatthukaran pathiri) took the bones of the sorcerer whose name was Mar Dehanā and placed them in the southern wall of the Kadamattam church. He made him a god (deyvamākivaccha), offered him burnt offerings (homam), [Hindu-type] worship (pūja) festive food-offerings (ulla ūtthu,t,ghošamāyit) and he showed many wonders and miracles. By sorcery, he caught the devils and conquered them. On those who stood against them [apparently against the group of the Kadamattam priest] befell many sorts of calamities and dangers.

So while he was doing these great things, this sorcerer taught another priest who was his nephew, to worship this sort of devils and to perform the burnt offerings and the worship (the pūjas). Then, from the time of the death of the senior priest until today there is the tradition that there always must be a priest to worship the name of Mar Dehanā, the sorcerer, and to maintain the aforementioned (customs). While this tradition was in force, it happened that there were no male children in that family. Then, members of the family (tharavad) of the Mar Thoma Metropolitans (metran) were adopted in the Kadamattam Pozhiyedutthu family. So until today the present Mar Thoma Metropolitan or, Mar Thoma V111 (1809–1816), is the one who has to venerate the devils of Mar Dehanā. Also, this man has somehow made others believe many falsehoods and he is a man who, having subdued the devils by sorcery, has wrought many miracles. Since he is such a man, many people, being afraid of opposing him, would keep silent. Those people who are in the Kadamattam family, are the worshippers of the devils and they are keeping a house as the seat for the devils (reference here is to Paulos Pathiri popularly known as kadamattath kathanar). This fact is known to all the Syrians in Malayālam and also

> to those who obey the Puttenchira and the Varapuzha Metropolitans (metran) and to the Nairs who are living near Kadamattam.
>
> Until now nobody from this Kadamattam family (tharavad) has become a bishop. The present Mar Thoma Metropolitan was not given episcopal ordination by other bishops and, therefore, to obey this man is very sorrowful. The bishop who, at present, is residing in the North, in the Chavakkad District (Chavakkatthu shīmayil) (shīma means a foreign country outside the Cochin Kingdom), is a very poor and humble man; still, there is the completeness of episcopal ordination in him. So I request the merciful Queen Sāyū (queen of Kochi) to save us by issuing an order to obey that man. I think that, if we have to obey the present Mar Thoma Metropolitan, it would be better for us to live on begging.

This document is extremely interesting because it shows the venom between parties who sought to separate from one another. For the time period that it represents, feuding was at its most violent.

Clearly, the document shows that church politics pervades the sense of ethics and values invested in marking a difference in belief. My visit to Kadamattath was on the assumption that interviews would help me to better understand the narrative materials I had, which are offered here as a description of the significance of oral traditions among the St Thomas Christians. Together, they corroborate the evidence that magic and sorcery have practical value for those who believe in them. They also suggest that faith is the catalyst when it comes to the Church's interpretation, regarding the transformation to a miracle through the gentle mediation of Mary. The parish priest, as we shall see, believes that Apocrypha is neither endorsed nor legitimated by the church, but nor is it denied.

Kadamattath village lies 30 km from Ernakulam town. The white church is extremely beautiful. It is ancient; the inhabitants of the village say it dates from the 6th century. Of course, there have been modifications, but the church certainly stems from the pre-Portuguese period. It is dedicated to Mary, who according to legend rescued the Kattanar or priest from the devil. The story goes, retold to me by villagers in 2009, that while Paulos Kattanar, sometime in the 14th century, was grazing his cows, the devil took him and they went down the well and entered *padallam* or purgatory. Having learnt the arts of magic, he escaped and with the devil and his allies chasing him, he reached the Church of Mary and managed to gasp 'ammae' (Mother), at which a rooster flew out of his mouth. This rooster is a predominant symbol, even today in this church, both as a creature to be slaughtered in sacrifice as well as in artwork present on the church walls. It is a phallic symbol of sorts, representing ego, sexuality, basic desires, the omen of crowing at the time of Peter's denial of Christ, and so on. Even in the creaking of doors in the church, I imagine that I hear the hollow sound of the cock crowing. The Church of Mary is crowded with miracle seekers. When I visit it (14 March 2009), it is Lent, and only Hindu devotees, who do not know that it is Noimbu or Lent have come to the church, hoping to sacrifice or slaughter the cock.

When 'sacrifice of the cock is acceptable', people bring the cock, which has its head chopped off, into that ancient well, and the rest is offered ritually, to the Kadamattath Kattanar. It is then cooked and presented along with five kinds of savoury foods (fried lentils) and with an offering of *madhyam* (alcohol) to Kadamattath Kattanar and then eaten by those offering the sacrifice. This is the Jacobite Syrian/Orthodox assimilation of the *chattan sewa* or service to the *chattan* described by Gilles Tarabout. The dominant culture of Hinduism is integrated into the larger tradition of Orthodox Christianity where, in this church, Mary is venerated. The Hindu aspect of the temple is the most interesting thing about it since it has the iconic aspects of the 5th century traditions where the symbols of the lamps, walls, tiled roofs seek to integrate it into the dominant culture of the region. For instance,

> Like domestic architecture, church architecture also borrows from the Hindu perception of the natural world. But unlike domestic architecture, it simultaneously draws from the Jewish tradition. The Christian church resembles in its internal structure the Jewish synagogue. However, the construction of the church takes place in the manner prescribed by the Thaccu Shastra (a book of rules in verse on building practice), and the rules followed are those adapted from the building principles for the temples. In the façade of the church, the

> cultural elements of Hinduism, Christianity, and the Syrian tradition are clearly in juxtaposition. (Visvanathan 1993: 9)

I ask the priest (Kattanar Joseph of the Syrian Jacobite denomination) about the distinction between magic and miracle. For him, the encounter between the devil and Kadamattath Kattanar and the consequent saving of his soul by his plea to Mary is a miracle or *albhoodam*. To this priest, the Kadamattath Kattanar is saved from the devil because of his plea to Mary. However, he is very clear that the church does not accept Kadamattath Kattanar's story as part of its orthodox canon. He is seen by the church to be outside of it. However, the young priest who is a parish priest, as well as a well-trained theologian, says that the church understands the transmission of local histories from 'mouth to mouth' and it respects tradition. The phrase he uses 'mouth to mouth' certainly communicates intimacy and familiarity as folk stories do. Legends, myths, the oral histories and records of communities are passed down very carefully, often suggesting 'by heart' or rote renderings which begin to have corresponding structures in narratives, whether written, printed or remembered. 'What then is faith? Can one evaluate or measure or weigh experience?' The priest asks me this when I interview him. People have miracles happen to them, which change their lives. He takes out a notebook from which he reads out several stories. Like many venerating St Mary in Orthodox and Syrian Christian churches, the Christian peasantry is mainly concerned with problems of fertility, bearing of children and their safe passage into the world. The people who come to him for advice are from distant places in Kerala as well as those who have jobs in America or the Gulf countries. 'It's not magic, certainly not,' he says. These are stories of faith, and of prayers answered. He asks me to stay in the village for a few days, and he will introduce me to the daily petitioners. Kadamattath Palli (church) according to him is the Church of Mary, and Kadamattath Kattanar a beneficiary of her great love.

There has been a tendency to schism in the Orthodox and Syrian Jacobite churches, taken together referred to as Yakoba (Visvanathan 1993). Here, too, that schism is historically more than apparent. The two 'parties' (or Katshis, to be translated as segments) after 8 years of a lock-out, quarrels and a court directive, now co-exist. They have a parish of 2,500 families, not counting the visitors. The priests take turns to use the church since a court order enjoined them.

Several steps below is the church which is built where Kadamattath Kattanar's home once stood. Next to it is an old well where the slaughter of roosters takes place. This ancient custom, which enjoins men and women to 'party' with Kadamattath Kattanar is a vestige of social custom for North Kerala, where women also may drink occasionally. The assumption is that it is a cultural practice, not leading to drunkenness or debt. It is part of the unrecorded survival of customs and histories of the Malayalis. The ritual cook who accompanies me to the well says that 'whisky and brandy are consumed' when I ask him what he means by *madhya*. When I say, 'Women, too?' he says, just a drop, a licked finger, that is all, communicating that anything more would seem scandalous to me. Quite often, anthropologists have reported that respondents tell them what they wish to hear. I instinctively laugh about Kadamattath Kattanar escaping from the devil; I can imagine him scurrying up the old well which we are looking into. The ritual cook says, 'It's true, not a laughing matter.' There is anxiety in his eyes, and that too is part of the tradition which suggests that when saints are insulted there is a backlash of bad luck. He continues, 'Anyone who feels they are bewitched can call on the Kadamattath Kattanar, and he will help them. Just say "Kadamattath" and he will help.' The priest I interviewed says that people of all religions come there, and they hope to find relief from agonies. He does not turn anybody away. The priest as counsellor is how I see him. Father Joseph listens to them and gives them advice. He makes me wait while he finishes speaking to two women who have approached him for a private audience. They have come from Verapoly and are Catholics, and yet, they speak with the parish priest of the Patriarch's Party of the Syrian Jacobites. He speaks with hundreds of such people, all of whom are either looking for miracles or have experienced them.

Because of the quarrels, there are four churches in the same vicinity:

1. St Mary's Church, (the original site of the 6th-century church);
2. Kadamattath Kattanar's house (now a church);
3. Patriarch's Party Chapel; and the
4. Orthodox Party Chapel.

The last two were built when the first two were closed. Once opened, by legal decree, each party used St Mary's Church and Kadamattath Kattanar's house alternatively every Sunday, since these formerly were the sacred and contested sites. Now, the chapels are used by those who meditate or pray, the Orthodox chapel having pictures of Parimalla Tirumeni, who is one of their most valued contemporary saints. Kadamattath Kattanar's skeleton was supposed to be found under the boards when St. Mary's Church was being renovated, but the 19th century church tracts digitalised for the monasteries by Istvan Perczel in the 1990s and the translation of the casket engravings (provided in the letter to me cited on the first page of this essay) suggest that it is the skeleton of a powerful sorcerer bishop from the Middle East that is interred. This iron casket (skeleton intact according to the priest) is decorated and lit up like a Christmas tree. It is located on the left-hand side of the altar in St Mary's Church, and to this casket or St Mary's tranquil presence encapsulated in the myth of patronage and protection, the people pray. William Dalrymple writes similarly of another church called Mannarkadu St Mary's Church. 'In the large courtyard of the church—newly rebuilt and enlarged around a medieval core—many of the worshippers had turned out to be Hindu rather than Christian' (Dalrymple 2009: 17–19).

This syncretism has been the virtue of religious faith. While ideologies and -isms constrain and bind in enclosures, faith and belief are more open, more osmotic, more tender in their mutual concern. Faith is personal; while it draws from collectivities and tradition, the real question of their viability depends on the larger structures which serve them, either in protecting or in constraining or in letting them be.

References

Baldaeus, Philip. 1996. *Description of the Great and Most Famous Isle of Ceylon*. Delhi: Reprint Asian Educational Services.

Barthes, Roland. 1985. *The Responsibility of Forms: Critical Essays on Music, Art, and Representation*. New York: Hill and Wang.

Bayly, Susan. 1989. *Saints, Goddesses, and Kings*. Cambridge: Cambridge University Press.

Bloch, Marc. 1954. *The Historian's Craft*. Manchester: Manchester University Press.

Brown, Leslie W. 1982. *The Indian Christians of St. Thomas*. Cambridge: Cambridge University Press.

Dalrymple, William. 2009. 'The Strange Sisters of Mannarkad'. In *Kerala Kerala Quite Contrary*, edited by Shinie Antony, 17–30. Delhi: Rupa & Co.

Das, Veena. 1977. *Structure and Cognition*. Delhi: Oxford University Press.

Farquhar, J.N. 1998. 'The Apostle Thomas in North India'. In Vol. 1 of *The Nazranis*, edited by George Menacherry. Thrissur: South Asia Research Assistance Services (SARAS).

George, V.C. 1964. *Apostolate and Martyrdom of St Thomas*. Ernakulam: St Louis Press.

Klijn, Albert F.J., ed. 1962. *Acts of St. Thomas*. Leiden: Brill.

Menacherry, George, ed. 1973. *The Thomas Christian Encyclopedia*. Madras: BNK Press.

Menon, Padmanabha K.P. 1924. *History of Kerala*, Vol. 1. Ernakulam: Cochin Government Press.

Moraes, G.M. 1964. *A History of Christianity in India*. Bombay: Manaktalas.

Morrison, Kathleen. 2005. 'Environmental History, the Spice Trade, and the State in South India'. In *Ecological Nationalisms: Nature Livelihoods and Identities in South Asia*, edited by Gunnel Cederlof and K. Sivaramakrishnan, 43–64. Ranikhet, Delhi: Permanent Black.

Mundakuzhy, Rev. Thomas P. 1982. *Our Church, Malankara St. Thomas Oriental Orthodox Church of India*. Mavellikara: St. Paul's Mission Press.

Panikkar, Kavalam M. 1959. *Asia and Western Dominance*. Bombay: Asia Publishing House.

Perumalil, Hormice C. and Edward R. Hambye, eds. 1972. *Christianity in India*. Alleppey: Prakasam Publications.

Podipara, Placid J. 1970. *The St. Thomas Christians*. Bombay: Darton, Longman and Todd.

Subrahmanyam, Sanjay. 1977. *The Career and Legend* of *Vasco da Gama*. Delhi: Cambridge University Press.

Vidal, Denis, Gilles Tarabout and Eric Meyer, eds. 2003. *Violence/Non-Violence: Some Hindu Perspectives*. Delhi: Manohar.

Visvanathan, Susan. 1993. *The Christians of Kerala: History, Belief and Ritual Among the Yakoba*. Madras: Oxford University Press.

Zaleski, Ladislas. 1912. *The Apostle St. Thomas in India*. Mangalore: Codiarbel Press.

2

Work, Gender and Parallel Politics

Flowers for household gardens, and the fish restaurant, which represents the coexistence of tourists, diaspora returnees and householders; June 2019. © Author.

The literature on 'housewifization' shows that capitalism and the market initially reduce the woman to passivity, and then as she enters the career and professional world, imposes on her a double burden of work. I shall look at the concept of androgyny in the Jungian sense in order to understand the positive quality of breaking sex-role stereotypes. In the second part, I attempt to understand Sr Philomena-Marie, a trade unionist of the fishing struggle in Kerala. I then compare Sr Philomena-Marie to another androgynous figure, Joan of Arc, and then elaborate on the general contours of artisanal struggles amongst the fishers on the Allapuzha (formerly Alleppey) coast.

Feminist Understanding of Occupation and Work

Carolyn Merchant, Claudia Von Werlhoff, Maria Mies and Ivan Illich have argued very forcefully that capitalism had rendered the woman a captive of the house. The labour of housewives goes unnoticed as shadow work, they are not seen to be part of the economy.

These authors have argued that in capitalism, women were seen as belonging to the domain of nature, and were to be broken, tamed, cultivated and civilised. Women who experiment with healing, agriculture, emotion and war were punished. Science and exploration were male domains; women could not innovate. Notions of the order were defined for them; the subduing of women's nature was the greatest expression of the hierarchy of gender. The housewife is the transformation of the creative energies of women into one systematic type of labourer, one who is concerned primarily with reproduction— that is—the birth of new members for the labour force, and their sustenance and nurture. This labour does not create surplus or capital, it cannot be sold on the labour market. It is, as one feminist has argued, love and responsibility. These are not in capitalist patriarchal ideology things of value, for value only arises from profit in the market. So, the histories of men are visible (Joan of Arc and the Slave Queen dress as men) while women constitute simply sex.

In a plea for return to motherhood and work, feminists like Sylvia Hewlett tried to handle the question of what gender neutrality entailed. While women enter the professional world (or the labour market) on an ostensibly equal footing with men, the domestic space still represented traditional hierarchies and differences. Women bore children, cooked and cleaned, while men controlled property, women and children. Both men and women went out to work, but women's earnings were a 'second' salary. Their official roles were continuing in a gender-defined way, but their commitment to the codes of work had to be neutral. Their real involvement in the powerful roles in society was seen to be negligible. What one required as a concomitant to gender neutrality of social roles at the workspace was gender neutrality in the domestic space. This would involve the socialisation of young children so that work allocation is not gendered. Boys, as well as girls, must be trained to cook, clean, wash, chop, rear children and earn. This was work, not women's or men's, but work that needed to be done in a shared and reciprocal way.

Why were women alienated from the control over production processes, although it was they who sustained the manpower required for the market? Women were seen to be objects of nature to be dominated rather than worthy of egalitarian interaction. They were the bearers of children, they made things grow, they understood the cycles of nature within their own bodies. By excluding women, men externalised that from which they were born, that which had to be a part of them.

Michelle Rosaldo (1974) underlines the fact that in most societies women may have power, but men usually have authority. Authority becomes a veil that separates and distances men so that they can control interactions as they wish. The 'natural' attributes of womanliness (ascribed status) are contrasted to the achieved status of 'becoming a man'. Because women are excluded from the domains of rationality and power by cultural stereotyping, they appear as the other. Women's status, Rosaldo argues, is achieved through their stage in a life cycle, from their biological function, and in particular from their sexual or biological ties to particular men. For Rosaldo (1974), the two extremes of this position can be seen in the witch, who sleeps with the devil, and the nun who is the bride of God.

Carolyn Merchant in *The Death of Nature* (1979) shows how Western science domesticated nature (and women) through the questions and methods of science. The earth was transformed from the image of a nurturing mother into a source and potential for economic interest. The disorderly elements of female nature would be subjugated, and women became passive dependents in both production and reproduction. Even today, the exclusion of women from knowledge about their bodies, their isolation in labour as if pain is demeaning and infectious is representative of scientific objectivity as opposed to empathy and subjectivity as experienced in traditional assistance at childbirth.

Nature and culture in such a perspective were no longer categories in a relationship but were now dual, external, divided and antagonistic. It was a fair description of the relationship between the sexes. Women, being identified with nature, became associated with animality just as were indigenous people in the colonies. Thus women, the enslaved and the animals all belonged to one class. Hannah Arendt (1958) writes that women and slaves were homologous because they were hidden away, belonged to someone or another, and their life was 'laborious' and devoted to bodily function. Arendt argued that the chief function of 'labour is the production of life' and therefore labour is associated with procreation. However, the least durable are those things that are needed for consumption, for life itself. If not used immediately by men, they perish. Therefore, the daily labour of women which contributed to subsistence was not inscribed in memory. Arendt said that work—what men did—was different, for it transformed things from matter into material, nature into culture, and was associated with the hands, skill and knowledge, rather than with the body.

Why then is labour, life-generating as it is, associated with passivity? Carolyn Merchant for the history of the West, and Leela Dube (1986) for India, have shown that women are associated with the earth which bears and nourishes the seed, which is the vital, life-generating active principle. Corporeality, substance and matter thus, in patriarchal societies, derive from the female—therefore also putrefaction and mortality, but on the other hand, quickness, the mind, the soul, celebreality is passed through the male. The passivity of women is continually reconfirmed through men's language. Leela Dube argues that a woman is alienated from her productive resources (like land, she belongs to someone) and has no control over her offspring. Illich (1981, 1982) would call gender neutrality fatal to the women's issue. What was required was complementarity, argument, conversation and understanding; where in Buber's terms the 'I–it' relationship characterising the subject as masculine and dominant, the object as female and passive should be substituted for an I-Thou or I-You relationship whose language is tempered by dialogue (1970). As Anna Kingsford, one of the early feminists maintained that women when kept back from articulating and achieving this were deformed and that in this, the men lost out too, for one sex cannot be handicapped without the other suffering (Maitland 1896).

Virginia Woolf's novels became an interesting exercise in articulating the theme of the suppression of women's work capacities. In *The Voyage Out*

(1982), Rachael's passion and proficiency in music while acknowledged may not be professionally used. Hewet, being the most sensitive and gentle of men believes that Rachael becomes 'less desirable as her brain began to work'. Hewet argues that women see men as horses do, 'They see us three times as big as we are or they'd never obey us.' In the end, Rachael must die—she represented the classic constraint upon individuality and being that masculinist societies imposed upon their women: talented and unprofessional, dying in the small cabin spaces that society provided for them. *A Room of One's Own* (1945) became a symbol of private space and autonomy, where women could find their own sense of being, write a new history of actions and events. I will not go into an analysis of Woolf's work here, except to mention that in *Orlando* (1979) Woolf destroyed this conception of women's being as conventional, peaceful and consensually embedded in patriarchy. She substituted a male-female figure who so light-heartedly, so brilliantly destroyed and ravaged all notions of women's being, transformed roles and rules, work and custom (see Chapter 11).

Woolf's work explored two central ideas about women and consciousness. One was the idea of androgyny. In *A Room of One's Own* (1945), she playfully and poignantly sketched a mythical account of Shakespeare's sister Judith, as talented as her sibling, but fated to die and remain anonymous, for, she was a mere woman. As in this lecture, she also spoke of the only possible way for women's emancipation—it was a plan for the soul. 'In each of us two powers preside, one male, one female, and in the man's brain, the man predominates over the woman.' Where there was harmony between the two forces, spiritual cooperation, a fusion, the greatest creativity is possible. While Woolf herself was housewife-ised and sanatorium-ised, through the character of Septimus Smith in the novel *Mrs Dalloway* (1966), she tried to show that God and nature speak in many voices and some have the gift to hear and understand. Her portrayal of *Orlando* (1979) became a powerful exegesis of the concept of androgyny. How terrible is the envy that Woolf feels for those male citadels into which women had no entry? In *Jacob's Room*, the contempt for women is well recorded. 'No one would think to bring a dog into church, a dog destroys the service completely. So do these women—though separately vouched for by the Theology, Mathematics, Latin and Greek of their husbands' (Woolf 1984: 30). *Night and Day* (1982) chronicles a greater resolution of the conflict between women's roles and work, between marriage and occupation. Work cannot yet be a career, but there is a greater celebration of cerebral endeavour and, to some extent, masculine adaptation to feminist strivings. Katharine Hilberry, in this novel, is a secret mathematician. 'No force on earth would have made her confess that. Her actions when thus engaged were furtive and secretive like those of some nocturnal animal.' It is Jacob of *Jacob's Room* who is the inheritor of history, architecture and learning—also of war and death.

June Singer (1977) in her valuable interpretation of Jung's work *Androgyny* argues that there is a natural biological opposition between men and women which is the basis of creativity. She develops Jung's notion of anima and animus to underline that every man has a feminine side while every woman has a masculine side, which is rendered unconscious by culture. The repression of the anima (in men) and the animus (in women) creates in both the longing for the other, as well as the awe, fear and incomprehensibility associated with the other.

The cultural stereotyping of emotions would then possibly end. Jesus, for instance, as a man, had no dilemmas about articulating a theory of love and care. Interestingly, though, C.F. Andrews who imitated Jesus in many ways was thought to be effeminate by some.

June Singer writes that 'The androgyne approaches the problem with the recognition that true change begins primarily within the psychic structure of the individual …. The androgyne consciously accepts the interplay of the masculine and feminine aspects of the individual psyche' (1977: 21). It allows us identification with others and what Jung called the Self. Singer distinguishes between various terms in order to define what androgyny is (ibid.: 16). Neither hermaphroditism, which is a lack of physical differentiation, nor bisexuality which is a lack of clarity in gender identification, the Jungian concept of androgyny expresses 'a natural unforced and uninhibited (male or female) sexuality'. Yet, neither tends to extremes. Men do not need to exude machismo, or women to pretend a naive and dependent character. 'Excessively polarised personality types' according to her thrive in cultures which demand repression of natural tendencies. Androgynous individuals lift these repressions 'not in order to prepare a way of living out sexual impulses so much as in order to permit what has been repressed to return and to be reintegrated into conscious awareness' (ibid.: 19). Consider Virginia Woolf's classic experience of an androgynous state, which Clarissa Dalloway feels, 'a match burning in a crocus, an inner meaning almost expressed.' It is a revelation that allows her to 'then feel what men felt.'

The androgyne consciously accepts the interplay of the masculine and feminine aspects of the individual psyche (Singer 1977: 21). In a stunning critique, 'Against Androgyny' Jean Bethke Elshtain (1987) demolishes arguments in favour of the concept showing how androgyny in feminist discourse has removed the mythic frames of the term. She believes that the presence of difference within the human frame has always been a cause of vexation (!) but that in the feminist discourse on androgyny, the fused body disappears. I think Jung's basic contribution is to reorganise the body in terms of the conscious and the unconscious which Singer celebrates and Elshtain completely ignores.

Androgyny has a long and complex history of usage which I am not in a position to elaborate on here. Why it becomes useful as a concept is because it so clearly negates gender neutrality. The latter does not allow for biological spaces to appear or to be clarified. Androgyny is more elastic, and that very flexibility also questions basic stereotypes which fix gender attributes in one way or another. Like any term, androgyny can be put to different uses, for different purposes.

I will now look at a specific case in order to understand how androgyny is a useful term for understanding women and creative work. I take the specific case of a woman, a Christian nun called Philomena-Marie who led the fisher people's struggle in Kerala in 1984. I shall also show the ambiguity of the term: at one level Sr Philomena-Marie functions at an androgynous level, at another level she sees her commitment to the struggle in a gender-neutral role as an official in the fishworkers union.

Sr Philomena Marie and the Fishworkers' Union

In Kerala, the fisherfolk's struggle against the capitalistic ravaging of the sea had drawn tremendous strength from Christianity. Some of Jesus' best friends were after all fishermen—Peter, for instance, whom we know as Cephas. Many of its leaders today are drawn from the church, though there are many internal contradictions. The struggle itself is about the opposition between capitalists and their trawlers which ravage the sea, over-fishing the waters, using destructive purse-seine and trawl nets without any regard for spawning seasons or ecological balance. In this sense, the sea is merely a commodity base. The fisher people contest this indiscriminate fishing and have been organising protest after protest without much success.

Sr Philomena-Marie begins to stand out in this struggle by her sheer insistence that she was ready to martyr herself, that she would fight until the cause was won. In this determination, she took on the state, the capitalists, the establishment church. She was jailed in the summer of 1984, and then soon after that, she began her twenty-three-day fast.

The bishops of the state after studying the participation of the radical members of the clergy in a Trade Union Movement resolved that fast to death was not permissible, nor participation in protests culminating in violence. They were to be warned about supporting radical slogans, warned against dangers to their faith.

Sr Philomena-Marie was forced to call off her fast, but she never lost her will to help the fisher people, to lead them in their agitations and to coordinate their work for them. In a speech in 1991, she said:

> When human rights are trampled, no one can stay neutral. Neutrality on such occasions is equal to a crime. From the experience of the struggle, we learn that justice is not given but taken by the concerted effort of the people concerned. The Church by her neutrality is supporting the existing political and economic system. When we struggled with the people ever ready to give up our life, the Bishops could see only disobedience, violence, entering into politics. The boat (trawler) owners go with the blessing of the Bishop. When poor people fight for their rights, they will be characterised as communists and Naxalites. The Church can only understand charity and the distribution of bread. (speech at Hyderabad 1991, cited in Visvanathan 1994)

How does one understand the power of this woman and her active involvement in the fisher people's struggle? I went to Valiyathura, a fishing hamlet close to Trivandrum on 9 June 1994. Sr Philomena-Marie helps to coordinate the work of the Kerala Swatantra Matsyathozhilali Federation (KSMTF) at its headquarters there. Sr Rose, her associate, showed me around the narrow margin of the village, hemmed in by large houses. The sea had eroded the coast very recently, so many of the fisher people were staying in the village school. There was malaria on the rampage, and the children were unable to go to school because these were the three hunger months: torrential rain, no work and no food. I could well believe Sr Philomena-Marie's comment that illiteracy predominates, for when school starts in June, the fisher people are incredibly impoverished. Not surprisingly, I was told that several pockets of Valiyathura were well known for their illicit distilleries and the hiring of wives and daughters as prostitutes.

It was 11 o'clock, a strangely bright hot day in the monsoon. The sea was sky blue and some of the fishermen were looking out at the surf, others were playing cards and some just stared at Sr Rose and me through eyes that were wretched and drunk. This is *Panna massam*—the bad months when the Arabian sea is usually turbulent and storm crossed, and fishing is by traditional discipline almost nil. Sr Rose has been with the Valiyathura community for eleven years and had begun embroidery classes for the girls 'in order to distract them from prostitution'. She uses a house on the beach, austere and old, with a desk near the window, from which you can hear the sea.

It was to this house that Sr Philomena-Marie came and then took me to her own KSMTF office: a bleak room overlooking a disused courtyard where the only thing of any interest was the existence of a scavenger cat looking for food under dry rustling heaps of palm leaves. We sat and talked for three hours. I report some of that conversation. She was born sixty-four years ago, she is small and slight and frail today, with an untidy greying bun, intense ardour for her work, and eyes strangely innocent.

She told me that there were many reasons that had brought her to the path that she is on. Like daughters of many traditional families, she was educated in a convent in Athirampuzha near Kottayam and then decided that she would like to serve God, through involvement with the sick and wounded.

She joined the Medical Missionaries in 1948 and understood the nature of professionalism where her work as a pharmacist became an end in itself. As she rose the bureaucratic ladders of her order, she went to Delhi in the early 1970s and got an MBA degree at the university. It was then that she learnt about trade unionism, and sitting in a class that was geared to the 'other' side of union politics (that is, management-biased) she understood what capitalism was. She learnt her union politics from capitalist texts by reading between the lines.

At the same time, those of her companions who were working in Latin America spoke of their encounter with liberation theology. Sr Philomena-Marie was forced to reflect on the dichotomies that faced her as an administrator and as a religious whose actual vocation was to work with the poor. She said, 'When I was a child I wanted to be a saint, I wanted to give my life to the poor.'

The safety of the interior of the convent felt too much like an upper-middle-class home. So, in 1978, she went to Anjengo, a fishing village near Trivandrum. There she met Fr Thomas Kocherry who was the priest for the local community but often went out to sea with the fishermen. This was her first experience of 'enculturation'—instead of bringing an institution to them (the established church), they lived with the poor and could identify with them. Life was simple here. They ate like the people, frugally, and lived ascetically in the small houses by the sea. Yet, what was most difficult was 'the feelings of superiority'. Sr Philomena-Marie said, 'It was a struggle, both theoretically and ideologically. We battled to be like them, not superior to them. Yet it was we who had all the answers, we had education and money, we were the leaders.'

The medical missionaries at Anjengo ran creches, and like Sr Rose in Valiyathura, did all that they could to alleviate the terrible poverty of the fisher people, and the consequent violence of their lives—excess of alcohol, illiteracy, fatalism. The Christian fishers were proud of their heritage, of the traditions linking them to St Xavier. They were pious and felt chosen in their life, to live alongside the beautiful sea. The very existence of the sea took away the squalor of their lives.

In 1979, there was a flood on the lake where the coir-workers, who were Hindus lived and worked. The Anjengo religious team helped and worked with them. The fishermen who lived across the road on the seaside saw that the religious people helped everyone regardless of whether they belonged to one religion or another. Then, soon after, the Boat Workers' Union was formed, because Thomas Kocherry and Joeychen Antony decided that they had to take on the responsibilities of asking for audited accounts on behalf of the boat-owners who had taken loans from the government. This nucleus joined with parallel unions in Kerala to become the larger group called the KSMTF.

It was in this way that the priests and nuns who were working with the fisher people slowly became part of the unions. They had to help with the bureaucratic structures, the accounts, the paperwork. In the KSMTF office, several cupboards that symbolised the universality of the bureaucratic order—the files, stationery, ledgers. 'We were not separate, we were part of the movement,' the nun kept reiterating. The relevance of power however was subtle and to Philomena-Marie frightening, as if there could never be true egalitarianism even in a movement like theirs.

In 1981, the trawler owners bypassed the enacted law. Thomas Kocherry and Joeychen Antony (the latter died tragically at sea at the age of thirty-eight) went on an indefinite fast. That year P.M. (as she is called) discovered the power of the people, of the federation. The years that followed, with the many commissions, brought the struggle to its logical climax in the fast of 1984.

In that year, when the struggle was at its highest, Sr Philomena-Marie volunteered to fast. She said, 'I don't believe in indefinite fast. That means nothing. One must fast until one gets what one is so desperately seeking, or fast to death.' There was a lot of antagonism from her superiors, but she was steadfast. She would stand beside the fishers, not behind.

First, she joined the picketers in order to be imprisoned 'Jail is the only recourse.' Thirteen of them—three nuns, six women, seven men, by union decision were chosen to picket the directorate and go to jail. They spent six days in jail in the company of prostitutes and distillers. Philomena Mary said:

'We became friendly with them, though there was a hue and cry in the local press about nuns locked up with *vaishyas* (prostitutes). Still, they told us their stories and we created a community through prayer and conversation. We had to have courage, especially to encourage the laywomen who were in the jail on behalf of the fisher people's struggle. The publicity was advantageous for us. While we were there, we learnt a lot. Some of us pretended to be sick and got a good view of the jail health services. After we came out, the union asked me if I would go on fast. Sr Alice, who was already fasting, was growing weak and had to be hospitalised. I was glad to go on a hunger fast. My father, mother and my brother came. My father was very angry. He said, 'You do exactly what you want all the time.' A long while ago, when I was a child, he had said, 'If you join a convent you'll only jump the walls.' My mother was sad to see me fasting. She said, 'Do you have to do this much.' I said, 'You have no right to ask this question. It was you who dedicated me to the people.'

After that, my mother stayed by my side all the time, going home only when she was forced to. After the 19th day, I was forced into the hospital by the police. There they physically forced me onto the drip, but I fought with tremendous strength. I don't know where the strength came from. They said, 'It is our duty to save you for your future work, for the people.' I resisted and continued my fast although my condition was fast deteriorating. The union asked me to stop. It was the 54th day of the struggle, the 22nd day of my fast. The movement was running out of resources—human and financial. Some of the leaders felt that they could not handle the situation. If I died, the people would go out of control. Besides, if I died, the union would be held responsible for my death. So, I stopped.'

Sr Philomena-Marie reached into the recesses of those bureaucratic stores and took out several reports of the KSMTF for me. The struggle goes on.

I will now look at androgyny, celibacy and dress to understand how a woman becomes an active leader, a symbol of the fishing movement which cuts across religious divides and becomes a forum for human-rights issues, and safety of the sea.

Sr Philomena-Marie is a woman who has devoted her life to Christ. The complexity of the relationship is implicit. She is certainly one of the 'wise-virgins' (Gospel of Mathew, Chapter 25, 1–13). This is one of the most poignant stories that Jesus told: it was of women who waited for their bridegroom in a state of preparation, and the parable highlights their joy in comparison to the anxiety and trepidation of the Virgins who were disappointed because they were not ready to meet the Lord. However, marriage—spiritual marriage—is about the meeting of the soul, and the understanding of the self and other. The metaphor of marriage is used in order to understand the intensity of desire, but when we say 'Virgin' and 'Bride', we are speaking of a consummation that is yet to come. In this sense, death presents the face of virtue, for it has lost its sting, and offers only the vision of resurrection and the union with the beloved.

The complexity arises, not with the love metaphors of religious union for these are to be found in all societies, but with the concept of androgyny. For Jung (1978), it represented the fusion of characteristics associated with masculinism and feminism in such a manner that it would create the whole being. It articulated the idea quite familiar to us now that psychological characteristics had social and archetypical undertones, and that the focus and development of one or the other was the basis of gender typing. How then could one use one's energies, psychic or religious in the most creative way? One sees this very clearly in the life of Jesus. I will not consider physiognomy, because the face represented is the desired face of Western heterosexual norms: he is always poignantly beautiful. But let us look at the androgyny of his nature—a child who is presented with gifts of perfume and gold, who is identified with the gentleness of pastoralism, and the careful art of carpentry, which combines both physical strength, accuracy and contemplative concentration. This Jesus grows up to be friends with fishermen and prostitutes, rich men and tax collectors; he is often with women and children, light enough to walk on water, capable of great and ferocious anger; he weeps quite openly and teases his mother; he cannot bear pain and humiliation and asks the God who is another form of his own self to take away the bitter cup. Weak and defenceless as he is before his father, he is quite different at the courts. This Jesus cannot then be stereotyped, because from one moment to the next we do not know how he will behave. What are the sources of his strength, his imagination (for he is always telling stories) and his courage?

Perhaps it lies in the body of his mother from whom he is corporeally constituted since apocryphally Joseph is only his foster father. If Jesus is physiologically and perfectly created but in a Godly way—for 'in the beginning was the word' and then 'the word became flesh'—we are at a loss if we search for him merely corporeally. The androgyny of his being does not question the right he has to his manhood; it only states that while being a man he could understand and empathise with women as much as with the Centurion's daughter, Lazarus, the lepers, the blind or Zachariah, who was always so ashamed. For centuries, this empathy, this understanding of the other in the essence of his or her being, has come down to us like the concept of love. This love however was culturally specific—it was not sexual (though the intensity of desire communicates itself in the story of Mary Magdalene) but appeared in the form of wisdom and peace. Jesus would through the symbol of his life and death and the visions his friends had of him define the intensity of spiritual existence and experience.

When Philomena-Marie leads the fishers, she symbolises the fact that she is a woman, a follower of Jesus, a Bride of Christ. However, she also leads them in another way, not because she is a woman or man but because she understands the rules of para-politics, capitalism and profit, of the servitude of the declassed. In that sense, she does not stand in for the bride of Christ—she is an official member of the KSMTF. She understands her job, is highly qualified in management theory, and her rhetoric does not carry any of the tones of gender or religion. She could be either male or female, nun or priest, Hindu or Christian (Visvanathan 1994).

One of the greatest problems of understanding work, as Ivan Illich and many feminist colleagues showed, is in the terms which neutralise gender. In the unbridled years of feminism, when women pitted themselves against male bastions it was important to believe that same is equal to equality. Yet, in certain issues of *Feminist Review* and *Signs*, some of the most poignant reviews have been about lost identity—what happened to motherhood, and being and celebrating womanly selves; did being a woman mean hating the 'other'; how would one then look at complementarity and division of labour?

Ann Snitow (1992) in *Feminism and Motherhood* has paradigmatised the shifts in feminist thinking, from the separatism of the 1960s to the anti-motherhood manifesto of the 1970s. Finally, she writes, 'In the 1980s we have apologised again and again for ever having uttered what we now often name a callow, classist, immature or narcissistic word against mothering .... We have embraced nurturance as an ethic, sometimes wishing that men would share this ethic without much hoping they will' (1992: 42).

In a completely different vein, Prue Chamberlayne analyses the emergence of *The Mother's Manifesto* and disputes arising out of it. The Manifesto was issued by women who were a part of The West German Greens in 1987. Their demands 'include collective provision for childcare, a revision of urban design, pay and pensions for home careers, flexible employment, increased leisure time and the facilitation of political activity for mothers'. According to Chamberlayne, many feminists believed the manifesto was reactionary and could even mean a return to Nazism, presumably to the kitchen, church and kindergarten. The Manifesto reflected the disenchantment with individualistic, capitalistic, competitive values which deny biological spaces to women. The debates on caring have become centre-space. German feminists echo the anguish of Ivan Illich, that gendering has led to greater inequality, that participation in the labour market has led to greater violation and loss of autonomy for women (Illich 1982; Chamberlayne 1990: 10). The sadness of the Manifesto, it seems, lies in that it wages an assault on non-mothers in a way that was waged by women against men or men against women in earlier years. German feminists like Giselda Erler say that as mothers, they feel 'marooned', relegated to a reserve as guardians of a dying culture. Mothers must be returned to the centre of societies, the quality they impart to the life of sharing, intimacy, uniting of body and soul, which have been destroyed by 'reason' must be valued once more. In the same way, such feminists do imagine the development of a new male tenderness and responsiveness through intimacy with babies as well as a rediscovery and extension of eroticism in experiences surrounding reproduction (Chamberlayne 1990: 11).

There is therefore the possibility of the transcendence of existing gender roles, and yet the retention of differences.

Joan Tronto analyses Carol Gilligan's famous theory of care as being both situated in women's experiential morality as well as transcending difference. Care, therefore, centres around responsibility and relationship rather than rights and rules; it is concrete rather than abstract and expresses itself in activity rather than in theory, engaging in 'daily' experiences and moral problems of real people in their everyday lives (Tronto 1987: 648).

What about 'caring' or pro-feminist men? Lynne Segal, in her essay 'Feminism, Socialism and the Problem of Men' (1989) quotes Jonathan Tonstram, who was an active participant in communities centred around socialism and women's rights. 'I feel it is vital for men to be more closely involved in child care if patriarchy and male violence is to begin to crumble. And that, however bleak our immediate political prospects, one thing that can happen now is that men can change' (cited in Segal 1989: 3).

Segal demands an analysis of masculinity which she feels is an area of conceptual deprivation. 'There are many different kinds of men and masculinities—gay, straight, gentle and tough, democratic and authoritarian—and these are all cut across by race, class, ethnicity and religion' (ibid.: 15).

That feminist experience contributes to theoretical holism is a point made over and over again. But Mary Louise Adams in her essay 'Identity Politics' (1989) argues that personal experience was used in the feminist cause as a means to liberation, but it should not cut feminists off from larger struggles. Similarly, Sally Alexander (1991) states that the first wish of feminist history was to uncover new meanings for femininity and women, to propel sexuality 'to the forefront of the political mind' was very similar to the goal of psychoanalysis. The latter attempted the discovery of a subjective history through image, symbol and language. She asserts that psychoanalysis and feminism arose together. (Early critiques of Freudian psychoanalysis came from feminist novelists like Virginia Woolf as *Mrs Dalloway* and *Orlando* clearly show.) Alexander argues that psychoanalysis preferred to focus on the mother–child relationship while feminism went into the debates about the rights of 'workers' and 'citizens', the rights of women in the public sphere (Alexander 1991: 128–133).

In this pursuit of questioning 'normality', feminists like Shiela Rowbotham have critiqued the concept of the good or 'normal' mother in an essay called 'To Be or Not to Be' (1989). She asserted that feminism's main contribution was to show that happiness could come from other things than mothering. Feminists came out honestly with their feelings, to show that motherhood could be both: oppressive or liberating; it were feminists who articulated the belief that 'motherhood must be freely chosen and socially transformed'. Yet by the 1980s of the last century, she concedes with Liz Heron that feminists were 'melting into motherhood' (Rowbotham 1989: 84).

In a brilliant indictment of maleness and the right to die in war, Genevieve Lloyd (1986) argues that heroism is for men, and in war, they transcend their love of life for the rationalist ideas of justice and freedom. Women, however, it is believed cannot overcome nature, or transcend death, because their role is to reproduce. Freedom and consciousness, then, are male preserves, but when a woman sacrifices her sons, she overcomes nature and becomes a citizen (like the Spartan mother who does not weep for slain sons but rejoices in the victory of her country at war).

Androgyny means overcoming the cultural parameters of what it means to be a man or a woman and raise the problem of common humanity. Work, then, is defined in terms of ability and interest, and the distinctions between men and women's work would at once be devalued. Androgyny then is about fearlessness and role choices that are not biologically insignificant. Anthropologists are familiar with instances of role reversal which augment cultural reasons for demarcating work as gender-specific. Trying to explain this in evolutionary terms would be as trying as asking why penguins and sea horses have gentle, loving nurturing fathers, while cats are so Oedipal-fixated that the tomcat sometimes kills his offspring.

Androgyny, as we saw, is not about bi-sexuality or hermaphroditism. It is not about transvestism though we will see that the latter becomes an important code by which androgyny often articulates itself. One of the complexities of androgyny could be substitutability, which sociologically is not a problem when applied to role behaviour. Substitutability is usually about roles and not persons. It argues that the case for resemblance is so high in tribal society that one tribal is alike another, one factory worker like another, though levels of skill or biographical characteristics may hugely vary.

So, if Jesus is acceptably androgynous in the Jungian sense, he only articulates in his person and character true consanguinity. Biologically we too are of cognatic descent but may be patrilineal or matrilineal in our societal and individual self-definitions. Each of us is composed of our father and mother in a genetic composition that is structurally universal, except in the case of mutation. Androgyny celebrates the differences and similarities that involves being human.

The case of Jesus is problematic only because his relationship with his father is philological, with his mother corporeal. (Visvanathan 1993 for a detailed analysis of the life of Christ as represented in 'The Eucharist', by the St Thomas Christians of one denomination, the Yakoba in Kerala.) His father is God, but his mother is only a saint. It is this cultural hierarchy that allows Fr. Tom Kocherry (another KSMTF leader) to be like Jesus, but Sr Philomena-Marie cannot. She must remain an (androgynous) woman.

The most interesting thing about androgyny is that it does not necessitate gender neutralisation. In this context, let us look at Joan of Arc. I shall draw my story from Vita Sackville West, Marina Warner, Tom Keneally, Bernard Shaw, William Shakespeare, though Joan-specialists know that this is a small cluster in the milky way of researches on her. Marina Warner's fascinating account of Joan of Arc focuses on her marginality in terms of social and political roles, and her clarity regarding her female biological identity (1991). Warner writes that 'the state of suspension, of indifferentiation achieved by a transvestite girl was confirmed by the Christian tradition as holy. Sexlessness is virginity's achievement and a metaphor for martyrdom, as hagiography bears out'. Warner disclaims the 'disorder of the androgyny of the neuter' in Joan's case (1991: 157). She says that 'in holiness, androgyny is not either this or that, it is the fusion—and Joan belonged to this order—the absoluteness of the way, the impregnability to relativism, which means their sovereignty over time' (ibid.: 158).

Warner asserts that Joan is the symbol of mobility, accepting neither her peasant birth nor her female condition or the limitations that would be a consequence of this (Warner 1991: 151). Having dressed as a boy, and while cutting her hair in the latest masculine fashion, Joan, yet 'never proclaimed herself a boy. Indeed she never once pretended she was male, since she referred to herself in the feminine gender, as La Pucelle, the Maid' (ibid.).

Joan constantly refers to herself as The Maid or The Virgin. What she conveys most stridently is the preparation for consummation, the Virgin Sacrifice by Fire. She must die so that her country may be liberated. What is most significant is that Joan does not menstruate—her 'womb is dead'—therefore, she may not conceive, but conceive only the deed or word or value. In this sense, Joan, Mary the Virgin Mother and Sr Philomena-Marie are homologous. Sr Philomena-Marie achieves the fertility and power of the word through celibacy.

The works of celibacy are well known to us through the lives of the saints in all the religious traditions, and specifically the life of Mahatma Gandhi. Sexual energy, in Jungian terms, is transformed into the energy required for self-realisation or political battle. Celibacy, like androgyny, is about the consciousness of one's own sexual identity, and the pain or the glory that arises from transcending or overcoming one's biological, psychological and social drives. Joan understood this well: she was, for one side, a saint, the Maid, the Virgin. For the English, she was a whore who led a dissolute life, who lay side by side with soldiers unafraid, a transvestite who used war to glorify herself. Most of the stories about Joan were about the fact that men were afraid to touch her, that they never wanted to touch her. Her virginity, her celibacy, her virtue, her 'integrity', as Marina Warner describes it, became the symbol which a ruptured France could heal. No wonder, then, that celibacy and androgyny can together combine, as in the case of Joan of Arc and Sr Philomena-Marie. It combines so powerfully, that they are able to lead the workers and be noticed only for the power of their vision. Charismatic authority, as therefore the least socially allocated grace, is an idea that settles upon a person, its power lies in the eyes of the beholder.

Any reader of the texts of Jesus would immediately understand the *advaitic* power of 'I am the Way, the Truth and the Life'. It is, as Ivan

Illich says in his book *Gender* (1982) that 'I is never gendered' because I is from the oral tradition. The listener knows immediately from the voice what the gender of the speaker is. In this sense, Christ's sayings do become patriarchally defined. Thus, Sr Philomena-Marie knows that she can be a friend of the fisher people as much as Jesus. But patriarchy as established conventions will not allow her to take the place of Christ.

Not surprisingly, when she is locked up in prison for trade-union activities, it is with the prostitutes. 'We prayed with them, made friends with them, shared their troubles.' That is a symbiosis of role identity with Jesus, impervious of gender. The newspapers scream that 'Nuns have been locked up with *vaishyas*' (prostitutes). For Philomena-Marie, the courage and love of Magdalene is the unarticulated theme of her compassion, which links celibacy with profligacy and makes the latter redeemable.

Joan, on the other hand, hated prostitutes and chased them out of the camps. Legend has it that the sacred sword that won her victory at Orleans broke on the back of one such prostitute, and then there followed her defeat and capture and death. For Philomena-Marie, prostitution, like alcoholism, is an occupational hazard arising out of the frequent economic crises in the lives of the fishers. What is important is to provide alternative modes of employment to women.

Joan dressed as a boy and was burnt at the stake for it because this was a role reversal, contrary to nature and so heretical. Yet, dressing as a boy meant that she could ride a horse, and ride to war. Sr Philomena-Marie dressed in indistinguishable fawns, dull browns—neither does she merge with nature, nor does she stand out. This contrasts with the brilliant colours of the fisherfolk. Her clothes mitigate her gender (they do not neutralise it or transmute it) because these are the colours one would not only associate with renunciation but also with bureaucracy.

So, in a world of men, Sr Philomena-Marie plays out her vocation. She is unafraid of prelates, capitalists, governments and death. She is of course thin (anorexic in the new equations between fasting and visions) and overworked. She oscillates between many roles. She nurtures a boy (married at eighteen), his wife and child because they cannot quite manage on their own. She races between one village and another providing medical help. She keeps the KSMTF office in order. Earlier, she stayed with a woman whose husband had died at sea and helped her reorient her life. Sometimes she gets thrown out of a Sunday-school classroom because the visiting prelate sees her trade- unionism as a bad example to young children. She eats her food with co-workers (nuns from a nearby convent) or with an office-bearer at the KSMTF. And she must cope with that abstraction—called a reputation—sometimes out there in the blazing limelight; at other times completely forgotten and marginalised as another Joan of Arc emerges in another part of India, taking the question of water in a different direction. She says, 'We are networking with other movements. We are in touch with Medha Patkar.' There can be no competition or jealousy in the emulation of saints, there can only be patience and reservoirs of heroism which sees martyrdom as the true androgynous term. This essay is not oriented towards asking for martyrdom for that would be a terrible act of lassitude and irresponsibility on our part, but asks to listen to the voice of the potential martyr and respond to the commitment to the cause, to be sensitive to the person who fasts, has visions, rebels, hears voices, and see in the androgyny of his or her being questions we need to really ask ourselves about what it means to be human. In the following section, I will discuss the modalities of everyday resistance and battles for survival among the fishers, where the intelligentsia that springs up is able to articulate their needs.

Writing for the Fisher People: Intellectuals, Intelligentsia and the Parallel Politics of Post-tsunami Interventions

Disaster management has become the keyword when we think about subsistence societies, and the lives of people who draw sustenance from agriculture, forests, rivers, seas, mountains and deserts. However, it is accepted that the key debates arise from the native intelligentsia, that is, those who belong to the community. It is only when we record their debates and their endeavour that we can hope to bring about changes in the conditions of poverty that so many of them still find their people in. There are many different kinds of voices that have to be analysed;

sometimes, these interlace, sometimes, they contradict one another. The task of the sociologist is to believe that there is a common good and that the voices of the people and their needs will be heard and understood. Globalised intellectuals often feel that the disappearance of peasantry and foresters and coastal labour is merely a punctuation mark in history, and those who can consume will consume, the rest will be ignored and debilitated. Labour history always salvages the voices of the oppressed, and it is in this context that a lot of the problems that I am going to pose here will be framed.

One of the most interesting formulations that Paulo Freire makes in the *Pedagogy of Hope* (1992) is that when speaking to fisher people, are intellectuals (read scientists) aware of the fact that the fishers are men of knowledge? Are scientists willing to accept that what they know about their work and environment is useful scientific knowledge? This is an old anthropological debate, perhaps best voiced by Marcel Mauss and Bronislaw Malinowski. Malinowski commanded his students in *The Argonauts of the Western Pacific* (1922) to notice that primaeval forms of survival are very carefully couched in oral traditions and that fishing and horticulture and trade in the Trobriand Islands were very organised and sophisticated. Yet, this theory of Malinowski was as carefully considered by the lay world as his critique of Freud, where he stated in *The Sexual Life of Savages* (1929), that if the mother's brother was the authoritarian figure in matrilineal societies, then it was the Mother's brother who would be the focus of Oedipal feelings and not the biological father for whom a man might indeed have feelings of love and longing, and regret that they were not in proximity! The evasion of common sense in writing theory only goes to prove that most people are happy to presume that men of science always have the upper hand, and the rest are always passive in their assimilation and implications to theory.

Paulo Freire showed in the *Pedagogy of Hope* that the fishers themselves believed that they were ignorant and incapable. They had to be persuaded that the decisions they made and the choices that were available to them made them powerful in the questions of everyday survival. In 2005, in a classroom interaction at the Institute of Mass Communications, Delhi, a journalist from Venezuela told us that peasants had used harmful insecticides and chemicals on their land for so long (three generations) that they were resistant to green activists because their 'tradition' was to use chemicals! The question of people's knowledge becomes problematic as soon as activists begin informing us that studies have shown that there are profits to be had with scientific interventions, never mind the damages, because that is part of the history of the modern world. This school believes that 'social problems' are due to 'social causes' of which science is innocent.

Is it possible that most people could never hope to know the sea as the fishermen do because, for them, she is their mother? This is a poetic question for scientists, and we must presume that scientists know things differently! Paulo Freire's method is thus of dialogue. He asks the scientists to tell him some things, which he as a social scientist does not know, and then he tells them something which they do not consider, like the problems of subjectivity and bias in scientific analyses. And in that dialogue, everyone leaves, knowing something more than they knew before. I must presume, then, that scientists working with fisher people would have the ability to listen, and in listening, they would understand the people better. This is what Kathryn Pyne Addelson in her book *Impure Thoughts* called non-hierarchical thinking. She says people must understand one another in terms of their worth and need. Addelson worked with a community of fisher people in a hamlet near Boston in 1992 and insisted on in her lectures to them, that they must believe in the power of 'regenerative communities'.

I will presume then, that both scientists and fishers have an interest in the ecological balance of the sea and the degradation of the environment. The emptying of the sea by industrialised fishing has been the concern of artisanal fishers and the 3-month ban in the monsoon something that they have been fighting for a long time. This one demand over so many years has not been respected has been the greatest disaster for them (in 1994). In 1981, the Babu Paul Commission according to the KSMTF website was silent on the aspect of sea-bottom trawling which hampered spawning; in 1988, after intense agitation on the part of the fishers, the Balkrishnan Nair Commission recommended a ban on trawling during the monsoon period, that is, for ninety days on an experimental basis for three years. The website informs us that the government announced a partial ban for forty-five days, and this partial ban continues, so the fishers continued to agitate for the ninety days ban. J. John, editor of the *Labour File*, says that the government violates the ban by allowing licenses to trawlers during the monsoon. He further underlines the fact that the rights of the coastal community and the nature of relief measures increases conflict, so that Dalits who are central to the economy of the country, whether of the coast or inland, are alienated. J. John demands a coastal policy on this, as well as the fact that macro-degradation brought about by disaster has exacerbated the difficulties of people. The destruction of mangroves and the question of housing and land rights is the central issue for government concern. The so-called immediate solution, to move the fishers out of their habitation and therefore make access to the sea more difficult, has been the paradox.

Disaster management consists of long-term demands. These are complicated by the changing face of social relations. The inability to make an impression on state and science establishments has meant that the survival-of-the-fittest clause (something which no mother would agree to as a principle of triage!) has worked, resulting in the imitation of trawlers by the use of motorboard engines and seine nets. Imitation results in the mitigation of the debates and this has been a weak link in the chain. The late C.V. Seshadri, who was the director of the Murugappa Chettiar Research institute (and whose work has been chronicled by Shiv Visvanathan and Rajni Bakshi), used a Paulo Freire method of interaction. While learning from the fishers, he used his pivotal place as a scientist, to furnish them with fish-aggregation devices, polyethylene catamarans with longer durability. One Injambakkam fisherman was still, in 2006, using the catamaran gifted to him by C.V. and the Chettiars in 1983. Agriculturally innovative experiments with vermicompost for organic farming were used by him in pilot seaside villages in 1995. There was also Spirulina as a diet-enrichment source, which was a fruitful use of algae grown in village tanks, to cure night blindness which C.V. tried out in seventy Tamil Nadu villages before patenting it. It is this kind of attitude that one requests scientists to have when training fisher people as we are told is their present task.

Writers have drawn the need for government workers (including scientists and development personnel) to be aware of the fact that the pre-tsunami conditions of the coastal workers were pitiful. *Labour File*, the monthly journal from Delhi had several essays on human rights and the plight of the poor immediately after the tsunami. What Henri Tipaghne and Patric Toomey brought out most powerfully was that the levels of poverty and stratification were such that the magnitude of the tsunami only eroded the pitiful condition of the fishers, but there were among the coastal peoples, others even poorer! These were the women, children, Dalits and the daily-wage labour that serviced the fishers.

The question of humanitarian aid was avoided by the communities themselves as a general principle. *Arra kayi ettuyadu, avaruka kitti,* translated as, 'Those who stretched out their hand, they got', many could not in fact, even manage to reach the aid-givers. Peter Thayil in Alleppey in the summer of 2005 informed me that aid-workers did not know who the fisher people were! One way to avoid this problem would have been to work with agencies at the grassroots. But we know that the differences in religion played a part.

Sridevi Srinivasan, a former JNU scholar and a well-known aid worker with international NGOs, who spent a day in a village in Cuddalore on 26 December 2005, found that the Dalits continued to be left out of the aid projects; people had recovered, but in some sense, the loss was apparent in their conversations, though it was not their habit to engage in nostalgia. She asked the question, in her communication to me, whether the nutrition expectations of the middle class were the core space from which philanthropy was to operate. In itself, the question points to the biases that people have towards others. What Sridevi Srinivasan writes is presented here since so much she says is relevant to those who work with the fishers:

> As I travelled on the East Coast Road that links Chennai to Pondicherry, I noticed three to four new hamlets close to the road. There was an unusual uniformity as far as these thatched hutments were concerned. These had been built after the tsunami for the fisherfolk. I thought to myself that this minor displacement might be the beginning of a bigger one (I heard that lobbies of realtors and businessmen had used the tsunami to throw people out permanently to buy up the land). As I cross Marakkanam, about 60 kilometres from Pondy, I noticed a

large number of signboards indicating fibre-boat manufacturing units. Many houses had fibre boats parked on their porch!

I travelled roughly about four kilometres from Cuddalore to reach a stretch of backwater. There is a fishing hamlet called 'Sothikuppam' across the backwaters. This hamlet is surrounded by the sea on two sides and is separated from the mainland by a stretch of backwater. There was no displacement or damaged houses in this hamlet. Twenty-two children died while they tried to escape through the backwaters forgetting that the waves could hit the backwater stretch too. (I noticed about 40 fibre boats anchored in the backwater stretch. My local guide told me that these were extra boats that the villagers had received from donors. Ones regularly used for fishing were at the seashore.) A boat is used to ferry people to and fro. This is neither a mechanised boat nor a rowing one. It is drawn with the help of a rope that is tied to the shores on either side. A middle-aged man and his little boy pull the rope with all their might to ferry about 11 of us and a motorbike! (I later learnt that this man belonged to one of the three Dalit families who do this job. Strangely only women passengers (about 1 rupee for both ways) need to pay—the reason being that it is women who take the catch for sale and hence earn money! I begin to wonder how much money this man would be able to make. I turned to a social worker sitting by my side and asked him. He said that they hardly earned enough to feed their families one square meal a day. I thought they probably would go fishing to earn a little more. But it was not so. The fishing community had exclusive and undisputed rights over the sea and all its bounty. Dalits were not permitted to go fishing. They were sometimes taken as assistants by the fishermen to lift heavy stuff and do odd jobs! The Dalits were not residents of this hamlet—they stayed across the backwaters, were not allowed to visit medical camps organised by various NGOs and were not given relief material at par with the fishers even though they were affected equally. A lady sitting on the boat with two of her acquaintances asked her friends why many outsiders were visiting their hamlet today. The other two mention that it was on this day last year that the tsunami struck and changed their lives. 'Oh really! Is it one year already?' she asked.

It is the first anniversary of the tsunami and I felt strange and sad to be visiting on this day. As I reached the hamlet, there was a lot of activity as a medical camp had been organised by an NGO. I first saw a group of young girls chatting and giggling. They were a group who had received vocational training from a community centre that has been set up by an NGO. They had learnt tailoring and embroidery. When I asked them how they were using it, they replied that it was not of much use and now they want to learn something else. They were excited about computers and wanted to 'learn computers' though none of them could reply to what they would with their knowledge of computers. A couple of these dozen girls had lost a sibling on that fateful day. They were not too nostalgic. They were enthusiastic about the opportunities available to them for learning new things.

Then I met a group of girls who had come from other hamlets in the Cuddalore district. One girl from Devanampattinam, probably one of the worst affected areas, said 'Our home is gone but we could not live in tents. So, we have built our home in the same place.' She was excited when I asked her if Vivek Oberoi, the actor, built their home: 'Little did we know that he was an actor. Only after he screened his movie *Saathiya* and told us he is a big star that kids and girls ran after him for his autograph! He asked kids to teach a few Tamil words too.'

Some other girls said they were still living in relief camps and were waiting for their houses to be rebuilt.

Local people in the village felt that they have got sufficient attention. But some questions torment me as I observed the happenings. A medical camp with just one doctor, one nurse and three paramedics was organised. The camp started at 11 am amidst much fanfare—the shutterbugs were capturing every moment to document evidence of the NGO's effective functioning! Three hours and 104 people were screened and given medicines and injections! I could not comprehend what kind of medical attention each individual would have received.

As I sat in one corner with a few girls and observed people, one old lady selling boiled peanuts asked me to donate a few kilograms of rice to her. She said that she had come to Sothikuppam 10 years ago. 'This community just does not give me food.' At the time she was talking to me, lunch was being served by volunteers of the NGO to their employees, paramedics and a few visitors like me. Her reference was to this denial of lunch by the volunteers to her.

Most of the young people of this hamlet were involved in some or the other activity of the organisations functioning there.

> A social worker told me how they went door to door in the hamlet telling them about nutritional facts and the basic nutrition required for the body. 'These guys just eat fish. They do not eat vegetables and cereals. We try to educate them about nutritional levels of various items and ask them to include it in their diet.'
>
> The talk about sustainable livelihood projects, psychological counselling and medical support filled the air. I could not resonate the same. How far can we penetrate these communities and change their character? Can we bring about homogeneity in lifestyles, their occupational strategies? Should we try to help the community support itself by objective interventions or dictate their entire way of life? Relief support in times of emergency is an absolute necessity and also a basic tenet of humanitarianism but the kind of haphazard support that I witnessed only disillusioned me. (Srinivasan, personal communication, 26 December 2005)

Sridevi's concerns have been sharply focused on by those who believe that the right to life and livelihood are the first concerns of those working with coastal people and communities. Thomas Kocherry, in the *Labour File* of March–April 2005 says that

> In all the countries, efforts should be made to legislate. Disaster Prevention and Management Authority. This Authority should be autonomous. All the available resources should be pooled by this Authority. This authority should be at the service of humanity in all the countries whenever such disaster happens anywhere in the World. The UN should facilitate this authority.

What the tsunamis of 2004 taught us was that regardless of state and federation, the earth is linked by the sea and the heaving magma below us. Here, I present data from the turn of the 21st century, when the fisher people attempted to adapt to capitalism, and set up imitative mechanisms to survive.

Workers of the Sea

I had met Peter Thayil, coordinator of the Fishworkers Development Forum in the diocese of Allapuzha, in the Summer of 1998. In an interview, he told me that 1984, which most people see as the landmark of the fisher people's struggle was not the beginning. In 1971, the Catholic fisher people's struggle was established. In 1974, it became known as the Latin Catholic Union, linking fishermen all over Kerala. Fr. Paul Arakkal was the first union president. In 1978, the term Catholic was removed. Therefore, it became known as the Akhila Kerala Swatantra Fishworkers Federation. It was at this point that Fr. Tom Kocherry began to emerge a hero.

For Peter Thayil, who represented a solid faction of support within the church's established body, Kocherry and others appear as secessionists in the 1980s because they brought in the excitement of liberation theology, which articulated the power of the poor, the praxis of the impoverished. They were gifted leaders who had influence in the world and a guiltless preoccupation with temporal concerns. Many of these leaders also belonged to orders which allowed *sannyasa*, while leaders like Fr. Paul could not wander at will; they were tied to a parish. 'So there was a clash, a clash of priests.' The bishops asked the fishermen, the leaders to compromise, to come together. Yet, Thayil argues that because of the differences among them, there was an abyss, and the whole movement went through a paralysis.

Thayil and his friends feel that because of large-scale unionism, which integrates fishers across the subcontinent, the movement in Kerala itself has become diffuse. If the Fishworkers' Development Forum is becoming an active force, it is because it answers the real ground-level needs of the poor for shelter, employment, medicine, schooling. Many of the benefits of the struggle were wrested from the government before 1984. These included pension (Peter said it was 75 rupees per month), insurance for sea accidents, education grants, housing loans and subsidised kerosene for outboard motors.

Fr. Paul, according to Thayil, fought substantially for many of these benefits by sitting on the road in front of the secretariat till he was heard. His supporters feel that fame has been bad for the movement, that the leaders became engulfed by publicity, and many of the local heroes went unsung. They feel that in the post-1984 scenario, there were only two main benefits: first, savings-cum-relief schemes and second, a trawling ban for 45 days, which means nothing. The ban must be for three months if the sea is to replenish itself.

The fishermen argue that there have been many commissions: the Babu Paul, Balan Krishnan Nair, Kalavr, Murari and Oscar Fernandes Commission. The Murari Commission Report is acceptable to the fisher people. The rest are biased towards trawler fishers. As one fisherman said:

> Why is this so? The IAS officers, the politicians, the government, in general, are ignorant and in league with capitalist trawler owners. We keep going to the Trivandrum Secretariat to depose. But there have been trawler owners who have become ministers. Further, so much money is involved. Licenses involve crores of rupees. Everyone receives kai kuli (hand tax or bribe). The bureaucrats are completely ignorant. Do they have even one fisherman in the commission? I can tell what fish is swimming in the water from a distance but these specialists cannot because they only have reports, papers, jargon. I know the sky, the currents, the water, its smell, its colour, its depth without measuring with instruments. We know the depth of the sea.

Thayil believes that the fisherman's knowledge is a resource that has not been utilised adequately in making decisions that affect their livelihood, community and lives. Other fishermen at the beach told me that they know the presence of fish from the way the crows fly, the movement of the waters, the shadows of the water, the sounds that can be heard from birds and the bubbles of air that appear on the water as the fish surface. A boy goes to sea only when he is fourteen or older, and the knowledge is passed on to his elders, and by his own powers of observation, since it is a matter of survival. 'The sea cannot crush us,' one man said, 'I know the wind, the lightning, the depths.'

The sea is empty now because of overfishing. The governments at the centre have been deeply implicated. An activist at the Fishworkers' Development Forum in Allapuzha called Justin, said:

> It was Congress which gave Sea Licenses. At that time, the BJP contested it. The BJP is now giving licenses. Only in Kerala do we have a Fisheries Minister. At the Centre, Fisheries are a part of Agriculture. We demand this because the entire coast of India stretches for 6,200 kilometres and the Kerala coast is

> 900 kilometres in length. Water encircles India, and its wells, lakes, ponds, constitute India. So, there is more water than land. And yet 50 years of independence has meant 50 years of avoidance of the fishing communities. (Interview, May 1998)

The sea is empty now because of overfishing. One fisherman said, 'Sivasankar Pillai made millions out of his novel on the life of the fisher people. Are you also going to do the same? I got up at two in the morning and I got nothing.'

Because of the intrusion of multinational and trawling interests, the fishermen feel their lives are over. The government receives foreign exchange, while the scarcity of fish leads to the decimation of the fisher people. Sardines, mackerel, tuna fish, ribbon fish are almost wiped out. Trawlers operate in *thearekadal*, the shallow waters which are 50 km from the shore, where the fish come for cohabitation. Trawlers are engaged in overharvesting the sea in its reproductive months. Commission after commission bypass the problem out of ignorance or corruption.

It is because of absolute ignorance and the General Agreement on Tariffs and Trade (GATT) policy agreements that the collaboration between government, multinationals and trawler owners is destroying traditional fishermen, Vijayan told me in Ponnapara. The woman who owned the house where he lived was a widow, one of the few who went to get fish from the beach to sell. Most of the other women stay at home, busy with household tasks as well as weaving coir ropes to supplement the erratic income their husbands bring. I have argued in an earlier essay 'The Fishing Struggle in Kerala' published in the *Seminar* (1994) that farmers and fisherfolk cannot be clubbed together. The sensitivity to their difference is imperative.

Vijayan said to me that the basic problem is that the central government has a financial perspective on everything, and the foreign exchange it receives through licensing trawlers or the export of fish is what it is solely concerned with. 'There has to be a social transformation. Multiculturalism is being favoured. Trawler fishing is a political collaboration, where even [the] IMF and World Bank are implicated as "development agents". This has to be changed. The relationship of the fisher people is with the sea and nature. Yet, there is a paradox.

The fisher people have themselves moved away from the *kattamaram* (raft) to the mechanised boat, which they term as the *vallum* or country boat. This is characteristic of Allapuzha, Kochi and Trichur, while in Thiruvanthapuram, the *kattamaram* is still in use.' The *vallum* in Ponnapra, Allapuzha district, are old, large country boats, with curved prows, deep black. They carry flags of different colours, and when they go out to sea, one feels oneself in the presence of an ancient maritime culture. But each boat has a motor and is dependent on the Honda and Yamaha Suzuki companies.

An old woman called Esther, whose husband and sons still go out to the sea said:

> We are a people who know only hunger and cold and debt. Since the coming of the 'engines' [mechanised boats], we have known only debt. The government is in league with the capitalists. The engines cost 1,40,000 rupees. Only the Yamaha-Suzuki motors can withstand the water, the Indian ones powder in no time, and despite the investments, on most days the men come back empty-handed. The cost of oil is hard to bear, the children of fishermen no longer want to follow this occupation. The strikes are endless, but there is no way out because the government does not hear our problems. We have no water, no electricity, no toilets. As soon as there is a haul, the debtors also appear. Nobody wants us to form cooperatives. This is a different matter from the Union. Everyone wishes to stand separately. When there is a shortage here from overfishing, people bring fish from Tamil Nadu. So, we are again losers. Here people are fishing from morning to night, from night to morning. What chance is there of the sea replenishing itself? The local fishermen have become our (their) own enemies. They have adapted their nets in imitation of the trawlers. The trawlers have to be stopped and the continual harvesting of the sea regulated.

John Paul, an activist in the struggle and a fisherman, put the problems of the movement brilliantly:

> Kocherry's problems are too abstract and political. The real problem is will the fisher people even survive? Each one of us is treated as a member of a political party. They come for votes at every election. We took out a notice reminding them of their promises: glasses

> (that is, spectacles) for the old; house loans which have not been given; subsidized machine oil which has been stopped. The coastal Regulation Act does not affect us. It will not be recognised; no fisherman has broken rules against nature or government. Each fisherman has his methods—he cannot leave his cove, the neighbourhood and group solidarity that he already has.

He argues that tribals and fisher people share the same conditions of degradation—economic and social. Yet, in deciding on the degradation marker, *daridram* or the poverty line, the government decided that the fisher people were 60 per cent above and 40 per cent below it. John Paul says that on the beach, 98 per cent of this occupational community is below the poverty line. He argues that their only income is from the sea. Out of 365 days, they get income on an average of 150 to 200 days. The remaining days they get nothing, even if they can go to work. The expense for taking out a boat with 35–40 workers is 40,000 rupees. The boat is usually owned by a *modulali* (capitalist) who may also be a commission agent—that is, he takes on the privilege of selling the fish. The fishermen catch and bring the fish to shore, then the agent takes over from him. He auctions the baskets; the fishermen say that out of 10 baskets, they keep aside two for the poor (and there are many beggars on the beach). Once the catch is sold, the fishermen receive 70 per cent, while the agent receives 30 per cent. Out of 70 per cent, the costs of the boat, petrol, tea for forty workmen, all have to be met by the fishers. The struggle of the fishers has been for human rights and equality. People like Philomena-Mary and Peter Thayil have communicated that livelihood and rights to commons such as the sea are ongoing battles.

As I have already discussed, after the tsunami, things changed considerably for the modes of livelihood were completely dismantled in affected areas, such as Ponnapra on the Allapuzha (Alleppey) coastline.

A lot of the problems of modernism is truly about the extinction of occupations. If diversity was the rule of nature, green activists are intent on preserving planet Earth and communities, which are in harmony with nature, we too must protect niche cultures. A lot of the 'aid' which the tsunami brought in its wake never reached the fishers. The groups who were given this money diverted it to other channels, other dependencies, other 'clients'. Patron–client relationships within the church and political parties are often based on traditional mechanisms of caste and class hierarchies. The fisher people say they got excluded because the power brokers doled out a small percentage to the fishers, and then diverted the rest of the tsunami funds to other needy non-fishers. Dalits continued to reiterate that they got nothing. The tension between the fisher people as Other Backward Castes and the Dalits is palpable.

Artisanal fishers appear in Ponnapra–Paravur as a forgotten community. Those whose houses were destroyed and not replaced live like perpetual refugees according to Thayil without toilets or medical help. The rest—144 families—have neat modern two-room dwellings with tiled roofs. The women go out as domestic labour and untrained helpers to the sick and old in private homes, with salaries of 1,500 rupees (in the year 2006) per month. Youth not trained to fish but with a school education are shop assistants. Manual labour is the other option, but as they say, that's not their world, and there must be a solution.

The 200 self-help groups, which Thayil coordinates for the Fisher Workers Federations, is the first step towards autonomy, till the sea is refurbished by nature or culture. These artisans can only hope to access traditional occupations in such a manner, as must presumes an organic perception of the sea by the state and scientists.

India remains one of the last enclaves of organic farming and fishing, facilities that are available to us as an asset. We must understand the significance of non-industrial farm produce and fish resource. It is a form of intellectual and social capital which the world tries to resuscitate for the wealthy through artificial means, but in our country, we are still inheritors of the best natural materials and resources like food. While the refugees of natural disasters receive attention, their real agony lies in waiting for surcease. However, their optimism in judicial, media and civil rights questions is matched with that of the activists working with and for them. The Farmers' Movement in the post-Covid era holds out against the oligarchy of industrialised agriculture which is in tandem with corporate houses and the right-wing state by demanding the freedom to cooperate across religion and culture.

References

Adam, Mary Louise. 1989. 'There's No Place Like Home or Identity Politics'. *Feminist Review* 31: 22–23.

Alexander, Sally. 1991. 'Feminist History and Psychoanalyses'. *History Workshop Journal* 33 (Autumn): 128–133.

Ardener, Edwin. 1986. 'The Problem of Power'. In *Visibility and Power*, edited by L. Dube et al. Delhi: Oxford University Press.

Arendt, Hannah. 1958. *The Human Condition*. Chicago: University of Chicago Press.

Buber, Martin. 1970. *I and Thou*. New York: Charles Scribner.

Carl, Jung. 1978. *Modern Man in Search of a Soul*. London: Routledge and Kegan Paul.

Cayley, David and Ivan Illich. 1992. *In Conversation*. Toronto: Anansi Press.

Chamberlayne, Prue. 1990. 'The Mothers' Manifesto and Disputes over Mutterlichkeit'. *Feminist Review* 35 (Summer).

Cobbe, Frances Power. 1895. *The Divine Law of Love*. London: Victoria Street Society.

Dube, Leela, Eleanor Leacock and Shirley Ardener. 1986. *Visibility and Power*. Delhi: Oxford University Press.

Elshtain, Bethke Jean. 1987. 'Against Androgyny'. In *Feminism and Equality*, edited by Anne Phillips. Oxford: Basil Blackwell.

Gilbert, Sandra M. 1989. 'Soldier's Heart'. In *Speaking of Gender*, edited by Elaine Showalter. New York: Routledge and Kegan Paul.

Illich, Ivan. 1981. *Shadow Work*. London: Marion Boyars.

———. 1982. *Gender*. New York: Pantheon.

Joseph, Cherian and K.V. Easwar Prasad. 1995. *Women, Work and Inequity*. Delhi: National Labour Institute.

Jung, C.J. 1973. *Memories, Dreams, Reflections*. New York: Vintage.

———. 1978. *Man and His Symbols*. London: Picador.

Keneally, Thomas. 1991. *Blood Red, Sister Rose*. London: Hodder and Stoughton.

Lloyd, Genevieve. 1986. 'Selfhood, War and Masculinity'. In *Feminist Challenges: Social and Political Theory*, edited by Carol Pateman and Elisabeth Gross. London: Allen and Unwin.

Maitland, Edward. 1896. *Anna Kingsford*. London: George Bedway.

Mani, Lata. 1991. 'Multiple Mediations: Feminist Scholarship in the Age of Multinational Reception'. *Feminist Review* 35 (Summer).

Merchant, Carolyn. 1979. *The Death of Nature*. Berkeley: University of California Press.

Mies, Maria. 1986. *Patriarchy and Accumulation on a World Scale*. London: Zed Books.

Mies, Maria, Veronika Bennholdt-Thomsen and Claudia Von Werlhoff. 1988. *Women: The Last Colony*. London: Zed Books.

Rosaldo, Michelle and Louise Lamphere, eds. 1974. *Women, Culture and Society*. Stanford: Stanford University Press.

Rowbotham, Shiela. 1989. 'To Be or Not to Be: The Dilemmas of Mothering'. *Feminist Review* 3 (Spring): 83.

Segal, Lynne. 1989. 'Slow Change or No Change? Feminism, Socialism and the Problem of Men'. *Feminist Review* 31 (Spring).

Shiva, Vandana. 1988. *Staying Alive*. New Delhi: Kali.

Showalter, Elaine, ed. 1989. *Speaking of Gender*. New York: Routledge and Kegan Paul.

Singer, June. 1973. *Boundaries of the Soul*. New York: Anchor-Doubleday.

———. 1977. *Androgyny*. New York: Anchor-Doubleday.

Snitow, Ann. 1992. 'Feminism and Motherhood'. *Feminist Review*, Spring.

Tronto, Joan C. 1987. 'Beyond Gender Difference to a Theory of Care in Signs'. *Journal of Women in Culture and Society* 12 (4).

Visvanathan, Shiv. 1995. *Unravelling Human Rights*. Paper for the Beijing Summit on Women, MSS.

Visvanathan, Susan. 1993. *The Christians of Kerala: History, Belief and Ritual Among the Yakoba*. Madras: Oxford University Press.

———. 1994. 'The Fishing Struggle in Kerala'. *Seminar*, November.

———. 2000. 'Workers of the Sea'. *Seminar*, January

Vyvan, John. 1969. *In Pity and in Anger: A Study of the Use of Animals in Science*. London: Michael Joseph.

Warner, Marina. 1991. *Joan of Arc*. London: Vintage.

———. 1993. *Alone of All Her Sex: The Myth and Cult of the Virgin Mary*. New York: Vintage.

Woolf, Virginia. 1982. *The Voyage Out*. London: Granada.

———. 1945. *A Room of One's Own*. London: Penguin.

———. 1982. *Night and Day*. London: Granada.

———. 1984. *Jacob's Room*. London: Granada.

———. 1986. *Three Guineas*. London: Hogarth Press.

———. 1988. *To the Lighthouse*. London: Granada.

———. 1966. *Mrs Dalloway*. London: Penguin.

———. 1979. *Orlando*. London: Triad/Panther.

3

The Vast Sargasso Sea of Indian English

Wall art in Jamaica, where there is a continuous refashioning of predatory English language, as in all formerly colonised countries; April 2016. © Author.

The political rhetoric of marginal fundamentalist groups, who pose as dominant groups holding the country and its people to ransom, appears most sharply when it attacks individuals for being aliens.

The question of time and history are central metaphors that push back the question of the past, the recognisable past to a point of no return. Oddly, the contestation of how this past is constructed is the central question of modernity. When a landscape is destroyed by natural or social means, a new metaphor is forged in concrete terms. The landscapes of modernism arising out of war and technological revolution have all communicated their idiom of rationality which may be contested by others. Here, I am concerned with how political ideologies can leave their imprint upon the mind upon forms of writing and literature.

In 1990, Ananthamurthy, the Telugu litterateur, spoke at the Nehru Memorial Museum and Library, Delhi of 'the co-existence of time'. He argued that every individual has many kinds of social lives which overlap and conflict with one another—some modern and rational, some feudal and caste-based. Today the domination of caste-based behaviour in national life organises the presence of orthodoxy of tradition in its oppressiveness. And citizenship and writing become two indexes by which this oppressiveness is to be analysed.

If the idiom of political hegemony centres the substance of its attack through the method of alienation, then it can only be a short-lived, violent and ugly mode as all fascist programmes are. State and rule, even in the forms of patrimony and kingship have always depended on the consensus of the people to be ruled. If lathi and cannon are the modes of legitimating coercion, in a democracy, the ability to protest will emerge and forge new modes of dissent. The politics of domination, however pervasive the cogs that operationalise the hegemonic core, cannot govern—it can only annihilate and its rule is entrenched only for the private profit of its mercenaries—money, status and power. Landscapes of memory will continue to express the varieties of ways in which human beings have solved the problems of discord—of lust for coercion and the destruction of the humane. Without a belief in the future, the present can have no meaning.

'Disaster, preservation, renewal, growth, revolution' are different modes of this transformation of the landscape and they 'connect our hopes and memories and sense of time flow' (Lynch 1995: 28). So also, human consciousness of time and events of peace and prosperity are not stable. By idealising the past, we cannot serve the present or future, nor deny that the substantial presence of poverty has been the lot of the people. The wealth of India has lain in the faith of the poor, an optimism which Gandhi understood only too well, surviving the avarice of the ruling classes.

The theme of my essay is thus to analyse what it means 'to be a foreigner in one's own country'. The term alien could be located in terms of those familiar concepts of sociology—to be a stranger, to be excluded, to be alienated, to be a non-citizen though one may have an

Indian Pan card (for tax records) or a ration card. It could apply to beggars, the poor, to people like me who had suddenly in the 1990s of the last century been marked out by the fundamentalists as alien for political purposes, to those who as foreigners accept citizenship and request that they be seen as that in order to marry, bear children, be buried here or to stand for elections.

Before 11 September 2001, an estimated 38,000, according to media reports, migrated to America every year on one kind of visa or another. In the land of chewing gum and rock, belonging depended upon the acceptance of the language as both monosyllabic and homogenising. In that context, it is interesting to note that a variety of separatist movements had their origin in America. Whether it is Hinduism, Islam, Sikhism or Christianity, the substance of this financial support from fundamentalist expatriates to drive the separatist wedge into India needs to be analysed.

Much of the political rhetoric of Hindutva's philosophy comes from asking the question 'When did you come?' and 'What makes an alien?' This could apply to an idea, a community, a party—any fact of identity that blurs questions of belonging as it is codified by the constitution. It seems apparent too that if this question was posed by the *dasyu*s (slave castes) of India who have been colonised now for millennia, the political imperative of throwing half the population out would be apparent and frightening. There is of course the recently propagated American laboratory and Indian media myth that upper-caste men are Aryans (whatever that means) and lower caste men and all women are *dasyu*s. The speculation around invaders, travellers, settlers is the stuff of archaeology and ancient history—all that we can do is analyse the masses of information that is put across and try to understand the contexts of its interpretation in objective or political terms. It has been made amply clear to sociologists, that to be objective, rational and analytical, is also now a self-conscious political act.

Now the central task of sociology remains singularly clear—that is to ask why people do the things they do. If the rhetoric of homogenisation has never worked except amongst political lobbyists, then the risks of diversity are interesting in themselves. The rights that human beings have are well defined in various charters and embodied in the welfare state. Michael Ignatieff has pointed out that:

> It is because money cannot buy the human gestures which confer respect, nor rights guarantee them as entitlements, that any decent society requires a public discourse about the needs of the human person. It is because fraternity, longing, belonging, dignity and respect cannot be specified as rights that we ought to specify them as needs and seek, with the blunt out institutional procedures at our disposal to make their satisfaction a routine human practice. (1994: 14)

If we are to understand what human needs are, then the production of literary fiction is one of the key spaces where desires and possibilities are fully suggested or left tantalisingly unresolved. The writing of expatriates becomes significant because each creates an imaginary world through words, and yet, communicates the immediacy of events. The *then* of myth and legend, of the past as tradition or as history becomes substantially offered as *Here and Now*. It is the here and now of literary fiction that makes each work survive long periods—decades or centuries, rather than the combustible conflagration of the time of the bestseller. Works written in 1930 or 1980 would appear in the year 2000 as fresh and open to interpretation.

Salman Rushdie's *Midnight's Children* (1981), Vikram Seth's *A Suitable Boy* (1993) and Amitava Ghosh's *The Glass Palace* (2000) are three memorable moments in the development of Indians writing in English which have been analysed by many literary critics. Why they interest me is because all three authors have made their home outside the subcontinent but visit often and see themselves as expatriates. If each of these three styles of writing is so far removed from one another, then it is interesting for me to locate within the sociological imagination how being a diasporan Indian, they can contribute to the writing of literary fiction. Ghosh's command over historical data and the ability to bring it closer to the reader, Rushdie's playful rebellious jibes at politics and hypocrisy, Seth's sensuous and intuitive control over the emotional worlds of human beings—these have been celebrated over and over again in the literary world, as well as in the greatest index for authors—the sale of books.

The expatriate has a house, friends, occupation, income in a country, but he dreams of home. He lives in a comfortable metropolis or university town—London or New York, has access to libraries, concert halls, museums, accessible to him in the sense that friends and critics are always around. Yet, there is searing loneliness about their lives which appear in the things they sometimes say or the unguarded melancholy of their faces on camera. The problem, of course, lies in the oscillation between the loneliness and solitude of writing. All craftspeople understand the chiselling of an object as a singularly lonely task and the moment of sunburst when the cameras flash and the stage is set for what is euphemistically called the 'book release'. The fact that a book may bomb or that critics hate it does not deter the author—each of these authors has written what are thought to be good books as well as a few over-rated books. Now, the survival of the author depends on his or her ability to withstand criticism and to write again.

Whether writing is biographical or not depends upon the author's ability to acknowledge the reservoir of memory he or she draws from. Researched, the novel becomes the keyword by which the success of the intellectual frame of the novel is acknowledged. Many writers would spend a lot of time reading, and the sources of that reading might or might not be acknowledged. The self-conscious author today documents his/her journeys and proves Barthes essay *The Death of the Author* to be a lie. The author seems continually available to defend his or her story. There has never been a time when the pressure to conform has not been imposed upon the author. How he or she deals with it is defined by the accidents of temperament and circumstance. How much of the love and death in the novel is autobiographical is left to the coterie of friends who gleefully or with melancholy recognise themselves or those known to them. But then does not every reader find resemblances in whichever book they read to people they have known or glimpsed? In 1928, Gorky wrote, in *Talks on Craftsmanship,*

> God has been created in the same manner as literary 'types' have, in accordance with the laws of abstraction and concretization. Characteristic exploits performed by a variety of heroes are condensed or 'abstracted' and then given concrete shape in the person of a single hero. Traits peculiar to any merchant, nobleman or peasant are similarly 'abstracted' and then typified in the person of some one merchant, nobleman or peasant—in other words, now a literary type is created. (n.d.: 31, 32)

Earlier he had argued that it is not enough to create a person, for this would have neither social nor educative features.

> If however the writer proves able to summarize the most characteristic class features, habits, tastes, gestures, beliefs and manner of speech peculiar to twenty, fifty or even a hundred shopkeepers, civil servants or workers, prove able to epitomize and condense them in the person of a single shopkeeper, civil servant or worker, he thereby creates a type, and that is art. (Gorky n.d.: 30)

Yet Gorky was always clear about the functions of literature—to inform, to educate, to entertain not in malice but through humane and generous anecdotes. This moral pressure was best conveyed in his critique of the 'sponge-like existence of younger modernist writers'.

He goes on to say that public duties were integral to a writer's life:

> If you sweep a courtyard, you will prevent harmful dust from getting into children's lungs, if you bind a book in good time, you will extend its terms of service, helping to make it of greater benefit to people, and saving paper for the state. Rough treatment of books causes tremendous losses to the state, because so many books are being printed, and after all, we are the State. (ibid.: 153)

Why I quote at length from Gorky is because of the biographical experience of having been given Gorky's 'Mother' to read when I was in Class III and all of Shaw's plays when in Class V (I rebelled against reading Shaw's Prefaces in Class VI). Certainly, I had no idea that my father who did not like *Anna Karenina* was setting out the agenda of what kind of literature I should be reading. Even now, the contempt that my father had for elitist emotions—philosophising about pain—is still hard to bear. Like Gorky, Marxist intellectuals like my father, could not bear the rift between the intelligentsia and the people—and it is exactly in this rift that Indian writing in English is located. The strikingly banal but brutal critique of elitist writing by M. Prabha, in *The Waffle of the Toffs* (2000) is easily available—funny, crude, authoritarian—it sets a norm clumsier than Gorky's well-crafted idealism. But every writer unlike every critic knows that writing has its will to power, and existentialist writers, who are primarily record keepers, rather than transformers of the world, understand the impetus of their quill. Take away their implements and they will invent another—but the work will get written.

It is here that I wish to analyse the work of a woman, Jean Rhys, whose book, the *Wide Sargasso Sea* (2000) remained alive despite her efforts to destroy it, forget it, evade it. The book appeared in 1962, though its first draft had been typed in 1938.

The *Wide Sargasso Sea* is an unnerving study of race and caste relationships in Creole society, of colonialism and accidents of history which one day would surely be the subject of detailed symbolic analyses. My problem is more specific. How does Jean Rhys understand her existence as a foreigner in England? Her father was a Welsh doctor and her mother, 'white' Creole. She was born in Dominica in 1890 and came to England when she was sixteen and spent what was a conventionally bohemian life moving between various frivolous positions. Suzanne Rouvier (in Somerset Maugham's *The Razor's Edge*) the artist's model, not quite a whore, but a practical companion to various aspirants in the Paris art scene would be an approximate analogy. But Rhys, encouraged by Ford Maddox Ford, who had also discovered D.H. Lawrence, was undoubtedly one of the most brilliant women writers of the 1930s. Then she fell out of sight. She lived for decades in obscurity and even had an unwitting obituary notice written for her. She died in 1979, having received acknowledgement when, as she said, 'It was too late.' She had received the W.H. Smith Award in 1966, was made a fellow of the Royal Society of Literature in 1966 and made a CBE (Commander of the Order of the British Empire) in 1970.

I am unable to engage with a biographical sketch of Rhys in order to answer my question. I will try to approach it through textual analyses. Why the problem seems evanescent to me is because so many of us who have never doubted that we are Indians are now being continually pounded with the question 'Who are you?' Asked often enough, it can push a person beyond the edge. When asked as anthropologists do, in a dialogic way, I see no problem with the question. Asked in psychoanalytical therapy or the quest for mystical resolution, this space can be one of the most profound areas of creative encounter. Yet, the political negotiations of identity are a fact of history, an emblem of social change, and fictional narratives sometimes capture this with a power of representation.

The *Wide Sargasso Sea* lies between the West Indies and the Azores, in the North Atlantic Ocean. Ships could become entangled in its weeds. It is the metaphor for calm and danger, for the ability to encroaching weeds that strangulate the beleaguered ship. The West Indies become a complex battling ground where indigenous, black, tribal, native, colonised, white, colonising all become fraught with multiple meanings as do the relationship between those who have mixed or pure French or English ancestry.

Rhys was in England and writing about Dominica, or Jamaica, which she blurred with artistic license. So let us use the West Indies or the Caribbean as an artificially organising term though the specificities of history and topography for the islands and their cultural landscapes may differ substantially. After all terms such as Bharat, Hindustan or India have been variable terms for a diverse and polyglot land, and 'subcontinental' identity is an even more problematic term.

So, Rhys' text begins with the assertion by the heroine Antoinette that 'the Jamaican ladies had never approved of my mother not just because of her beauty but because she was a "Martinique" girl.' Black people jeered at the mother and daughter, but as servants in the house, they had tremendous power over their half-caste masters. It was the house and the garden that communicated a great sense of power—the power of the land, the past and memory.

> Our garden was large and beautiful as that garden in the Bible—the tree of life grew there. But it had gone wild. The paths were overgrown, and a smell of dead flowers mixed with the fresh living smell. Underneath the tree ferns, tall as forest tree ferns, the light was green. Orchids flourished out of reach for some reason not to be touched. One was snaky looking, another like an octopus with long thin brown tentacles bare of leaves hanging from a twisted root. Twice a year, the octopus orchid flowered—then not an inch of tentacle showed. It was a bell-shaped mass of white, mauve, deep purples, wonderful to see. The scent was very sweet and strong. I never went near it.

Sitting in England, such a para was written—the intensity of the past surfaces, and much of diaspora writing captures what are seemingly visible details of topography in order to communicate how haunting the past and its dreamtime seems to the writer. But what is diaspora, and who is diasporic? As a Malayali who was born in Delhi and who often writes about Kerala, this chatter about diaspora as an alien is empty for me. The diasporic makes himself or herself at home and is at home; she or he sends out deep roots in less than a month of his/her arrival and is here to stay. People are pushed out, have their heads bludgeoned in—but they fight to stay, or they fight to return.

Antoinette's mother is driven mad by a holocaust of hate—the slave-owner attacked by night, her retarded son by her first husband killed, her house burnt down, her second husband helpless as the house burnt down. Antoinette remembers,

> But now I turned too. The house was burning, the yellow-red sky was like sunset, and I knew that I would never see Coulibri again. Nothing would be left, the golden ferns and the silver ferns, the orchids, the ginger lilies and the roses, the rocking chairs and the blue sofa, the jasmine and the honeysuckle and the picture of the Miller's daughter. When they had finished, there would be nothing left but blackened walls and the mounting stone. That was always left. (Rhys 2000: 24)

If ruin and the memory of a foundation are all that the survivor has, and the memory of things that once had a pattern of normality, then the tragedy of the present lies in that continuing absence which, like the ghost of an amputated limb, thrashes in the victim's memory. As Rhys writes in the second paragraph of the first page, 'My father, visitors, horses, feeling safe in bed—all belonged to the past.' The tragedy of the coloniser is the moment of seduction—when the native, the Creole, or the woman has been lulled into a state of secure concupiscence. Rhys uses the imagery of sexual love as represented by the white male in relation to the Creole woman to understand this peculiar form of submission. The violence of seduction lies in its mutual pleasure and the shattering quality of boredom annihilates both. Significantly the coloniser and the colonised blame one another, seeing their autonomy either in the past or in the future as an obliterated dream.

> 'Why do you hate me?' she said.
>
> 'I do not hate you, I am most distressed about you, I am distraught.' I said. But this was untrue, I was not distraught, I was calm, it was

> the first time I had felt calm or self-possessed for many a long day… I watched her holding her left wrist with her right hand, an annoying habit.
>
> 'Then why do you never come near me?' she said, 'Or kiss me or talk to me. Have you any reason?'
>
> 'Yes,' I said, 'I have a reason' and added very softly 'My God.'
>
> 'You're always calling on God,' she said. 'Do you believe in God?'
>
> 'Of course, of course, I believe in the power and wisdom of my creator.' (Rhys 2000: 81)

Having driven his wife to insanity, the colonialist Rochester leaves her in England.

> When I first came, I thought it would be a day, two days a week perhaps. I thought that when I saw him and spoke to him, I would be wise as serpents, harmless as doves. I give you all I have freely I would say, and I will not trouble you again if you will let me go. But he never came. (ibid.: 116)

*

> All the people in the house become ghosts for the madwoman in the attic, voices and memories without substance. 'All the people who had been staying in the house for the bedrooms doors were shut, but it seemed to me that someone was following me, someone was chasing me, laughing'. (ibid.: 112)

In the end, there is a conflagration, and life appears as a series of vivid images of the sky, orchids, the green and gold of ferns and moss against a burnished landscape of a fire run amok, and everything destroyed. Words capture this in an afterlife, where everything is redrawn, as images of a life once lived.

Homesickness is so terrible that nothing is real, only the past beckons. Amitava Ghosh's consummate obituary on the Indian-born American Shahid Aga captures it in almost Sontagian detail. The corollary to such homesickness is madness and death. Yet, many of us live in this strange, beckoning world of the past or another land—it is not merely the stuff of an expat's longing. The Macaulayised Indian fiction writer knows the bylanes of Bloomsbury as well as the *galis* of

Chandni Chowk—not very well, but the map is real and haunting. Sitting in Delhi or Brooklyn, Calcutta calls forth. No human being can be devoid of this intense longing and that has always been the stuff of literary fiction. Claiming citizenship, identity, home, nation is always a tenuous and self-conscious task.

English is certainly the language of colonialists. But so are Sanskrit, Persian, French, Portuguese and Computer Java. Ask any illiterate tribal or peasant. The history of India has been a long and chequered history of crossings and wanderings and conquest, by sea or water, by air or ideas. Our vocation as sociologists disallows the possibility of engaging with fiction or speculation unless they appear as collective representations. Indeed, the debate around hierarchies and the complexities of language and dialects will always continue. Sociologists are generally wary of nondualism, just as much as theologians. If everyone believed in the possibility of inclusion, then many people, particularly theologians and empirical anthropologists, would be without a trade. Sociologists glean off the gatherings of diversity and resilience.

If English is seen merely as the language of power, uncontested power, then the reality of the Indian subcontinent would fail us completely. The truth is that English is alive and kicking despite boards painted by local painters which might leave one breathless by their spelling. The reasons for this are three.

English is a language of power because it has the power to mediate. It belongs to no one, so it can be used by all. There are hilarious confrontations recorded by our scribes, where Hindiwalas send letters in Hindi to Tamilwalas who reply in Tamil. So, often, English intercedes as a third language. Further, it is a language that has colonised the world so that American dictionaries exist in computer software, but American is only a dialect of English like the pidgin spoken in many parts of the world. Emily Dickinson wrote in English, just as did Henry James or Mark Twain, Poe and Melville and Thoreau. They were Americans writing English, a similar status which many of us in our country have in a way—*Indians writing in English.* The language of state and statecraft are in the hands of those who rule. When the French left India, or the Portuguese did, some small enclaves like Pondicherry, Chandernagore, Goa, Daman and Diu remained behind as symbols, museumising in time, the urban, linguistic and culinary significations of a robust slice of history. In 1989, at a public lecture given at the Centre for the Study of Developing Societies, Raimundo Panikkar once asked an audience in Delhi, 'If French colonialism had survived or Portuguese colonialism had, what are the ways their language and culture would have affected us?' The accidents of history—premeditated sometimes, though that sound like a malicious contradiction—left the British as a master race for four centuries. But the interesting thing is that the resilience of the Indians has come from accepting the institutional regimes that were imposed upon them, whether by force, custom or consent, and to continue to carry on their lives as best as they could. This is a history of millennia, and it is about a culture of poverty. Yet would one accept the tenuousness of rule, if there is injustice? The Indians have made an art of maya, which allows them to imagine better worlds wherever they are. So, English has survived, even with the poor, because it is the language of opportunity, it is the language of globalisation. The Malayali nurse, the UP bhaiya, the Baul singer … the list is endless, who has not made it good in a globalised multicultural world with the rudimentary knowledge of the English language?

The second reason for the survival of English is that it is a language of commerce. This is independent of it being a colonising, imperialist language of state machinery in global interactions. Banking, trade and e-commerce have united the world in a form of capitalism that survives on hedonism. Advertisements have used English in the most remote villages and obscure towns to sell what they have to. E-commerce means that spellings and grammar are not primary, a heartwarming dyslexia has overtaken the world. Young people understand that visuality and orality are more compelling than grammar—the meaning is the message and the form is to spit at the erudite and literati. These are some of the grand gestures of modernity and not to be frowned upon in a ferment of rage over what constitutes the pure form. Democracy is about the marketplace, the forum is still dominated by young healthy and wealthy males or older stable powerful established males, but it looks like the brevity of words and the simplicity of the message—power, money, sex—remains the uniform code. Women, when they push into the system, must either catalogue intention, or behave like 'the boys'. Ernest

Hemmingway, well-known as a great hunter, always had a young healthy huntress travelling by his side. He was the boss and wrote, she carried the guns and communicated that she could shoot. English as a language of sport or business has made its compelling legitimacy known to the world.

The third problem is that which directly pertains to us, English as a literary language. Multinationalism implies that today, people belong to many different worldviews simultaneously. It is impossible to belong anymore to a compartmentalised world. I am sure this has been the history of the world if not of groups or individuals for centuries. In 1930, after the collapse of the pepper trade with the West, following the First World War, my grandfather's business went awry. He was a man given to sharp and compulsive dealings, a self-made scholar of sorts. My grandmother told me, when I was ten or twelve years old, that Grandfather had an English penfriend, a woman who sent him books from England. Perhaps I had asked her where those blue and brown calf-leather gold-embossed volumes of Shakespeare, Marlowe, Donne, Browning had come from. In 1968, when my grandfather had suffered a near-fatal stroke, he returned home for a brief period before death. He was hopelessly in a state of senile dementia, but he recognised his family, was shaved and tonsured by his barber every day and would lie quietly in bed. Yet, whenever it began to rain, he would get up, take a wicker shelf with a dozen or more English books and put them out in the rain. My grandmother who would frequently check on him while he lay serenely on his rosewood couch watching the rain would suddenly notice the English works of prose and poetry out in the verandah catching the rain. Then throwing a towel over her head she would rush out and drag them in. Was my grandfather saying something about Macaulay's shelf of English books? It was my grandfather who had made my sister and me sit next to him on the verandah while a woodpecker rapped a home for itself in the *thoon* or column of wood holding up our roof. We recited 'A lily of the day is fairer far in May' over and over again till we knew it well. I had been eight years old when he taught me that verse, a grand gesture from a man who didn't like children over much and was by nature strict and careful with time as he was with money.

Now, while the debates go on about multinational companies, *bhasha* writers, awards, 'Rushdie's opinion'—I am very puzzled. A love for language when rural or forest peoples singing songs to the seasons or their gods or wives or crops comes from the contexts of their lives. A love for English or Sanskrit or Greek or Telugu comes from just such specifics of contexts. For me, there was no reincarnational sense at 6 when I thought to myself, 'I know when I use a word wrong in English. I just know.' It was my third language in early childhood, not as decreed by the state—but by the contexts of my upbringing. Malayalam was first since my parents, my sister and my Ayah (*chedathi*—or classificatory older sister) all spoke Malayalam at home. Hindi was equally significant and most loved because it was the mother tongue of most of my friends in the neighbourhood. English was my third language learnt at school—a parrot language that went 'Ann sing to mother', 'Mother sing to Ann', 'Father comes home', 'Ann sings to Father' and on for pages and pages with watercress, pianos and heaven knows what else. Was it divorced from my reality? Of course, it was—but children are not sceptics, and we were as trusting of the English language text as we were of the Hindi language, one which said that Shastriji, who would be a revered prime minister extolling the *jawan* (soldier) and the *kisan* (farmer), known to the world as a very simple wonderful man, had swum a river to reach his school. Children believe in the other and the plausibility of many worlds. So, I learnt the English language and in time it became the language of greatest significance. My paternal grandfather had an English penfriend perhaps, but my maternal grandfather had learnt English by travelling for 11 km in a bullock cart every morning as a young man to the nearest town to learn English at a missionary college in the later part of the 19th century. He was a village schoolteacher who taught Malayalam to sixth formers (or fifteen-year-olds), as they were known then.

My point is that languages when alive cannot be hierarchised. Langue and parole are conceptual tools—in reality, the symbiosis between speech and grammar is as woven as the tongue to the palate. Distinctions only allow for greater interlacing and greater power. For users like me, English is a *bhasha* language and I am a *bhasha* writer. Hierarchies of language or dialect, of great and little traditions, are festoons of the state. Like Timon of Athens, the state feeds the chosen ones—trips abroad, feasting and awards—and when the money dries up, no one is happy. Writers may or may not get money, and radical and bourgeoisie writers are equally pleased when patronised. Writers never scoff at money. Why should they? It is that which allows them to live, gives them the pleasures of autonomy and generosity. Yet, I am drawn to the idea that there are thousands of writers and singers of tales in all parts of our country who continue to write and sing, invent and perform, even when the resources of welfare or patronage fail them. Writers and storytellers do not choose to be poor, hungry, dying, miserable—but if they are forced into situations like those, then they would still try to write.

English-language writers rarely suffer abysmal poverty. What they fear is a lack of press. It seems mandatory to be recognised (even notoriety as a bad writer seems all right) in order to be seen as a professional writer. These are self-created hierarchies, and not as dangerous as state crafted ones, where the Indian writer of English language fiction is always a diasporan. There is a tragedy to that stance. Success as a writer in English, for the state, comes from one's distinction as an Indian writer domiciled in a foreign country. Conclaves held will list NRI writers as the most significant contributors to literature in India. One can well understand the angst of *bhasha* writers. Yet, we know that most people do the work they do because it helps them make a living (pay the rent etc.) or because it is a job and everyone must be employed according to their status or their family's expectation, because they like the work that they do, or because they are forced to engage in some gainful employment. Why must writers feel that they absolutely must achieve awards, distinctions, large sums of money, or feel that they've lost out? Most probably this feeling is an artificial hunger, induced by a globalised society. How could we hunger for coffee if coffee bushes hadn't come our way, or tea, or vanilla bushes or chillis or tomatoes or potatoes or gulmohars or jacarandas? One could extend it to the horse and cow I suppose if one didn't feel one was treading on some politically dangerous ground, like that of the Harrapan horse. One should '*chipko neem azadraktha*' (hug the indigenous margosa as a political act) and hope for the best. I think the new preoccupation with being recognised is as new as television coverage and media attention. The masses of our people cannot read yet and do not have the money to buy a newspaper for themselves. It is these shocking contrasts that make us what we are.

If we look at Amitava Ghosh's book *In an Antique Land*, some of these existential problems I have raised are dramatically and sociologically posed. Ghosh is confronted with the possibility that the subjects of his study are more curious about him than he could have imagined. Yet although they are 'simple peasants' they are amazingly perspicacious. They ask him, in a staccato voice a relay of questions that leave him completely dumbfounded, and they ask these questions over and over again, centring around 'the divinity of the cow among Hindus' and 'the cremation of the dead'. What happens to this research scholar from a British university is the sudden realisation that there are categories of translation that must take place when one tries to decipher a culture. His secular and now suddenly foregrounded Hindu identity, his understanding of language, English, Bengali, Egyptian, his modernism, his return to the archives to decipher the relationship of Arab trade and commerce with the Malabar coast all suddenly leap through print. It is puzzling that the language of time asserts itself here—modernity and tradition, the past interfaces with the present in cunning ways. Would Arab traders in early medievalism use the Western calendar while corresponding to one another, to date their missives?

Sociology and Literature

What is literature? All writing that lasts and is relevant over large periods without seeming outdated constitute a body of literature. Sociologists have produced great literature. It is impossible to read Marx's *German Ideology*, for instance, without coming to terms with the sheer brilliance and clarity of his style. Even with the crumbling of communist states here and there, Marx's writing is read the world over, both for its understanding of capital as well as how the narratives of history and peoples are articulated. There may be fewer takers for the view that Emile Durkheim or Max Weber provides the same quality of colour and vibrancy. Yet, as a body of literature that survives time, the resilience of sociologists as litterateurs cannot be denied. To write about marriage and children, property and death is the subject of sociological recording. To write well about the everydayness of existence is another talent entirely. But to be a sociologist one must be a writer. To teach, one must write. One must read great works of sociology and be in a position to want to write—to change the world one must wish to write, and one must wish that everyone else can read and write as well.

Feminist theory is a distinctive type of sociology that produces its own literature. Many of the criticisms that come from those who call themselves objective, or biased in some other time-honoured way are significantly around the questions of the sociology of emotion or affect. Is sociology equipped to study affect? Anyone who reads Max Weber would immediately respond to the questions of rationality, values and ethics (and the varieties of combinations of these) to say that indeed this is possible. *The Protestant Ethic* (1953) arises out of the regulation of desires as does modern bureaucracy. Yet the empirical sociologist's questions arise from the maverick nature of social life and activities. Providing order to reality is only our second methodological task; the first is to observe, record and compare. Feminism uses the method of bringing that which was silenced to the fore. It contributes substantially to how a kind of recording takes place that allows balance to be restored. If sociology is the science of combining wisdom and community, then objectivity demands that we see women's voices as crucial to the endeavour of describing what reality is. Sociology, though abstract, is concerned with realism. While we are indebted to the founding fathers of sociology, the search for the voices of women continue in loyalty to the objective pursuits of our art. This is no shifting canvas, there is a certain structuralist paradigm that comes alive: that is the search for meaning. In that sense, recording the voices of women is not significantly or merely a woman's task; men are as much part of the venture, and the solidarity and support of men in the task of reconstructing the fabric of sociological narrative are integral. Women's names, women's work, women's contribution and the deficit in the structure which contributes to their oppression must be highlighted. It is in this context that one is grateful to the gender studies programmes in many universities where the shared tasks of analyses have been made evident to men and women faculty as well as students. If there are dangers that men will again speak on behalf of women, it is a risk that we must take, and some of us as women scholars feel that we can safeguard these risks by recording in newspapers, journals or women's meetings, the dangers of assimilation.

The writing of fiction, I find, is one of the most interesting metalanguages that sociology can use and that it is a legitimate form of writing. Sociology has never been doubted by universities, wherever sociologists have appeared as writers of fiction. I first began to write fiction because of boredom and the fear of death. These are sociological principles that are catalysts to human behaviour, active and creative. The sociology of fear, boredom, corruption and Pandora's gift to the world, curiosity and hope … are difficult to handle through the statistical method. To write prose, poem, essay or play that delineates the human condition, that is easier to do. Yet, unlike writing sociology, this kind of writing demands an empty mind. Its creativity arises out of fallowness. This particular condition is available only to the wealthy, the protected or the renunciant. I fall into any of these categories, only marginally. Like seasonal labourers who go out to harvest a crop, the season of work for me as a writer comes into being only when I'm on a paid holiday from teaching, scripts, doctoral submissions of students. Such times of fruitful pleasure are rare for me. So, I enjoy my busman's holiday when I go on fieldwork or recuperate from nervous exhaustion or go on a seminar tour. The chances are that after a break like that, I will write forty pages. I am fairly committed to writing, so somehow that one short story or that chapter out of a novella does get written.

A lot of the work that I have done focuses on record keeping as a form of social criticism. I believe that the task of the sociologist is as radical critic and that in the description which compels verification as its accompaniment, much can be achieved. Those who wish to read what is clearly stated can act upon its assumptions. With fiction, the task is much more subtle, and a lot is said between the lines. This sets up a great deal of controversy because people read texts of fiction very differently from each other, each according to his/her/their need, and often each according to his/her/their whim. No fiction writer believes that his or her work can be standardised through critical readings. We all form part of concentric rings, each one with a job to do and our responsibility to our differing audiences is hard to gauge.

As a sociologist, I have been interested in working with the Weberian idea that we are actors and agents, that we can transform the world. This creates a methodological space for the analyses of biography. Much of the work I have done presumes against the generally held sociological idea that any one person can change structures. I feel hesitant to say this because I am not sure how it works myself. It draws from the idea of the exemplary hero. I believe that the catalytic agent is able to draw from various sources within him or herself to take on situations where pathologies have become 'normal'. This presumes that loneliness is an acceptable human and social condition.

It also presumes that such individuals are well able to understand the relationship between themselves and society; while being detached, they are also interventionist. All my reading has led me to believe that there is no one point of view and that we are enriched by these ambiguities and differences. The next essay 'Joan of Arc' draws from various commentaries and novels and Bernard Shaw's play to reassemble the identity of Joan, who became a symbol of resistance to the extent that even Charles de Gaulle identified with her. By collaging various representations, I show the reader how a young girl integrated various levels of the estate system, the king, knights and clergy, soldiers and peasants to lead the French to victory. Her dismissal and death, once she achieved victory for the Dauphin has been written about many times. Novelistic and dramatic incarnations have always depended on historical and archival materials, in this case, deposition in the Inquisition records of the early 14th century as Vita Sackville West showed.

References

Ignatieff, Michael. 1984. *The Needs of Strangers*. London: Vintage.

Lynch, Kevin. 1995. *What Time Is This Place.* Cambridge, Massachusetts: MIT Press.

Prabha, M. 2000. *The Waffle of the Toffs*. New Delhi: Oxford and IBH.

Rhys, Jean. 2000. *Wide Sargasso Sea*. London: Penguin.

Said, Edward. 1995. *The Politics of Dispossession*. New York: Vintage.

4

Joan of Arc

Joan of Arc constantly represented in cathedral mnemonics and literary narrative in the context of constantly being refashioned and remodelled according to need; February 2011. © Author.

Joan exists. She changes in form but not in substance from one century to another to suit the needs of her readers, appearing as a witch in one and saint in another. The story is so familiar—a young maid who heard voices and went on to lead soldiers into war and victory, and then to support the coronation of the Dauphin at Rheims; then betrayed, to die by fire.

The story sketched like that sounds simple, and there has never been any doubt from the perspectives of nationalism and patriotism that Joan was a saint. Why did it take so long then, for this fact to be realised? It lay in the ambiguity of her being—a woman, dressed like a man, serving to unite through warriorhood a France that was severed. She heard voices—what manner of voices were they—evil or good, hallucinatory or real? Prayer, miracles, bells and churches all figure substantially as symbols in the course of her short, brilliant and tragic career. Joan never thought of herself as having magical powers, but she did think of herself as Jesus' sister, a peasant whose blood was to be sacrificed for the sake of her king. Why did Cauchon, Bishop of Beauvais, hunt her down? Vita Sackville-West, who has written a detailed and logical chronology of Joan's days in power and the final betrayal, says that Cauchon had been in the pay of the English, had been driven out of Beauvais and a fugitive at Rouen, had 'time to reflect upon the wrongs he had suffered even as an indirect result of the triumphant campaigns' of Joan.

She was delivered to the Inquisition in January 1431 and burnt at the stake on 30 May 1431. The central axes of the Inquisition were her clothes and the 'voices'. The jurists of the Inquisition and the University of Paris declared:

> That the woman commonly named Jeanne La Pucelle shall be denounced and declared as a sorceress, diviner, pseudo-prophetess, invoker of evil spirits, conspiratrix, superstitious, implicated in and given to the practice of magic, wrongheaded as to our Catholic faith, schismatic ... and in several other articles of our faith, sceptical and astray, sacrilegious, idolatrous, blasphemous towards God and his saints, scandalous, seditious, disturber of peace, inciter of war, cruelly avid of human blood, inciting to bloodshed, having completely and shamelessly abandoned the decencies proper to her sex, and having immodestly adopted the dress and status of a man-at-arms, for that and other things, abominable to God and men, a traitor to laws divine and natural and to the discipline of the Church, seductress of princes and the populace, living in contempt and disdain of God, permitted herself to be venerated and adored, by giving her hands and her garments to be kissed, heretical, or at any rate vehemently suspected of heresy, for that she shall be punished and corrected according to divine and canonical laws .... (Sackville-West 2001: 304, 305)

They asked her to retract, or she must be considered a heretic, sorceress, schismatic and apostate. She recanted on 24 May 1431 but on 30 May was burnt.

Three sets of concepts emerge: (a) androgyny and dress; (b)church and state and (c) visions and voices.

This androgyny was not implicit in her being—it was slowly put together, constructed by herself and those around her as suitable for going into war. Was she beautiful? This question is constantly posed. Jean D'Aulon, Joan's squire stated that she was young, beautiful, shapely. Shaw (1978) calls her 'sexually unattractive' which he attributes to her power which repelled male desire, but he agrees that a representation of Joan must define her as wonderful of face. Joan never saw herself as a shepherdess or a cowherd, though, certainly, sometimes she might have carried out these tasks, but they were not her profession. She said that she was given to using the spindle, weaving and helping her mother at home.

St Michael first visited her when she was twelve years old. Here, she was looking after sheep when a youth appeared to her and said:

> Jeanne, you are destined to lead a different kind of life, and to accomplish miraculous things, for you are she who has been chosen by the King of heaven to restore the Kingdom of France, and to aid and protect King Charles, who has been driven from his domain. You shall put on masculine clothes; you shall bear arms and become the head of the army; all things shall be guided by your Counsel. (Sackville-West 2001: 55)

The visions appeared frequently, accompanied by light. She heard them for five years according to the letter written by Perceval de Boulainvilliers to the Duke of Milan and reproduced by Vita Sackville-West (ibid.: 54).

Joan's account is simpler:

> I was in my thirteenth year when god sent a voice to guide me. At first, I was very much frightened. The voice came towards the hour of noon, in summer, in my father's garden. I had fasted the preceding day. I heard the voice on my right hand, in the direction of the church. I seldom hear it without seeing a light. That light always appears on the side from which I hear the voice. (ibid.: 56)

*

> The spirits who habitually appeared to her were three—the Archangel Michael, St Margaret and St Catherine; Gabriel and other angels appeared too but these were most constant. They came in light; she could feel them and touch them. They had soft and beautiful voices and appeared particularly if she was in a wood, and when bells chime. One of the witnesses writes when she was in the fields and heard the bells ringing, she bent her knees. (ibid.: 61)

She left Domremy, her native village, first in May 1428 and then finally forever in January 1429. She left without her parents' knowledge. Her father had already had dreams of Joan's warriorhood and had threatened to drown her if ever she ran away with soldiers. Her father was to die of a broken heart at the end, but her mother would work hard to reinstate her (Sackville-West 2001: 61, 62).

De Metz and Bertrand de Poulengy, knights in arms, would recognise the visionary in her and swear allegiance. She was dressed in her shabby red dress when they met her. They had heard of her aspirations and de Metz asked her, 'must the King be driven from the kingdom and must we all become English?' To this, she replied: 'I should prefer to be spinning beside my poor mother, for these things do not belong to my station, yet it is necessary that I should go and do these things, since God wishes that I should do them' (Sackville-West 2001: 90).

Joan, according to Sackville-West, asks Robert de Baudricourt to take her to the Dauphin:

> Still, the very fact that so steady and solid a soldier as Robert de Baudricourt thought it worthwhile to despatch the girl, escorted by two of his own lieutenants and by a royal messenger, postulated that she must in some way be worthy of despatching; also it was an age when visionaries were common, though not usually very effective; it was an age where superstition was rife, faith paramount, and Charles himself a devoted son of the Church. (ibid.: 119)

It is now that the question of clothes arises. How was she to travel? They were to travel 250 miles of war-torn country to meet the Dauphin. She wore clothes taken from a servant but later on, it would be a mail of gold.

She arrived at Chinon with short black hair, dressed in a black tunic. She had travelled safely in the company of the gentlemen soldiers De Metz and Poulengy who slept side by side with her, never desiring her 'by reason of the virtue they divined in her' (Sackville-West 2001: 110).

Vita Sackville-West (2001) and Thomas Keneally (1991), realistically portray her as peasant and sturdy, and both are quite preoccupied with the physical aspects of her being. She wept continuously, ate sparingly usually bread soaked in watery wine (a representation no doubt of her continual longing to hear mass). They describe her ability to wear heavy armour and even to sleep in it; to hold a sword and yet not use it, corroborating the phallic symbol of the unused sword with her own bound virginity. Yet, Keneally raises the other question of what Joan felt, and running through the subtext of *Blood Red, Sister Rose* is the question of her desire, her longing which had to be controlled for love and sex so that France could be free. By playing upon Joan's emotions when she whips prostitutes out of camp or when she promises a waiting wife the assured life and return of her husband from war, Keneally underlines that celibacy does not mean an absence of desire. It burns in her like a flame, which must consume her, and in identifying with Christ, she becomes through her consent a sacrificial victim which allows Charles to attain his kingdom. This prophecy of her death, both King and Maid understand.

Georges Duby (1977) has shown how the 11th century saw the decline of kingship in France, as the knights, marauding and chivalrous, gained power. The crusades became the symbol of the fusion of church and state, where the loot of war was given to the church. The churches became richer, and Christ became King. The churches grew larger, more dominant. So, for Joan, the 'sacredness' of kingship echoed the divine kingship of Jesus. Rheims was where Charles, the dispossessed, would be crowned. In this very symbolic moment of uniting kingship and Christ, Charles is displayed as a victim, for whom Joan was a logical substitute, as she questioned the hierarchies as given in the estate system. She a woman, united through war, king, knight and peasant—and the Inquisition and the violence of the clerics against this attempted homogenisation resulted in her death. She showed that the conventional opposition between the haves and have-nots disappeared when it came to nationalism. The peasants who were used to the exploitation and death of the countryside would now ride into war with her and a legion of aristocracies to rid France of the English. She would be the arc: the bend in the river, the bridge, the ship, the church, becoming every symbol of safety and sustenance that a prophetic virgin could offer. At this very moment, the maid becomes the meeting point of town and country, the nucleus that collapses the Estate System in such a way that medieval Christianity, patriarchy, textual and theological power are all as much under siege as the citadels of the English. Prophecy is more dangerous to conservative structures than witchcraft, and Joan had to be transformed from being heroic to be merely misguided so that she could be punished.

Rheims is the turning point. Once Charles is crowned king, he loses interest in Joan, and the rest follows as systematically and deliberately as murder. Joan's voices, having accomplished their mission, logically clamour for the sacrifice. Blood must be spilt; this is the semiotic consequence of her amenorrhea. Even in death by fire, however, her heart and her guts did not burn or atrophy according to the legend but running with blood were thrown into the river.

Thus, for two years, briefly, Joan broke the boundaries between what was characterised as the implicit features of the estate system: religious/warrior/production functions. In her being, worship, combat and labour were fused. What had justified their existence as separate categories were their functions. Joan showed that she, a woman could collapse all of them and be victorious. What was then the basis of her prophecy? It was an understanding of structures, roles, events, circumstances and the will to act upon these. Intuition and reason combined fearlessly and communicated itself in the clarity of her position, her speech. A peasant, a woman led a king and won for him a crown. The strategy lay in her belief that God existed, and that she had a will. Both existed autonomously and in relation to each other and gave her the courage to face the fire.

And yet, despite the miracles accompanying her death, is the understanding that she was a woman, afraid, cold, isolated, confused. And it is to a description of these last months that I shall now return.

Vita Sackville-West writes that the conclusions of the trial were preordained. All the large and impressive structures of medievalism and orthodoxy ranged against her: the Holy Catholic Church, the Court of the Inquisition and the University of Paris. One cardinal, 6 bishops, thirty-two bachelors of theology, 7 doctors of medicine, and 3 others were present to interrogate Joan (Sackville-West 2001: 287). She was, thus, a prisoner of great importance. She was alone, illiterate and tired after eight months of captivity. Her voice came through this anguish with absolute clarity, and reports say that she had a beautiful voice, a womanly voice: 'Do you consider yourself to be in a state of grace?' they questioned her, and she answered, 'If I am not, may God put me there, if I am may He keep me in it' (ibid.: 290).

It was a religious conclave, to decide whether she was a witch. She knew of the biases, and she was reported to have told Beauvais: 'Oh, you write the things which are against me, but not the things which are in my favour' (Sackville-West 2001: 293). She handled the Inquisition with the same intensity and impertinence that had characterised her military strategy—her ability to cut into the heart of the problem of tactical warfare.

Joan had begun the proceedings of the trial with the same trenchant and obdurate courage for which her captaincy at Orleans had made her famous. 'Perhaps you may ask me things I will not tell you' (ibid.: 296). This applied particularly to the Revelations which she would tell no other person, even if her head was to be cut off. They accepted this modified promise to tell the truth and nothing but the truth but then proceeded to bombard her in such a way as to confuse her, to dodge from one problem to another, hoping that she would contradict herself. Her voices had appeared even the day before she came to court.

> 'The voices told me to answer boldly.' (She repeated this sentence four times).
>
> 'How do you know that it is Saint Catherine and Saint Margaret who talk to you,' they asked.
>
> 'I have told you often enough that they are Saint Catherine and Saint Margaret—believe me if you like.'
>
> 'Does St Catherine speak English?'
>
> 'Why should she speak English as she is not on the English side?'
>
> 'What did St. Michael look like when he appeared to you? Was he naked?'
>
> 'Do you think our Lord has nothing to dress him in?'
>
> 'Had he any hair?'
>
> 'Why should it have been cut-off?' (ibid.: 300)

Joan had insisted on the reality of her revelations, and that was enough for the Court to indict her.

Having settled the significance of hearing voices whom they did not believe to be sacred, they focused on her male dress. Joan herself says contemptuously to the courts that dress was a small thing, among the smallest. The rationality of dressing like a man was that she ran less danger of rape than if she went about dressed as a woman. This secularism was thought to be abominable. The Inquisition held on to deuteronomy for advice on attire, and to Paul (I Corinthian, XI) for legitimating women's long hair as her crowning glory. Jeanne saw herself as Jesus's sister, who systematically broke the rules of the orthodox in order to lead the peasants and artisans against the close-knit hegemony of Pontius Pilate, Publicans and Pharisees.

They asked her, 'Since you ask to hear Mass, would it not be more seemly that you should hear it in women's clothes? Would you rather take woman's clothes and hear Mass or retain man's clothes and not hear it?'

She answered, 'Guarantee that I shall hear it if I dress as a woman, and then I will answer.'

The examiner gave the promise.

> And what would you say, if I had sworn and promised our King not to abandon this dress? Nevertheless I answer you, have a dress made for me, reaching the ground, without a train, and give it to me to wear at Mass; then on my return, I will resume the one I have. (Sackville-West 2001: 303)

For her, the counsel of voices was the one to whom she gave legitimacy and she substantially proved thereby that private judgement, will, intuition and revolution were more important to her than the Association of Believers called the Church—and this individualism was seen to be the power of the witch, to contest the collectivity for individual profit. The nation as secular, a composition of differences was so clear in her articulation, as well as in her aim and motivation; but it was not a valid desire in the medieval age when state and religion were thus combined. This is why Bernard Shaw (1978) calls her Protestant because it is indeed an early voice of direct encounter with God mediated by voices of angel and saint. She loved the church, but her politics was profoundly located in the freedom of spirit. Yet as Shaw remarks, this will to freedom was never arbitrary, it was conditioned in the understanding of the divine. Joan's answer is implicitly that of complete trust and a cerebrality characteristic of prophecy. Shaw describes this attitude with the verse 'Though he slay me, yet will I trust in Him; but I will maintain my own way before Him.' Vita Sackville-West records that when threatened by the fire, Joan said, 'I will say no more about that. Were I to see the fire, I would still say all that I have said, and would not do otherwise.' The clerk wrote in the margins 'Superba Responsa' (Sackville-West 2001: 307).

One of the most curious turns of the trial is the so-called 'invention'. On 27 February 1431, the judges asked her if they had seen an angel above the king's head when she first recognised him and gave the sign of her potential warriorhood. Joan replied, 'By our Lady, if there was one, I was unaware of it and did not see it' (Sackville-West 2001: 309).

By 10 March 1431, she said that 'there was an angel, she curtsied to him, went down on her knees, and took-off her cap'. 13 March saw her elaborating the story further, for as she was probably exhausted by the Inquisition's desire to hear a story, she invented it. It is a gauche and muddled story for according to her, the angel brought the crown through the door to the King (a distance 'the length of a Lance'). She follows the angel into the room and said to the King, 'Sire, here is your sign, take it.' She believed by the time she produces this version that other people had seen the crown (ibid.: 311).

What Sackville-West has called an invention, or at best an allegory, Marina Warner describes as the substitutability of metaphorical language. A king was not a king without a crown given to him through God's intermediaries on earth. The angel at Chinon, whom she first said gave the Dauphin the sign of his crown, and the archbishop of Rheims, of whom she spoke later, are in this respect interchangeable. When Charles was crowned at Rheims, which had been Joan's greatest desire, she wept and said,

> Gentle King, now the will of God has been accomplished who wished that I should raise the siege of Orleans and bring you to this city of Rheims to receive your solemn consecration, showing that you are the true King, that you are he to whom the Kingdom of France should belong. (Warner 1991: 70, 72)

Why was Rheims so important for Joan?

It was Saturday, 16 July 1429. Rheims had its foundation stone laid in 1212, and through the years of war had interrupted it since 1381, work was resumed in 1427 and was nearing completion. Lacking spires, for the occasion enormous fleur-de-lis were substituted. The stained glass had been present for almost a century. Bishops, kings and queens crowned and sceptred were represented in the nave. This church was destroyed in 1917, bombed by the cruelty of another war.

Auguste Rodin wrote a book called the *Cathedrals of France*, first published in 1914, in which Rheims is described, and I turn briefly there, in conclusion. The set of notes are a pilgrimage, to all the great churches, an attempt to inscribe in writing what was to be destroyed by war. Rodin wrote:

> How masterpieces are masterpieces: I know and what joy I have in knowing, in exactly the same way great souls are great souls. It is by rising to what is indispensable in the expression of their thoughts and feelings that both man and artist worthily fulfil themselves. A masterpiece is of necessity a very simple thing which comprises, I repeat, only the essential. (1965: 7)

Further, he says, 'One learns much by studying sequences, correspondences and analogies—for the same law governs moral and emotional life' (ibid.: 11, 12). The cathedrals of France are the collaboration between human beings and nature and need we say it, the sacred. He writes, 'The Cathedral is a synthesis of our country. I repeat: the rocks, forests, gardens, Northern sun, all these our condensed in this gigantic body. All of our France is in our Cathedrals, just as all of Greece is summarised in the Parthenon' (ibid.: 14).

As Rodin enters one of these churches at the triumphal arch, he sees a little girl and describes her as 'a lily of the valley in flower' to whom sensual pleasure is yet a stranger: 'If this young girl knew how to look and to see, she would recognise her portrait in all the portals of our Gothic churches, for she is the incarnation of our style, of our art, of our France' (ibid.: 50).

Does he realise that he is remembering Joan? He describes her as having simplicity, integrity, tenderness, intelligence (ibid.: 51).

For Rodin, beauty exists only if it has a conscience and Rheims conveys this. 'Rheims Cathedral evokes the enlarged figure of a woman kneeling' (ibid.: 161, 162). Further, in the next line, he says, 'I observe that the cathedral rises like flames.' Then he speaks of the bells—'the great voice of the bells'. Joan, when in power, would ask for church bells to ring for her as she prayed for half an hour at a time. Somewhere, as Rodin goes deeper in, it becomes a forest, dark and impenetrable—he understands terror, fear of being 'closed in' just as Joan must have when she jumped from her prison and neither escaped nor died. Rodin recollects his panic:

> I advance. It is an enchanted forest. The tops of the five columns are no longer visible. The pale lights that cross the balustrades horizontally create informal dance. Here one is in heaven by day and hell by night.... But the horror controls itself, imposes order, and this order reassures us. (1965: 183)

Joan then, her life and work have become like the churches of France, as permanent across destruction, myths of the meeting between secular and sacred, nature and culture, male and female. She is the church, not as Virgin Wife or as Virgin Mother, but as Virgin Sister. Perhaps, finally, she is like the Arc of the Rainbow, refracted light, always difficult to understand, but synthesising difference in a complex way.

There are two ambiguities that I have not been able to handle here. One is her closeness to Gilles de Rais, the original Blue Beard, a heroic soldier and sadist lover. They fought together, knew each other well. Keneally captures the understanding that lay between them, that Joan always understood the possibilities of evil, but acted instead like a spiritual catalyst.

Second, there are the prostitutes. Joan hated them, drove them out, broke her sacred and prophetic sword on the back of one of them. Legend has it that she lost her powers after that. Was this the mythic way of resolving the dualisms of morality?

In the next essay, I look at the debates around language, and the subtexts of colonialisms of various kinds, where the individual as both biological as well as symbolic being, is located within the social structure. Mission history gives us an anvil from where we look at the questions of marginality and survival of the lone traveller on distant shores, bringing with him the multiverse documents of his identity in the search for belonging. In the essay 'Ringeltaube and the Natives: 1813 and the Narratives of Distress', I will draw the attention of the reader to mission-history debates to show that it was the Danish Mission which first began the substantial introduction of English education, and through the Church Missionary Society, the relationship between English education and the Indians became compounded. The relation between

English education, mission history and secular education has been dealt with by me earlier in several essays on sociologising missionary history (1998, 2000, 2007). In this essay, I discuss the biographies that went into the pioneering work of translation and compounding of grammars and dictionaries in local languages, where now-forgotten figures appear in dramatic detail when the sociologist or the historian abstracts lives from the archives.

The curious thing about writing fiction, or in this case 'probable history' as Natalie Zemon Davis calls it is that total historical veracity is never a focus or a prescribed virtue. This is a very different mode of history writing from the Collingwood perspective of the detective historian, where accuracy is the ultimate objective goal. Probable histories work with the assumption that subjectivities are archetypes. What is more centrally focused is that ideas should be paramount—new ways of thinking about the past and the present are demarcated. Nothing more is expected.

References

Duby, Georges. 1977. *Chivalrous Society.* London: Edward Arnold.

———. 1981. *Age of the Cathedrals: Art and Society 930-1420.* Chicago: Chicago University Press.

———. 1983. *The Knight, the Lady and the Priest.* Harmonsdworth: Penguin.

Keneally, Thomas. 1991. *Blood Red Sister Rose.* London: Sceptre.

Kunze, Michael. 1987. *Highroad to the State: A Tale of Witchcraft.* Chicago: University of Chicago Press.

O'Keefe, Daniel Lawrence. 1983. *Stolen Lightning: The Social Theory of Magic.* New York: Vintage.

Rodin, August. 1965. *Cathedrals of France.* London: Hamlyn.

Sackville-West, Vita. 2001. *St. Joan.* New York: Grove Press.

Shaw, Bernard. 1978. *Saint Joan.* Delhi: Orient Longman.

Visvanathan, Susan. 1997. 'Representing Joan of Arc'. *India International Quarterly* 24 (4).

Warner, Marina. 1991. *Joan of Arc.* London: Vintage.

Zemon-Davis, Natalie. 1975. *Society and Culture in Early Modern France.* Stanford: Stanford University Press.

5

Ringeltaube and the Natives: 1813 and the Narratives of Distress

This essay is concerned with the Tranquebar mission as a site of spiritual striving. Whose striving we might ask, and what were the motives of such men as Ringeltaube, whose name means curiously enough, some kind of wood pigeon with a ring around its neck. One can well imagine the curious task of the missionary, constantly struggling in this double-edged identity—he is out in the woods and must carry messages! There's a constant dialectic between missionaries and natives, a process of adaptation or repulsion, the historical details of which I have chronicled in earlier essays (Visvanathan 1993, 1998, 2000, 2007). This essay is concerned specifically with describing the quest for religious exaltation on the part of the missionary, and the sense of distress he feels when the two book-ends of his monologue are unreceptive. I speak here of the missionary board of directors, on the one hand, and the natives on the other. It is true, that the anxieties faced by a man like Granges (he died at the age of thirty-one) are exactly about the questions of physical survival, and the problems faced by Ringeltaube are about the dignity of the missionaries' daily work and studies, but they merge into one voice in the intensity of striving to spread the word of the Gospel.[1] The descriptive entries on the diary in the SOAS archives, London, are as follows:

1 I offer here some of the evidence, which I collected from the School of Oriental and African Studies (SOAS) archives, London in 1997. The materials were in a box, not then on microfilm, and I feel grateful for the opportunity to have read them in the original, remembering even now, the thick edge of ink on brittle paper and the curlews of the elegant script of a man for whom English must have been a foreign language.

Box South India 1808, a Missionary Pioneer 1807–1810

> The diary of Augustus des Granges of Vizagapatam
> Written between May 1807–June 1810, the year of his death at 31.
> Business to be transacted
> To pour or impart merit to another.
> Sailed with Ringeltaube from Copenhagen
> Arrived Dec 5, 1804, Tranquebar
> July 1805 went to Vizaqapatam
> June 12 1810—died there.

What were the problems that poor Granges faced? Let us read his diary for its description of life and times in the early years of the Tranquebar Mission, significant because it asserts that he sailed with Ringeltaube from Copenhagen, arriving in Tranquebar on 5 December 1804.

Journal of the Missionaries Cran and Des Granges from 26 June to 8 September

> Since we enclosed our last journal which we left with the Brethren at Madras to be forwarded to Europe, the Lord has continued to deal graciously with us. He has placed us in a situation where an extensive field of labour presents itself to our view, sufficient to occupy the most diligent endeavour of a thousand missionaries in one language. This makes the place in which we are of unspeakable importance for a Missionary station as the language can very easily be attained here, from whence missionaries may proceed to any part of the interior. We should have continued to study the Telinga language at Madras had we not been informed from good authority that the dialect spoken there differed considerably from that spoken to the North and in the interior. This we have since found to be true and think it would not be good for Missionaries destined to labour in the Telinga county to study the language of Madras. (2)

Early in his missionary career, Granges had stumbled on the tensions that exist in South India, where language subtleties were at the heart of identity and difference. Susan Bayly's work *Saints, Goddesses and Kings* (1989) has shown how boundaries, as we recognise them, were not as sharply defined and that linguistic difference was one of the clearest symbols of the pre-modern period. Granges writes in his diary:

> June 26. Spent the day with our brethren .... Received from them the Magazines, Missionary transactions etc; which were sent us by the Society, for which we return our grateful acknowledgement. These will be of great service to us as many Gentlemen derive much pleasure from the perusal of them. The good effects likely to be produced by lending them to persons of influence in this country we trust will lead our friends to send us two or three copies by every opportunity. Gave the two brethren our Public Journal to preserve. Wrote to Mr Ringeltaube of the arrival of the brethren, enclosed the letters directed to him from his friends in England, together with the general letter from the Directors, and requested him to inform us which of the publications he preferred, promising to convey them to him on receiving an answer. (Bayly 1989: 3)

What was the relation of the Missionary Society to these men who had left home and family and travelled to south India? They would have got off the ship at Allapuzha (Alleppey). The Missionary Register (MR) for 1818 describes the port thus:

MR March for 1818: From the Introduction of Editorial

> Allepie is situated about 60 miles north of Quilon, and 120 of Cape Comorin. It is the principal, if not the only place, at which the East India Company's ships call to take in pepper and other spices. The soil is a deep bed of sand, occasioned, as it is supposed, by the sea returning, which it does very fast. It has retired several yards within the last four or five months. Indeed the whole of the coast, from Quilon to Cochin, is a kind of narrow island separated from the mainland by what is called the backwater. There is no harbour, but a mud bank of about ten miles in length from north to south, and extending three or four miles out to sea, protects the anchorage. It is said that a vessel may lie at anchor the whole of the monsoon without danger.
>
> The inhabitants of Allepie are numerous; some say between 13,000 and 14,000, others many more. Allepie itself, therefore, appears to be a fine field for usefulness, especially when we consider that its

> inhabitants consist of Moormen in general, of Parsees, Gentoos and Roman Catholics.
>
> Roman Catholics are numerous, especially among the non-caste Portuguese. Colonel Munro remarks on this subject.
>
> Allepie is quite central with respect to the Syrians and the Roman Catholics. It is a large commercial place, inhabited by men of all countries and religions, and there are scarcely any Brahmins or Pagodas. (100)

Colonel Munro, a friend of the missionaries, would hope to establish a mission base there. That story is recorded by me in *The Christians of Kerala* (1993). Although the tenacity of those who saw in evangelisation the principles of a homogenised empire is yet to occur (Visvanathan 2000), the statutory concern of administrators was not present during the time of Granges and Ringeltaube, and it would cause them physical and emotional torment. Clearly, in 1805, nobody recognised them, nobody wanted them, and they were hard placed regarding their daily survival. Granges' diary is indicative of how hard it all is! There were contesting mission stations, the people were completely ignorant of the benefits to be had from converting to Christianity and the weather was hot! There were different languages to be learnt! Granges writes in his diary, preserved in Box South India 1808, School of Oriental and African Studies, Church Missionary Society Archives, London:

Box South India 1808, a Missionary Pioneer 1807–1810

> In the town where we now reside there are above 20,000 inhabitants all perishing for lack of knowledge. Within a few miles of us on all sides, there are numbers of large villages where thousands of heathen living in the grossest idolatry claim our piety and compassion. This place is nearly central which makes it the most favourable for branching out into any part of the circars. We have hundreds of miles right or left of us where we may labour with freedom and where we shall have no Brother to complain that we interfere with their mission. It being on the coast and continually cooled by the sea breeze makes it advantageous for the health of Missionaries on their first entrance into the country. By having the Missionary station on the coast they will necessarily be

> detained there a year or more learning the language which will tend to inure them to the climate without endangering their health.

He describes in his diary that when Brother Cary and his associates came to India, they had to 'remain concealed', but in 1805, the directors of the East India Company have been persuaded to be protective of the missionaries.

By 1810, Granges is dead, and we shall look at Ringeltaube's printed declarations about his circumstances in the Missionary Register of 1813 to find out the circumstances of missionary life. He says, for 1815 in his journal published by the Missionary Register as:

Ringeltaube for Travancore South India 1813–1816, 7 January 1813–20 January 1816

> July 1. The famine beginning to rage utterly. I found I must devise some employment for the poorest of our Christians in that part of the country where I lived. I could discover no scheme to commensurate with my small means but that of planting and watering several thousand trees. Many have survived the horrible drought and I have devoted them for the future support of widows and orphans. Such measure attached the people to the church. Where widows and orphans are neglected, the death of the father in general carries the whole of his offspring back among the idolatrous relations.
>
> July 28. Got our associates official letter dated Jan the 15th, 1814, so full of paternal kindness that it did attract me anew to them in preference to any other connexion however respectable. Notwithstanding I could not help being wounded at heart by one paragraph which is the following, 'The directors who while they propose to you spiritual comforts would not be mindful of your temporal supply, apprehending that your stated income may not be sufficient, define that you would henceforth draw as long as you see if needful, for one hundred and fifty pounds a year, and not hundred as before and they will take care to inform Messrs Hunter Hay and Co. to honour your drafts to that amount. The Director will also continue to refund such expenses given to catechists as you see fit according to former directions.' (16)

> The words as long as you see it needful proved a snare to me in as much they undoubtedly implied that I as a labourer was to be the judge whether I should take my hire. If so I ought to be likewise the judge, whether I should continue my services. Now the longer I have considered the subject the more I am convinced that under all existing circumstances it would be best for the Society the Mission and myself to resign my work into other hands. This has not been a hasty but a most deliberate resolution which more and more gained strength by all meditations, prayers and concerning Providences. It is plain that our society by enjoining the duty of ceasing to be burdensome to them at some future period or other entertains a fallacious hope that this is to take place. It is also plain from what has been officially communicated to me that whilst our society is planning some new and expensive missions the question has been seriously discussed whether some of the missions now under their patronage should not be given up. I have no doubt when our directors shall feel the whole weight of expenses that must shortly come upon them if their East India Missions are to become at last effective, they must throw up some of their less interesting establishment. And most likely that in Travancore might appear sufficiently provided for in order to bear no longer on the Missionary Societies purse. Such considerations made me anxious concerning my lot in old age. The fate of Mission under so uncertain auspices and finally the honour of our society when dire necessity shall force them, against their wishes to reduce their expenditure! Consequently, when afterwards Providences occurred which seemed to be so many hints from above that should suffer the mission to pass into other hands I more easily surmounted my scruples and feeling on this occasion than I could have done if our society had pledged themselves unconditionally to my support for life. All societies that wish to have faithful servants make it a pleasure, duty, to stand by their messengers, their widows and orphans without presenting similar prospects of ultimate destitution. (16)

Ringeltaube writes of the generosity and invariable protection of Maj. General Macaulay and Col Munro which were of the greatest assistance:

> The former gave me 1000 rupees to build churches just when I wanted the money, and without the seasonable gift, my Directors having not yet made any provision, the Mission in Travancore would have died in the cradle. The latter held his hand over me when a less indulgent character would have created much uneasiness. May the Lord reward them and build them houses, as to the midwives in Egypt, who feared God and would not give their aid to the Pharoah's exterminating decrees.
>
> But all this would have signified nothing at all if our Society had not allowed me a stated salary and a gratuity. The salary enabled me to stick to my proper calling, to be a missionary and nothing but a missionary. Had I been obliged to live by a boarding school, it would have required the whole man to do justice to that. Directors will find that Missionaries who keep boarding school cannot rove about to convert the heathen. To act as Minister in Government pay at an outstation is also a confining business. A missionary that must sell his liberty on Lord's Day for 25 star Pagodas a month is truly to be pitied. The same may be said of all employments that are binding. But a missionary who derives all his support from his society is at liberty to go and seek Christ's sheep where they are, to superintend them constantly and gradually to form them into decent flock. Without this close superintendence our sheep in Travancore would have remained as wild as mountain goats. I therefore entreat our Directors to make it a settled thing that their missionaries might not to entangle themselves in the affairs of this life. (Missionary Register, *Church Missionary Society, 1813–1816*: 38)

How painful for Ringeltaube to describe the poverty in which the missionaries were constrained to live out their lives, knowing that they were living on the charity of their patrons. One is reminded of the Weberian discussion of the well-paid mandarins of China or the well-fed Brahmins of India and the strong contrast that the pecuniary catechist here provides. Dennis Hudson has very early in the debates around missionary history, referred to the differences in wages between European missionaries and native ones (Visvanathan 1993). It is in this context that those residents inclined to support missionary work, such as Munro, were such heroes to the missionaries as the Missionary Register for February 1815 proclaims:

> In Travancore the Resident Col. Munro, not only assures us of his patronage of Missionaries but has actually written to have two sent to him.
>
> In a word could you send me a dozen missionaries by the very next fleet, I could dispose of them instantly, I trust on the entire satisfaction of the Committee .... (82)

In November 1816, the Missionary Register records that:

> The letters of Major Munro in a reply contain important information. He readily accepted the invitation to become a member of the corresponding committee, offering a liberal donation of one hundred pagodas, and a monthly subscription of five pagodas during his stay in India. (462)

By 1817, as the Missionary Register for March 1818 records, Munro had even provided land and house to the missionaries, at Alleppey with the promise of a church. Colonel Munro writes to Mr Thompson under the date of 22 January 1817:

> One object is to establish sure foundations, what I may term the Head Quarters of the Travancore Mission, and I think that Allepie is, in every view, the best place for the purpose.
>
> A large house and garden occupied by the Missionaries have been presented to the Mission, as a free gift in perpetuity, by the Government of Travancore. I am very desirous that a respectable Protestant Church should be erected in the garden, where there is ample room for it, and a burying ground appropriated. I have put a subscription in circulation, in order to obtain funds for building the Church. I have obtained from different sources, about 1500 rupees, and this sum, with such further aids as we may procure will provide for the erection of the Church.
>
> A school has already been opened by the Missionaries and in a few months, we shall have at Allepie a good Church and School, and in fact, all the foundation of a Mission.
>
> At this place and also perhaps at Cotym, I propose that all the new Missionaries, who may arrive, shall fix their residence, and prosecute their studies, until they learn the language. (MR 1818: 101)

Let us return to the travails of Ringeltaube, which are chronicled for 1815 in the Missionary Register. He has conquered the problem of learning the language, but he says his listeners are deaf. He writes:

> October the 3rd. Set out for Palamcottah to try a change of air which so restored me for a season without however giving me back that strength of voice and limb which is necessary to a Missionary who is continually travelling among a people that is very hard of hearing—then another great Providence appeared. I was greatly involved in my circumstances when unexpectedly Messrs Hunter Hay and Co sending me an account and stated that our Society owed me Star pagodas 270 in consequence of particular items which I might draw for. For this I sincerely praise the Lord, whose opportunity is invariably our extremity. (MR 1813–1816: 19, 20)
>
> October the 22nd. Set out for the Western congregations. People began to flock to the Church since I got the fields. My churches being extremely damp and windy, I soon got my asthma with a dry cough that tortured me both day and night. Without waiting for Colonel Munro's answer, I wrote off myself to missionaries A and R inviting them to take charge of this mission. I used every argument that was consistent with truth and sent a copy to the Resident. (ibid.: 20)

So much ill health and suffering! Brijraj Singh's sensitive and very readable biography of another and better-known missionary *The First Protestant Missionary to India, Bartholomaeus Ziegenbalg (1683–1719)* discusses the grievous illness that Ziegenbalg suffered and describes that he was treated with a potion of iron-filings which did not cure him but indeed killed him. Ziegenbalg had arrived before the famine and had commented on the 'greenness of the land and the excellent irrigation system which ensured a plentiful supply of water' (Singh 1999: 45).

The language referred to as Malabarese is a general term, as is the description of the land. Singh writes:

> Ziegenbalg was well aware that Tranquebar was located in the land of the Tamils, or, as he called them the Damuls. Nevertheless, in accordance with the European custom of that time, he always referred to the area as Malabar. We should not confuse his Malabar with

> India's southwest coast or with Kerala, remembering every time we come across this word in his writing to mentally substitute it with the modern Tamil Nadu, Malabarians (or occasionally Damulians) with the Tamil people, and Malabrick or Damul with the Tamil language. (Singh 1999: 45)

While the later Protestant missionaries had the support of the residents, Ziegenbalg was aware of how hard life would be without money. He had to pay his tutors and amanuensis. Tamil manuscripts were extremely expensive to buy. Schools cost money. The converts needed financial support. The building of the Jerusalem Church was paid for almost entirely from the pockets of Plutschau and Ziegenbalg (ibid.: 28).

As Dennis Hudson had argued in his doctoral thesis on Tamil Catechists (1970), the costs of missionary living were higher than the native catechists had. Brijraj Singh shows us why:

> When he went to Madras in 1711, he alternated between three modes of transport: walking on foot, being carried in a palanquin, and riding on a horse. This meant that he had to take along with him palanquin bearers and an ostler to look after his horse, as well as a cook, a water bearer, porters, and a personal assistant. (ibid.: 29)

Singh also quotes from Stephen Neil's monumental study of the history of Christianity in India that at the end of his career, Ziegenbalg had employed a Danish teacher, a Portuguese teacher, two Tamil teachers, a matron for the girl's school, a Tamil catechist, a Portuguese catechist, two female cooks, a matron for the Portuguese girls, a house servant who also acted as a gravedigger, two water carriers, two gardeners, a workman, two Tamil clerks, one accountant, a doctor and a washerman. He had a wife, whom he never mentioned in his memoirs, though he had known her from his youth, and children, most of whom tragically died, except a son who came back in adulthood to India as a director of the sugar factory in Fredericknagar (the present-day Serampore). His widow married the Deputy Governor of Tranquebar and went back to Europe (ibid.: 39).

Ziegenbalg had had his enemies. There was Wendt, who on the board of mission in Denmark, thought Zieganbalg was very materialistic, and ought to be emulating the life of the ancient apostles. Ziegenbalg had a wife and children with him, and he ate European food and subsidised the life and death rituals of the poor, the Sudras and the Pariahs, whom he had brought into the Protestant church. Consider the expenses, Brijraj Singh suggests, of learning the Tamil language:

> During the period that Ziegenbalg was at work on his dictionaries, he devoted at least eight hours daily to language learning activities. In a letter of 22nd August 1708, he tells us that every morning he reviewed previously learned Tamil vocabulary from 7 to 8 o'clock, then from 8 am to noon, he read Tamil texts with the help of a poet and up to six amanuenses. From 3 to 5 in the afternoon he again read Tamil in a similar way; then in the evening from 7 to 8 he got another reader to read Tamil books out loud to him but now the books were chosen for their simple style such as people needed in their daily converse. (Singh 1999: 71)

What Ringeltaube considers is just the same concern for survival and learning, his own and that of the people whom he works for! These early missionaries, as D. Dennis Hudson notes, were interesting for their ability to set up spaces for cultural dialogue, which were perhaps not as stridently hierarchical as the British missionaries of the latter half of the 19th century (Hudson 2000; Visvanathan 2000). Thus, the Halle Tranquebar church provides us with important insights into the nature of the early history of Christian missions in India. They suggested as Henriette Bugge reports, 'an attitude to non-European peoples which was strongly influenced by the enlightenment but which was destined soon to be suppressed by the Protestant missionary ethic' (1994: 56).

The task of anthropology is to record! Thus, it is interesting that the missionary's accounts had been the mainstay of so much arm-chair anthropology. It is impossible to imagine Emile Durkheim's classic *The Elementary Forms of the Religious Life* (1965) without being concerned with sources. The impetus was always to presume, in the era following emancipation, that the colonist and administrator's reports could be replaced with a new objective form. The history of missionary studies is as concerned with the 'otherness' of those who are within the fold as Gauri Viswanathan (1998) describes it, as much as with those who are outside of it. Mainstream sociology has presumed that within its methodology itself, we know the assumptions of what we construe as objective behaviour. However, the parameters of our science continue to change, and new missionaries appear beckoning the way to greater objectivity. I see this as an interesting play of biases, and it has been recorded in mainstream literature over and over again. If bias and its controlled impetus allow marginalised individuals to communicate what was previously silenced, it is all for the good.

Gifts given by missionaries to natives is one framework with which the analyses must proceed. Marcel Mauss' work, *The Gift* (1969) is significant, in terms of the reading of the term 'gift'. This anthropological classic deals with the attributes of gift-giving as reciprocity, redistribution, contract, chicanery, bribe, taxation, tithe, donation, alms and blackmail. One could use flattery, fear and withdrawal of privileges, or giving of them as part of this ensemble. It is useful in this context to view anthropology from the perspectives of similar such exercises of mapping of identity for archivalisation as well as the pursuit of development. We would have to remember the gifts of tobacco in the simplest instance that Evans-Pritchard makes to the Nuer in order to glean important information, and in the other instance, the death of Michelle Rosaldo in the field. Renato Rosaldo's book *Culture and Truth* (1989) is essentially a methodological text on love and death among practitioners in the field. James Clifford's classic text on contemporary anthropological method has a photograph of Marcel Griaule photographing Dogon territory, and while doing so, his ankles are held by his colleague, to avert the danger of him falling over the cliff (Clifford 1988). Anthropologists like George Stocking are concerned with the moral community that anthropologists are forced to conform with, their every action being read by others, in the display of the tension between subjectivity and objectivity. Between love (for the discipline) and the possibility of death (an occupational and existential hazard in every walk of life!) lie according to the analysts, the question of initiation.

This initiation into the customs of the people, in order to understand them, implies the suspension of the believing subject, but equally involves the dialogic attitude of empathy. This is in strong contrast to the missionaries of Christianity, who always communicate the antagonism to the other's perspective, and the desire to transform the subjects to their own path. A distinction must be made between the Gospels and the Letters, for the term 'the Bible says' is a generalising imperative. If the whole is to be taken, then the injunction to have only one tunic and one pair of sandals must be taken as seriously as the command to spread forth and evangelise. Should the Church, wherever it is, take this seriously many of the accusations of aggrandisement and mission would disappear. Jesus in the marketplace of the synagogue then becomes less of an abstraction! Let us look at Ringeltaube's witness to the dire straits of the missionary in the early years of evangelical enterprise. He wrote:

> Still of greater importance was my gratuity. This enabled me to exercise a good deal of charity in as much as it relieved me from travelling expenses. Postage, building, repainting, planting, watering and other disbursements are considerable, being very necessary and helpful to the Christians. Through the straightness and uncertainty of my income, I was obliged to remain unmarried. Accordingly, I wanted little, and could (ibid.: 38) maintain the character of a charitable Father to his distressed children. It can be proved that every missionary who had some command of money and took charity into his plan has had more or less success. Whilst a needy or saving man could never get on, I had a command of 200 pounds (my salary included) which providence led me to carry to a different country—where I was perhaps the richest and most charitable man for many miles around. All this money 200 pounds per annum spent among my poor Christians either in wages or little charities to the sick, the aged, the helpless, the widows, the orphans. Where I lived the money went further than 400 pounds would have gone in a place where Europeans possessed of wealth and rank reside. At Madras, Vizag, Calcutta, Bellary, Pallamcottah, Tanjore, Trichinopally, this small sum would have availed nothing. Had I been married the case would also have been desperate, as I must have scraped together a trifle for my widow and orphans. That I must come to a resolution to exercise charity to my Christians the people taught me themselves. Some declared that formerly in Tinnevelly, Tanjore, Madras, much

> charity had been given and intimated that I purloined what was sent for their use. Others apostatized and sent me word, they had done so because in their bitter distress I did not assist them. I think they were not to be blamed. They see me every day eating a fowl with my rice. (I have positively eaten above 3,000 fowls in Travancore.) This is a luxury that they are startled at and dare not think above once a year. Whilst I thus feed like an epicure, I see them perish round about me with hunger and disease and button up my pocket without giving them the smallest gift. Can such a man love them? Can he be a teacher of a merciful God? It is positive that such a close being is hated by them and they shut their hearts and ears against his discourses. Let it not be said your Christians are Rice Christians and Hypocrites. Rice Christians certainly are, for all their bones, sinews, muscles, their blood and their brain is composed of Rice, the poor creatures have nothing else to eat. But not all of them are Hypocrites. True and distinguishing love makes no hypocrites, it carries an argument along with it. (Missionary Register 1813–1816: 39–40)

His sense of the relative condition of prosperity he found himself in is the basis of his identity as represented some 300 years later as being praiseworthy and noble. *Ringeltaube the Rishi* is the title of a book written about him by W. Robinson, published in 1902. Hans-Werner Gensichen, in a brief biographical note, describes him as one who was in 'total disregard of comfort and prestige'—this was to 'attract people to faith in Christ'. He convinced them to 'waive all views of temporal advantage and not to imagine that they would be exempt from the Cross' (Gensichen n.d.: 572).

Stephen Neil describes him as 'a man devout and humble but restless and volatile, who carried eccentricity to the point almost of absurdity' (Neil 1985: 323).

Yet, as Said writes in his brilliant collection of essays on *Exile*, that we contextualise the work of a writer from those things taken for granted, such as residence, nationality, a familiar locale, language, friends and the work of interpretation is to read the work and the worldly situation. He writes, 'For if you feel you cannot take for granted the luxury of long residence, habitual environment, native idiom, and you must somehow compensate for these things, what you write necessarily bears a unique freight of anxiety, elaborateness, perhaps even overstatement' (2001: xv). In this reading, the case of Ringeltaube's high-strung and desperate cries can be laid to rest as normal reactions to desperate conditions of work and life. In the next essay, I am concerned with how British colonialism is interpreted through archival materials pertaining to the mnemonics of power, how funds are accrued so that lodging for the administrators in Simla is obtained and organised.

Chapter 6 'Summer Hill: The Building of the Viceregal Lodge' takes the reader to how the British built a summer palace for the Viceroy and his retinue in Shimla. It had been the privilege of the colonial masters to look for hill stations where their officers and staff could go with their families to escape the intensity of heat in summer wherever they were. I show how complex the bureaucratic demands of the colonial office were in relation to the supply of men, materials and money. Of course, the women had an important task to be supportive to their husbands, and accompanied them, keeping diaries of the work that they did, and the observations that they made were immensely useful to archivists and the documentation of colonial legacies. I juxtapose a fictional account at the end of the essay which I wrote while in Shimla at a workshop on documentary and fiction writing. As a course instructor invited to a writing workshop by Rukmini Bhaya Nair I wished to show that when we work with legends or accounts drawn from memory about historic personages, we are fabricating. This does not limit its wide reach, as the reader can well distinguish between fact and fiction. However, fictional accounts, while not being history, nevertheless, work towards augmenting objective accounts and linear chronological histories.

References

Bayly, Susan. 1989. *Saints, Goddeses and Kings*. Cambridge: Cambridge University Press.

Bugge, Henriette. 1994. *Mission and Tamil Society*. Richmond: Curzon Press.

Clifford, James. 1988. *The Predicament of Culture*. Cambridge: Harvard University Press.

Durkheim, Emile. 1965. *The Elementary Forms of the Religious Life*. New York: Free Press.

Durkheim, Emile. 1973. *Moral Education*. New York: Free Press.

Ellerton and Henderson. Missionary Register, 1813–1816, 1817, 1818. London: L.B. Seeley.

Evans-Pritchard, E.E. 1974. *Nuer Religion*. Oxford: Oxford University Press.

Gensichen, Hans-Werner. (n.d.). 'Ringeltaube'. In *Biographical Dictionary of Christian Missions* by Gerald H. Anderson. New York: Simon and Schuster, Macmillan.

Hudson, D. Dennis. 1970. 'The Life and Times of H.A. Krishna Pillai, 1827–1900: A Study in the Encounter of Tamil Sri Vaisnavism and Evangelical Protestant Christianity in the 19th Century'. Unpublished PhD dissertation, Clairmont: Clairmont Graduate School.

———. 2000. *Protestant Origins in India, Tamil Evangelical Christians, 1706–1835*. Richmond: Curzon Press.

Mauss, Marcel. 1969. *The Gift*. Norfolk: Routledge and Kegan Paul.

Missionary Register. *Church Missionary Society, 1813–1816*. London: Ellerton and Henderson.

Neil, Stephen C. 1985. *A History of Christianity*. Cambridge: Cambridge University Press.

Rosaldo, Renato. 1989. *Culture and Truth*. Boston: Beacon Press.

Said, Edward W. 2001. *Reflections on Exile*. Delhi: Penguin.

Singh, Brijraj. 1999. *The First Protestant Missionary to India, Bartholomaeus Ziegenbalg (1683–1719)*. Delhi: Oxford University Press.

Stocking, George. 1985. *Observers Observed*. Wisconsin: University of Wisconsin Press.

Viswanathan, Gauri. 1998. *Outside the Fold, Conversion, Modernity and Belief*. Delhi: Oxford University Press.

Visvanathan, Susan. 1993. *Christians of Kerala: History, Belief and Ritual Among the Yakoba*. Madras: Oxford University Press.

———. 1998. *An Ethnography of Mysticism*. Shimla: Indian Institute of Advanced Study.

———. 2000. *The Homogeneity of Fundamentalism: British Colonialism in India in the 19th Century, in Studies in History*. Delhi: Sage Publications.

———. 2007. *Friendship, Interiority and Mysticism*. Delhi: Orient Blackswan.

6

Summer Hill: The Building of the Viceregal Lodge

Summer Hill, where Viceregal Lodge, a castle, calls in any number of tourists from all over India, with its narratives of the coexistence of past and present; October 2015.
© Author.

The glass house on Summer Hill, with its horticultural and botanical diversity in the hands of its gardeners; October 2015.
© Author.

My attempt here is to analyse for the reader, the sequence of purchase of land, electrification and costs of building the Viceregal Lodge, Summer Hill, Shimla. As a cultural anthropologist interested in questions of labour, I would like to highlight the problem of expenditure, and the problem of degradation of labour. In the first part, I use the conventional academic exercise of collage of primary and secondary materials to provide a view of the past, and its interlacing with our present. In the second part, I use 'fiction' to tell the same story, manoeuvring the reader to a different view, where description need not necessarily imply legitimation or consent, to rule or be ruled.

Purchase of Properties, Costs of Building and Electrification of the Viceregal Lodge

In a letter to the Marquis of Salisbury, who was Secretary of State for India, Lytton and his team wrote that the municipal committee of Shimla had been expanded for purposes of conservation and improvement. For this purpose, he said a new order of bureaucrats had been appointed, and these officers were primarily, one superintending engineer and two executive engineers with supporting staff, who were under the direct control of himself and his staff. These men were now busy checking the details of water and drainage projects and were pre-eminently hired to make sure that accommodation would be made ready for the 'coming season'. He adds that 'the general instructions to the Superintending Engineer will be found in our letter to that officer, No 383 M, dated November 7th, 1876, which is also one of the enclosures of this dispatch' (No. 34 Public Works 1877).

These houses and the other buildings on the estates which were planned would eventually serve for several of the public offices. In the meantime, until a residence for the Viceroy could be built, they were intent on making certain additions and alterations to the building called 'Peterhoff' at an estimated cost of about 10,000 rupees. Lytton argued that this would not only give a necessary increase to the accommodation that was required for the public offices but would, render the house more suitable and convenient for occupation. However, he continued:

> These additions and alterations will not however make 'Peterhoff' a really well arranged or suitable residence, and it is necessary to build an entirely new house, and as will be understood from the 3rd para of our Resolution, measures have been taken for securing the only eligible site which the limited space in Simla affords, and for purchase at a cost of about 7,000 rupees the surrounding private estate.
>
> The expenses connected with the arrangement will be in addition to the sums of 10,000 rupees and 50,000 rupees set down in the 3rd para of our new Despatch No I, dated 14th January 1876, as the probable outlay that may be anticipated on general sanitary improvements, public offices and clerks' quarters. The precise addition will be duly reported after the necessary plans and estimates have been submitted, but we may here notice that on the estates which we have acquired

> during the current and past years there are various houses (occupied for the most part by the Viceroy's staff) for which rents are paid, so that a considerable portion of the outlay incurred is even now remunerative.
>
> Nothing has yet been settled in respect to the financial arrangement which will have to be entered into with the Municipality, nor as to the precise share to be borne by that body in the execution of the several works, but these points will receive our attention during the ensuing season at Simla, and as desired by Her Majesty's government, we shall take care that every project is fully scrutinized in detail in view to ensuing the utmost economy.
>
> (Signed Lytton, H.W. Norman, A. Hobhouse, C. Bayley, J. Arbuthnot, A. Clarke, John Strachey. [No. 34 Public Works 1877])

It is stated in No. 34 Public Works 15 March 1877 that while Peterhoff was being expanded and renovated, steps were afoot to procure more land:

> As to permanent arrangements, it is under consideration to build a viceregal residence on the 'Observatory' or 'Bentinck Hill' between the present Observatory House and Squires Hill. But whatever precise site is ultimately selected it will be necessary to acquire the other estates on Bentinck Hill.

Pamela Kanwar in her study *Imperial Simla: The Political Culture of the Raj* (2005) gives us a detailed report on locations and historical configurations of the early years of colonising Shimla. She writes that Shimla was first sighted and recorded by two officers who were mapping the terrain. It was Captain Charles Pratt Kennedy, who was posted as Garrison Officer until 1821 and then became the political agent with supervisory powers over the hill states, who first built a residence. Kennedy is described as being a dandy who was quite at home dominating over the local elites, even sending them to prison and fining them or hanging them when he thought it necessary. For 14 years, he made Shimla his 'royal estate' and contributed to the town's growth. He is associated with the introduction of potatoes in the hills.

Kennedy's house, according to the journalist Vipin Pubby, was the first retreat for those looking for a change of routine (1988: 20). The town was later in demand among those who saw it as a sanatorium. Land for house construction was leased 'free of rent' from the rulers of Keonthal or Patiala, depending upon the site chosen. 'Begarees (landless forced labour), building material and wood were also secured from them, and the transactions recorded in Kennedy's office' (Kanwar 2005: 16). Begar or forced labour was finally abolished in 1929 through the work of Samuel Evans Stokes, who was close to Mahatma Gandhi (Pubby 1988: 87).

Lord Amherst had chosen Shimla in 1827 for his summer camp and he spent two months there, leaving before the rains. Pamela Kanwar writes that he came with an entourage and 1,700 coolies. Much of the colonisation of the hills was also about the networking of roads. Coolies were often not paid and there were complaints of non-payment of wages from local zamindars. The subjugation of hill territory depended on the making of these roads as Kanwar observes:

> This road was not permanent because it takes several years before paths cut into hillsides can stabilize into roads. The monsoons often wash segments down into khuds while landslides carry stones and segments down on to the roads. While Kennedy did much to lay down roads, and this was noted by the administrators, he was refused a request for a special allowance. He was also responsible, as we saw, for introducing potatoes into the villages of the hills. (2005: 23)

Kennedy had been host to Lord Amherst and many others. Jacquemont, a visitor, is quoted by Pamela Kanwar as writing that they were well fed and received champagne, hock and delicious mocha coffee at dinner as well as receiving the Calcutta journals at breakfast (ibid.).

Kennedy's work is reported to have taken only one hour after breakfast, but it was his imagination that unfurled, that saw the houses, bazaars and roads as they came to be (ibid.: 24). The British officers saw Simla as a sanatorium, but then, it must be remembered that foot passengers, horses, mules, ponies or cattle, travelled over 41 miles of mountain road. Coolies were rounded up, but even with sedan chairs and porters, the hill climb to Shimla was extremely difficult (ibid.: 25). Captain Mundy, an aide-de-camp, wrote that in 1828, hundreds of mountain labourers and coolies were employed for cutting timber, laying blocks of stone and erecting buildings (ibid.: 17). There were often scuffles with the Raja of Keonthal and his men, who did not want their forests cut. The Raja said, 'If I give all my trees how will my subjects be able to live in my country?' (ibid.).

In 1837, with the Afghan question, Lord Auckland saw the significance of Shimla politically and moved there. The trips were not yet official, but Auckland's visit was not a holiday trip, for his staff travelled with him. Emily Eden, his sister, wrote in her journal on Good Friday, 13 April 1838:

> This dear Simla! It snowed yesterday, and has been hailing today, and is now thundering in a cracking, sharp way that would be awful, only its sublimity is destroyed by the working of the carpenters and blacksmiths, who are shaping curtain rods and rings all around the house. It has been an immense labour to furnish properly. We did not bring half chintz enough from Calcutta, and Simla grows rhododendrons and pines, and violets, but nothing else—no damask, no glazed cotton for lining—nothing. There is a sort of country cloth—made here, wretched stuff, in fact, though the colours are beautiful—but I ingeniously devised tearing up whole pieces of red and white into narrow strips, and then sewing them together, and the effect for the dining room is lovely when supported with the scarlet border painted all around the cornice, the doors, windows etc. and now everybody is adopting the fashion. (1978: 127, 128)

In yet another note, dated 22 April, she writes:

> I am quite well again now, thank you, and have begun riding and walking again, and the climate, the place, and the whole thing are quite delightful, and our poor despised house, that everybody abused, has turned out the wonder of Simla. We brought carpets, chandeliers and wall shades from Calcutta, and I have got a native painter into the house and cut out patterns in paper, which he then paints in borders all round the doors and windows, and it makes up for the want of cornices. Altogether it is very like a cheerful middle-sized English country house, and extremely enjoyable. I do not mean to think of the future (this world's future) for six months. It was very well to keep oneself alive in the plains by thinking of the mountains or to dream of some odd chance that would take one home—there is no saying the inventions to go home that I had invented—but now I do not mean to be imaginative for six months. (ibid.: 128, 129)

The relief at being in Shimla was patent. When she had arrived after the interminable journey, she exclaimed:

> Well, it really is worth all the trouble—such a beautiful place—and our house, that everybody has been abusing, only wanting all the good

> furniture and carpets we have bought—to be quite perfect. Views only too lovely; deep valleys on the drawing-room side to the west, and the snowy range on the dining room side where my room also is. Our sitting rooms are small, but that is all the better in this climate, and the two principal rooms are very fine. The climate! No wonder I could not live down below! We never were allowed a scrap of air to breathe—now I come back to the air again, I remember all about it. It is a cool sort of stuff, refreshing, sweet, and apparently pleasant to the lungs. We have fires in every room, and the windows open, red rhododendron trees in bloom in every direction, and beautiful walks like English shrubberies cut on all sides of the hills. God! I see this to be the best part of India. (Eden 1978: 125)

In the website of 'Exhibitions at Victoria Memorial Hall, Calcutta', which chronicles the achievements of Emily Eden, drawing from her letters and paintings, it is established that Emily Eden's paintings are preserved at the Victoria Memorial at Calcutta. J. Dickinson published her paintings. Emily Eden was the author of two novels, *The Semi-Detached House* (1859) and *The Semi-Attached Couple*. According to the website, on 21 October 1837, Lord Auckland, accompanied rather reluctantly by his sister, set out from Calcutta on board the 'Meghna' a flat or long barge towed by a steamer. They alighted at Benares and went on foot to Shimla.

Emily Eden writing of the servants accompanying them on the barge from the Sunderbans describes the nights on the barge as hot and sleepless: 'The native servants sleep any and everywhere, over our heads, under our feet, or at our doors; and as there are no partitions, but green blinds at the sides and grating above, of course, we hear them coughing above' (Eden 1978: 5).

In Shimla too, the servants were often ill. In the entry for 29 April 1838, she writes:

> All the native servants are, or have been sick, and I do not wonder. We have built twenty small houses since we came and have lodged fifty of our servants in these outhouses. Still, there were always a great many looking unhappy, so I got J to go round to all the houses and get me a list of all who were settled, and of those whose houses were not built, and I found there were actually sixty-seven who had no lodging provided for them. I should like to hear the row English servants

> would have made, and these are not a bit more used to rough it. There is not one who has not his own little house at Calcutta, and his wife to cook for him; so they feel the cold and their helplessness doubly, but they never complain. (Eden 1978: 144)

Indira Ghose, in one of her chapters in her book *The Power of the Female Gaze: Women Travellers in Colonial India* (1998), discusses Lord Auckland's sister Emily Eden who set sail in October 1835 to assist him in his duties when he became Governor-General. The narrative of 'Up the Country' describes a political journey made by Auckland in the company of his sisters from Calcutta to Shimla between 1838 and 1840. Ghose writes that Emily Eden's hallmark was irony, and describes the march to Shimla.

> Accordingly, a vast imperial machinery was cranked into action for the tour, with a cavalcade ten miles long led by the Governor-General and his sisters on elephant and on horse-back, followed by armies of elephants camels and horses and their grooms; next the British members of the party, on horse-back in carriages or in palanquins; then came bullock carts loaded with household goods; eight thousand soldiers in all and trailing at the end, crowds of camp followers, including fakirs and robbers. (1998: 73)

Fanny Parks who joined the cavalcade had said the cost to the exchequer was 70,000 rupees. Emily finds the march uncomfortable with 12,000 people with tents and elephants, camels and horses, but says, 'What can one do?' (ibid.).

It was in Shimla that Emily Eden found herself to be supremely happy (victoria memorial-cal.org/rx eden Exploring India: The Travels of Emily Eden 1837–1840). Other viceroys and their families were to follow. Ellenborough and Hardinge visited Shimla in 1842 and 1846 (Kanwar 2005: 260).

Ellenborough, before his visit, released funds for the improvement of roads. Lord Dalhousie found Shimla overrated, though the 5-day journey did not seem such a chore. He too was overwhelmed by the festivities and balls, concerts and entertainment available in Shimla, though he saw that it had a 'wonderful political advantage as administrative views went' (ibid.: 27).

Vipin Pubby quotes one of Dalhousie's letters of 1851:

> We have had a terrible fortnight of festivities. Balls without numbers, fancy fairs, plays, concerts, investitures—and every blank day filled up with a large dinner party. You may judge what this 'hill station' has grown to when I tell you that 460 invitations were issued for the last ball at Government house, and most of them came.

Further, Dalhousie wrote:

> Balls here, balls there, balls by the society; amateur plays, concerts, fancy fairs, investitures of the Bath and co and co. I quite sigh for the quiet of Calcutta. (Pubby 1988: 24)

The summer palace was necessitated however by the need for continuous work, where five days of work in the plains was equivalent to one day in the hills. Ian Stephens writes, 'The memory that sticks in my mind is of those coolies pulling and humping terribly heavy loads on their backs up-hill slopes' (ibid.: 42). The exodus involved tonnes of baggage, heaps of files and dispatch boxes beside the families of the officials.

Further, Andre Wilson describes the passage of officials as:

> There were colonels and clerks of departments and other men so tremendous in their spheres. Assistant Deputy Commissioners, still relatively unburdened with the cares of highest office, cantering lightly along parapet-less roads skirting precipices, and the ton weight of a post office official requiring twenty groaning coolies to carry him. (ibid.)

The increase in population after the opening of the railway was 24 per cent. In 1899, it was 24,179 and in 1898 it was 30,405 (ibid.: 44). The reservoir was constructed in 1880. Prior to 1880, there were only the natural springs or *baolis*. The church reservoir, which lay below the ridge held 12,00,000 gallons, the Sanjauli Reservoir carried 1,00,000 gallons. A third reservoir was built at Saog in 1904. The cost of these reservoirs was Rupees 6,06,000. A pump installed then, was still in use when Vipin Pubby wrote his book. Rainwater storage was made compulsory by the British. The Europeans received 25 gallons each and were allocated 10,00,000 gallons. The Indians received 5 gallons and totalled 1,80,000 gallons. Major General Beresford and Mr Pook suggested pumping water from the Sutlej, but this was refused.

The cost then was Rupees 25 lakhs. Pubby writes that the idea was revived at the cost of Rupees 35 crores. Incinerators were in existence, which not just burnt the garbage; they provided steam and electricity for heat (Pubby 1988: 46). The number of houses increased from thirty houses in 1830 to 290 in 1866. The number of occupied houses in Shimla in 1881 was 1,141 (ibid.: 20). The details of planning and building were closely documented by administrators in their dealing with bureaucrats and engineers.[1]

A letter from Maj. Gen. W.A. Crommelin to W. Smith says that:

> The Resolution of the Government of India in the Public Works Department dated 3rd November 1876 a copy of which is enclosed, will make you acquainted with the general scope of the duties which will devolve upon you, and of the works which will have to be carried out in connection with the superintendence of the new Circle of Public Works which may be styled the 'Simla Imperial Circle'. (No. 34 Public Works 1877)

The Circle was to be under the direct orders of the Government of India, and Mr W. Smith was expected to correspond directly with the Secretary to the Government of India in the Public Works Department.

The works to be engaged could be summarised as follows, according to Maj. W.A. Crommelin:

> Additions to 'Peterhoff' to render it a more convenient temporary Viceregal residence, until a permanent structure can be provided.
>
> The construction of a permanent Vice-Regal residence on the Observatory or Bentinck Hill
>
> Water supply for the whole settlement.
>
> Quarters for public offices and clerks.
>
> Certain major works for the improvement of the drainage and conservancy of the settlement.
>
> Peterhoff, Inverarm have been acquired. Negotiations are on foot for Landsdowne House, Squire's Hall, Morvin
>
> You will understand from the Resolution that a sum of 2 lakhs has been authorized to meet immediate requirements, and that the

1 This essay uses the documents on microfilm at the National Archives, Delhi, titled No. 34 Government of India, Public Works Department, Civil Works ACC no. 1480 R no. 535. Since it is a collation of materials in the Archives, there are no specific page numbers.

> accounts are to be dealt with by the Examiner of Military Works Accounts who is located at Simla. It is desirable that you should arrange with the Examiner for the subdivision of the above and subsequent grants under certain main heads of outlay such as
>
> Purchase of house
> Improvement to property
> Original Works
> Repairs
> Establishment
> Tools and Plant. (No. 34 Public Works 1877)

In the carrying out of the tasks with regard to the 'formation of the new circle' the duties of the Executive Engineer of the provincial division were not to be interfered with. The specific interest was to 'transfer to your charge the house which have been purchased already for the Government of India and which are at present under the charge of the Provincial Executive Engineer, but this will not be done until your arrangement are fully matured' (ibid.).

In the same document, it is recorded that Lytton writes to Marquis of Salisbury:

> Referring to our Despatch No 34 P.W of this date, on the subject of the proposed improvements at Simla we have the honour to inform your Lordship that we have selected Captain H.H. Cole to prepare the designs for the new Government House and the other public buildings and offices.
>
> Captain Cole, after inspecting the sites has gone home on leave, and will be in London, at the time when this Despatch reaches your Lordship; he proposes to prepare certain of the designs during his stay in England, and we request that, if your Lordship sees no objection, he may be allowed to employ a draftsman to aid him in the manual part of this work, and to leave him more free, than he would be without this aid, to employ his own time in the most useful way. We enclose for your Lordship's information, copy of a report by Captain Cole on several points of detail relating to the Vice-Regal residence, with the remark that the suggestions of this officer are generally approved by us.
>
> Captain Cole has also requested permission to purchase some books on architectural subjects. (Signed Lytton et al.)

The British Government of India had decreed that 'Simla shall be for the greater part of the year, the Headquarters of the Supreme Government. It is indispensable that the present make-shift and unbecoming arrangements should cease'.

Till then, as we saw, houses were rented for accommodation, but these were expensive. Summer residence for the Viceroy was to be built at a cost of over Rupees 13 lakhs—Rupees 13 lakhs and 20,000 was asked for. 'Peterhoff', where the Viceroy stayed previously was thought to be unhygienic and too small. Three members of the Viceroy's family fell ill there due to typhoid. When native chiefs visited Shimla in the summer, it was believed that the Viceroy would require a space in which to interact with them. They had been put up in tents, and such inhospitality to local chiefs was thought to be unbecoming of the British in India. Accusations of extravagance came from the home office. Lytton was forced to write:

> We presume that you refer to the appointment of a Superintending engineer. Our object in making this appointment was to have an executive officer of experience who, besides conducting our own work, would be associated with the Municipality, and advise that body on the important actions which they are about to undertake. We shall take care that the appointment does not last longer than is absolutely necessary. (Signed Lytton, P.P. Haines, R.C. Bayley, A.J. Arbuthnot, A. Clarke, E.B. Johnson, B.B. Johnson, W. Stokes.)

Lord Dufferin, who was to be in time a resident in Shimla, wrote to the Home Government.[2]

> The total cost of the new house (excluding the furniture and mural decoration) and its accessories completed as sanctioned by us was estimated at Rs 6,05,131, and on the strength of this estimate work was commenced; but unexpected difficulties were met within securing the foundation which have entailed an additional expenditure of Rs 54,798 owing to increased depth and massiveness; and of Rs 12,306

2 The documents on microfilm at the National Archives, Delhi, titled No. 34 Government of India, Public Works Department, Civil Works ACC no. 1480 R no. 535.

> in retaining walls for securing the approaches to the house. (No. 34 Public Works 1877)

The cost of furniture and murals was thought to be Rupees 2,00,000. The letter was signed by Dufferin, Roberts, Ilbert, Hope, Colvin, Chesney (the Reply to the Governor-General, London, 23 December 1886).

There was stiff resistance from Viscount Cross, that he had not been informed in time.

Dufferin in his letter of 15 March 1887 records his regret that formal sanction was overlooked while pursuing the matter of congenial accommodation for the Viceroy.

Electrification of the Viceregal Lodge

The correspondence of 26 August 1887 from Shimla communicates the anxiety of the planners about whether to use gas, candles or electricity while lighting the building. Installation of electric light was seen to be more economical with regard to maintenance. Lord Dufferin wrote to Viscount Cross:

> We have decided that the most satisfactory arrangement is that the house should be lighted by a full installation of electric light; and it appears to us that besides the advantage of coolness and cleanliness, the employment of electricity may be considered to a great extent as an insurance against accidents by fire, which would be more likely to occur if the house was lighted by gas, kerosene or candles. (No. 34 Public Works 1877)

Since no provision for expenditure on this was claimed earlier, it was now requested. The sum of Rupees 1,50,000 would, it was thought, cover the entire cost including freight, carriage in India, erection of all machinery, lamps and appliances connected with the installation. Dufferin requested the participation of the electrical engineer of Buckingham Palace Mr Massey to supervise the contract with manufacturers.

In another document, titled No. 50 Public Works Simla September 2nd 1887, available in the National Archives, Delhi and addressed to

Viscount Cross, who was Her Majesty's Secretary of State for India, we receive the following information:

My Lord,

In the 7th paragraph of your Lordship's Despatch No 61 P.W of the 23rd December last, a request was made that copies of the designs and estimates of the New Vice Regal Lodge in Simla should be forwarded, for the information of Her Majesty's Government. We regret the delay which has occurred in complying with this request, it has been mainly due to certain alterations in the design which have suggested themselves as the work went on, and which have rendered it necessary from time to time to amend the estimate and to alter the plans.

In paragraph 5 of our dispatch No 45 P.W of the 27 September 1886, we stated that the estimated cost of the building was 6,87,051. The estimates which we now forward show the manner in which that total was reached in juxtaposition with each of the items which go to make up that sum, the corresponding items, as they now stand, have been shown. The total of the present estimate which is comparable with that mentioned in our dispatch of September last is 8,69,676.

The excess of 1, 82,625 on the entire estate may be divided as follows

Excess on "works" 1,22, 287

On establishment 53,032

On tools and plants 7,306

1,82,625

Passing over the first of these items for the present we should explain that the excess on Establishment is almost entirely due to the fact that the building has taken a long time in construction than was anticipated. It was at first thought that it would be completed by the beginning of the current season, but it is now certain that it cannot be ready for occupation by His Excellency the Viceroy before next year. To a certain extent the extra work, to which we will presently refer, have tended to increase the establishment charged.

The excess to the cost of the Lodge itself is to a great extent, due to a strike among the cartmen which has entailed increased expenditure in the delivery of stone. It is essentially due also to a variety of petty causes which led to excess either of quantity or rates on some of the sub-heads. (No. 34 Public Works 1877)

Lord and Lady Dufferin's New House

In Raja Bhasin's lucid account *Simla: The Summer Capital of British India*, we find an entry by Lady Dufferin in her journal entry dated 15 July 1887:

> D took Hermie and me all over the house in the afternoon. We climbed up the most terrible places and stood on single planks over yawning chasms. The workpeople are very amusing to look at especially the young ladies in necklaces, bracelets, earrings, tight cotton trousers, turbans with long veils hanging down their backs and a large earthenware basin of mortar on their heads. They walk about with the carriage of empresses and seem as much at ease on top of the roof as on the ground floor; most picturesque masons they are. The house will be beautiful, and the views all around are magnificent. I saw the plains distinctly from my boudoir window, and I am glad to have that open view, as I shall not then feel so buried in the hills. (Bhasin 1992: 55)

Doz, described by Raja Bhasin as being the most amusing of diarists in Shimla, says the summer palace was 'the spacious medieval stronghold of greystone on Observatory Hill, which is both a joy and an expense forever'.

Raja Bhasin documents Lady Dufferin's views. She was the first occupant, and shifted into the palace on 23 July 1888, describing it as follows:

> The entrance hall is the great feature of it. The staircase goes up from it, and there are stone pillars dividing it from a wide corridor leading to the state rooms, and both hall and corridor are open to the top of the house, three stories. This gives an appearance of space and height which is very grand. The corridor opens into the ballroom with a large arch; and a similar arch at one end of the big drawing-room, which is a lovely room. Furnished with gold and brown silks, and with large bow windows, and a small round tower recess on it. Sitting in it you look down the ballroom the colouring of which is a lighter yellow. It is a very fine room, and outside the dancing space there is plenty of room for

> sitting, as the wall is much broken up into pillars, leaving a sort of gallery around it. At one side is one of these high panelings of teak, along the top of which are shields and arms or the coronets of all the Viceroys, and of the most celebrated Governor-Generals, and above that Spanish leather in rich dark colours. The curtains are crimson. There is a small drawing room, furnished in blue. These are all on one side of the hall .... My views are, as I have said, quite splendid. D's room is rather dark and serious looking. The colouring of mine is a bright sort of brown, and it has a very large bow window, and a tower room recess, which is nearly all glass, like the one in the drawing room. The girls will have a similar sitting room above me, and all our bedrooms are equally nice. (1992: 57)

Parties had been a routine of life in Shimla quite early. The Lawrences, well known for their quiet and companionate marriage, found the routines giddy. John Lawrence's wife had documented this very clearly:

> There is not much to say about our domestic life at Simla. To me it seemed one long round of large dinner parties, balls and festivities of all kinds. My husband did not, at Simla go for the long early rides of which he had once been so fond, and which he still kept up when he was in Calcutta. It seemed strange to us to be once more together here at Simla for it recalled many happy memories .... Few of the friends of those days were left, and a different generation had sprung up. (ibid.: 46)

Transport of Valuables and People

The road to Shimla was a hard one, and Raja Bhasin's book describes the nature of the transport used. Transporting all that the British needed for their comfort is a matter for cultural analyses. However, as late as 1904, Sir Frederick Treves describes the scene on the Hindustan Tibet Road:

> It was on this road that I met the man with the planks. They are the hill men of the poorer sort who carry planks of sawn wood into Simla .... The men are ill-clad and the sun and rain have tanned them and their rags to the colour of brown earth. They bear the planks across their bent backs, and the burden is grievous. They come from a place some days journey towards the snows. They plod along from the dawn to the twilight. They seem crushed by the weight of the beam and their gait is

> more the gait of a stumbling beast than the walk of a man. They move slowly. Their long black hair is white with dust as it hangs by each side of their bowed down faces. The sweat among the wrinkles on their brows is hardened into lamentable clay. They walk in single file, and when the path is narrow, they need must move sideways. In one day I met no less than fifty creeping wretches in this inhuman procession. Each dull eye is fixed upon the scuffled road or upon the plank on the stooping back that crawls in front. To the beams are strapped their sorry possessions—a cooking pot, sticks for a fire, a water gourd, and a sheep's skin to cover them from the frost at night. If there were but a transverse beam to the plank, each one of these bent men might be carrying his own cross to a far-off crucifixion. (Bhasin 1992: 34, 35)

Ferdnand Braudel in his classic *The Mediterranean and the Mediterranean World in the Age of Philip* (1996) writes that mountains are often described as half-wild, their residents are hardy, the villages always semi-deserted, for people have to leave to find work. Men carrying loads described so vividly in the preceding paragraph appear even today. In the 19th century, one of the most significant problems was of course the question of labour, 'begar' being the appropriate title for the kind of appropriation of work from the surrounding hills.

How were goods and materials transported? Pamela Kanwar has some interesting motifs in her book on Shimla. The British had created many hill stations, the largest number in the foothills of the Himalayas (Kanwar 2005: 35).

In 1864, 484 persons were transported from Calcutta to Shimla for six months. Four lakh rupees incurred in the transportation was not thought to be a great sum. John Lawrence believed that one day of work would equal five days in the plains. The town expanded with the years as viceroys and governments continued to visit Shimla every year. A railway line was constructed in 1869. There was a cart road from Kalka to Shimla through Dharmapuri and Solan. The Ambala–Kalka link was extended in 1891; twelve years later the first passenger train arrived at Shimla on 9 November 1903 (Kanwar 2005: 39, 40). Shimla transformed itself from being a sanatorium and holiday town into becoming an official town. While there were questions about extravagance, yet, by 1880, Pamela Kanwar argues that the British saw Shimla as a certainty in terms of seven months of real bureaucratic time (Kanwar 2005: 45). The town grew according to the needs of the people living in it, or what she calls 'the exigency of time' and of 'Viceregal direction'. The lower bazaar was seen to be untidy and ugly. It was a residence for Indian clerks, camp followers, shopkeepers, carpenters, cloth merchants, cooks, bakers, artisans, domestic servants, coolies and porters (ibid.: 57). In contrast to the lower bazaar, was the Mall, which was a public area for the British, and this was cleared of sweepers and coolies every evening from four to seven (ibid.: 63). Along with the maintenance of roads, sewage networks, water supply and the maintenance of forest cover of rhododendron and oak, was the sustained conservation measures for the water sources (ibid.: 65). This would be re-read by Kanwar in terms of the fluctuations of population in the summer and winter months (ibid.: 132).

Raja Bhasin cites Rudyard Kipling writing to his Aunt Edie, a letter from Lahore, dated 14 August 1883,

> Privilege leave, as I may have told you before, gives you the pleasant duty of enjoying yourself in a cool climate for thirty days and being paid 20 pounds for that duty. The month was a round of picnics, dances, theatricals, and so on—and I flirted with the bottled up energy of a year on my lips .... Simla is built around the sides of a mountain 8,444 feet high, and the roads are just ledges.

Yvonne Fitzroy, who accompanied Lord and Lady Reading as a member of their retinue, was not a camp follower in the uncritical sense. She writes:

> Simla must be the meanest of Imperial capitals. Seen from a distance between April and June, before the rains have worked their annual miracle, it clings to a mangy hillside, a forest of tin roofs, rickety wood and discoloured plaster. The gothic crime of the Secretariat dominates the centre, the Victorian ardour of Viceregal Lodge its western limit. The forests of pine and deodar have been very largely destroyed, and the houses crowd as thick as the trees they have supplanted. The northern hills are bare and brown, and the ultimate snowline contributes the Himalayan touch with which we exiles dazzle the envious hearts of Pimlico. (1926: 90)

Later, her impressions are even more complex:

> At a discreet distance, Viceregal Lodge possessed a cathedral-like silhouette, rather impressive, but on near approach it revealed all the eccentrities of a Scottish hydropathic. It sat on a peak, the views it commanded became, in due course, superb; it was built of grey stone, quite porous, an idiosyncrasy of which we reaped the full benefit during the monsoon. Within, I do believe it was really far uglier than it looked. You could have found fault with it to eternity and then not have reached the limit of its crimes; on the other hand it was so large, so gilded, so perfectly complacent, that in the end you grew near to accepting it at its own valuation! (Fitzroy 1926: 191)

She complained that 'Simla, in particular, is little more than a vast boarding-house, every bit as depressing, and its houses owe nothing to humanity in its building and little in the living'. Yvonne Fitzroy called it the 'dislocation of English life in England' (ibid.: 191, 192). Writing from the vantage point of the 1920s, she says:

> I never heard a scandal worth remembering, and a few worth believing; tongues were busier in malice than in wit, and its record of wickedness would be found tedious by the average flapper. Which is not to deny there was scandal in plenty, what else would you expect of a community with hardly any interest in life but the social. (ibid.: 193)

There were odd sorts of dances and balls, memberships in eccentric clubs of those who dared to consort with the unworthy publicly, such as Knights of the Order of Black Hearts. She continues:

> The summit of achievement was, I think reached only last year in the great Chinese ball given by Their Excellencies to cheer the monsoon-laden minds of Simla. As a spectacle I have never seen its equal in either hemisphere, and even the monsoon abetted by dropping a grey veil over the exterior eccentricities of Lord Dufferin's Scottish stronghold. Within the entire house was transformed, lit only by countless lanterns with a dias of imperial yellow, and two huge red-lacquered pailows or gateways. The walls were adorned with panels on which Chinese dragons raged and curled, and the costumes were limited to those

> of China, Japan and Burma. Indian guests were present, such as the Maharajah of Patiala. The Indian servants were reviled for being slow and cunning.
>
> Preparations for any and every party were always incredibly complicated by the Indian servants, who though they sometimes by force of numbers achieved miracles, are never to be hurried, and above all things, reverence the brain saving device of habit. They are engaging enough even if of a mentality that defeats the understanding, but for their proper appreciation you should lead a life of leisure. (Firzroy 1926: 195)

Yvonne Fitzroy was on the staff of Lord and Lady Reading's retinue, and she described her time in service as that of a 'hurrying life, the living of which was so like running backwards on a moving staircase; you were always at the top, however desperately you tried to get to the bottom!'

Barbara Crossette in *The Great Hill Stations of Asia* writes of the Viceregal Lodge that:

> At the time it was built, however, it quickly became symbolic of Simla's hierarchical professional and social system. A summons to a viceroy's reception or dinner was something to die for. Once in possession of the engraved invitation card and starchly outfitted in formal evening clothes—and medals if he could muster a few—an ambitious officer or colonial administrator of middling ranks would travel the three or four miles from Simla town to the viceroy's baronial hall in both hope and trepidation, aware that a casual remark or the wrong answer to a viceregal quest from him or his wife could ruin a career. Commenting on the serious social climbing that went on at such formal events, the journalist William Howard Russel described the Simla scene as 'ball after ball, each followed by a little backbiting'. (1999: 56)

Since the fear of proximity and mixture always existed, the caste, class and race systems were jam-packed with taboos. Crossette writes:

> At the top were the Brahmins and maharajas, who also bought property at Simla until the British began to fear they were amassing too much of it and tried to stall the process with red tape. Indian rulers

> paid formal calls on the viceroy or a lower official befitting the ruler's perceived place vis-à-vis the imperial hierarchy. Gifts were exchanged. Indian professionals and rich merchants from several higher Hindu castes bought homes and became influential in the affairs of the town as their numbers grew, although most local businesses were relegated to the Lower Bazar which still tumbles down the cliffside below the Mall. (1999)

Yvonne Fitzroy writes that there was 'much mutual entertainment' and that they would each represent their communities. 'We in India, may not be the flower of our kind, but by us will our kind be judged' (Fitzroy 1926: 214). This mutual entertainment was clearly in terms of the acceptance of colonialism by the upper castes, from whom the National Movement found its propagators. Madame Blavatsky was a guest in Shimla of the founder of the Indian National Congress, and there is a record of this in the Theosophical Society archives.

In the last section, I present a short story written by me during an Asia Pacific Writer's workshop, hosted by the Indian Institute of Advanced Study, Shimla and Indian Institute of Technology, Delhi in October 2008. I was invited there by Rukmini Bhaya Nair to be a creative writing instructor in the uses of oral history, at a writing workshop. I wrote the story while Robin Hemley from the University of Iowa, another instructor, asked participant writers to close their eyes and imagine their grandmother's kitchen. It was a case of moonlighting on my part, while the rest were busy with the assigned task of using the reality principle to create backdrops for writing fiction (13 October 2008).

Voices in the Morning

The council sat around the table. Lord Dufferin had just had the worst nightmare of his life. He had stumbled down the stairs, his dressing-gown tassels caught in the complex web of wood. The man had stood there facing him. His face was quite the most warped, like the rough and pitted texture of old wood which had not been polished and planed. He stood for fear and death and the terrible litany of labourers' woes. He had not been paid for the winding staircase. He had not been paid for the panelling. It went on and on. The labourer was of course a ghost. Lord Dufferin did not doubt that. Labourers never met him. They always met the bailiff.

The Council looked at Dufferin. They wanted to know about the actual cost of electrification of the Lodge. They enquired about the new estimates for the cost of the gardens.

Upstairs Lady Dufferin was getting dressed to meet the Council. She could hear their voices:

Gentlemen, I assure you, the costs will be met from the money allocated.

The Chandeliers, sir, are too fragile. You must do with Burmese glass, not Belgian ones.

Sometimes she got quite nervous hearing their voices, rising from a steady burr to a constant crescendo. They were men with some power, these accountants.

Who were they but impoverished Scots? She often thought of the sky at home. How different, how grey, how full of tears. And here the sun blazoned, and at night the sky was burnished with stars. Of course, silly Duff was beginning to see things. They all did that. After a while, the heat melted their brains, especially on those hot white days of light in autumn.

Last night he had floundered into her room. He had that puzzled look that was typical of men who see death. What was it?

The workers! They want payment!

Well, it's fine work. You should pay them. We can cancel dinner for the Council and let them eat in their lodges.

Lodges! The Council! My dear, do you believe that I can permit you to even think of such a thing?

The kitchen is in disrepair. The ceiling is crumbling. It will fall into the soup..

Think of another place in the Lodge to cook then.

If you don't pay the workers, they will die and haunt me. The children can hear them weeping. It's true that they have nothing to eat.

We'll discuss this tomorrow. For the moment, my dear Lady, can we now think of what you will cook for the Council.

It's too early to discuss with the staff. And not if you look at me like that, with hollow eyes, with smoke billowing out of your ears.

The children were sleeping of course, while the argument over what was to be made for the Council continued. Their voices were raised, and the children woke up. It was a strange space of complete annihilation. Lady Dufferin walked out, and the mountain seemed to be a shadow in the glow of the autumn sun. It seemed to darken in the haze of the oncoming heat. She walked for miles, full of that odd and wary sense of loss of being which followed every quarrel. Sometimes she thought that life was an abyss when all she had to do was appear in a space of tranquillity that was consumed by all.

The labourer sometimes appeared as a coffin carrier to Lord Dufferin. Curiously, he recognised him in the oddest circumstances as heralding death. Fear would rise like the sea in an endless ebbing, a threat of return, a lost country. The labourer spoke to him in a dream from which he could never quite awake. That's how he once realised that in the language of dreams, nothing needs to be said.

Lady Dufferin woke up sometimes in her room knowing that the house was haunted. It didn't frighten her. The labourer was Duff's visitor. Hers were different. She would open her eyes, and Duff was somnambulently standing over her bed.

What did he say, darling?

The same thing as yesterday.

Not being paid? Don't you have any other conversations?

No.

She would wake him up, as he stood blinking at her. They would kneel and she would pray, in her clear soft voice. She was used to him, his eccentricities never bothered her, everyone laughed at him—his rude speech as they called it, his monosyllables to hide his accent, his constant excuses and apologies to those who were more powerful than him.

You must not be afraid of him. See him as Jacob's angel, wrestle with him, I'm sure the ladder to heaven will be yours.

I'm sick to death. If only we could go on furlough.

But the wiring is still being done. Electrification is what you have always wanted. Do not give up now.

The air was cold and swirled around them. It was a world that was familiar to them, and yet they felt sealed inside in glass as if it would break and destroy them. They had travelled so far, by sea and by road. They had met one another as shadows in the odd circumstances of their marriage. They had been deposited here by history, charmed by fate. The large canvas of their dreams lay in the sharing of power. She, the constant chatelaine, and he the keeper of keys. It was curious that while she was the quiet one, afraid of company, afraid of people, she would take guests around this great stone castle. It was a place where people loved to gather, to eat, to drink, to talk, to dance, and it was only by invitation. There was no occasion when anyone could come uninvited. No moment thus went unsupervised. It seemed to her that they were prisoners of their invention, prisoners of a grandeur which was so hollow it left them enchanted and removed from real things.

She had her ghosts too. They spoke to her in her head. Some of them were cruel, mocking her for her simple faith. She knew that her language was different from theirs and yet she had learnt to speak it. Sometimes, she forgot her language, she thought now in images. Pictures floated in her mind, always within the frame of the bay window, where she sat for long hours. Peterhoff floated in the images of the past; how uncomfortable it had been, the *khansamas* always cross. Here it was the same. However hard she tried, she could never get away from the peeling ceiling. Everything was perfect, till the new coat of paint began to detach itself and fall into the food. They had not noticed it at first, imagined that it was crystallised salt, but then suddenly one evening, her son had crunched on mortar. And on days of unutterable crises such as those, she would appear, the lovely Lady Samantha. She was the perfect embodiment of lazy afternoons in Shimla. She was the gentlest of people, with grey-blue eyes, and streaked gold-brown hair. She lived in a turret in one of the older buildings near Lower Bazaar. The turret was rented to her by a writer who made it clear that he wanted no favours, only her friendship. Samantha Sutton, with her wealth, and misplaced title, and her Cockney accent, over which she had a veneer of languor and affectation. She drove Lady Dufferin mad, who, however, was forced very often to include her in their parties because everyone liked her. But now back to the immediate question, What time was lunch?

References

Bhasin, Raja. 1992. *Simla: The Summer Capital of British India.* Delhi: Viking.

Crossette, Barbara. 1999. *The Great Hill Stations of Asia.* New York: Basic Books.

Eden, Emily. 1978. *Up the Country.* London: Curzon Press.

Fitzroy, Yvonne. 1926. *Courts and Camps in India, Impressions of Viceregal Tours 1921–1924.* London: Methuen and Company..

Ghose, Indira. 1998. *The Power of the Female Gaze: Women Travellers in Colonial India.* Delhi: Oxford University Press.

Kanwar, Pamela. 2005. *Imperial Simla: The Political Culture of the Raj.* Delhi: Oxford University Press.

Pubby, Vipin. 1988. *Simla: Then and Now.* Delhi: Indus Publications.

7

Romain Rolland and Gandhi

A sculpture of Gandhi in Nikosia, Cyprus signifying the constant presence of the ideology of non-violence in a country often faced with inter religious tensions; November 2018.
© Author.

Romain Rolland first heard of Gandhi through his friend D.K. Roy. The entry in his diary, published in *Collected Works*, for 23 August 1920 described Gandhi as a 'magnetic lawyer' who was influenced by Tolstoy. 'He preaches passive resistance to them and turns them away from violence' (Rolland 1976: 3). In 1921, Tagore visited Rolland in Paris (diary, 19 April 1921) and told him that non-resistance was the way in which in India, 'all invasions shattered themselves'. Rolland believed that non-resistance would be dangerous in his context, given the nature of the political climate which Europe was experiencing in that decade. He argued that there are two sorts of pacifism. One sort is based on renunciation and is a forced passivity, the other type is based on 'calm trust in one's strength, out of a superabundance of vitality' (ibid.: 4). Europe was then moving into a stage of great insecurity and we know that much of Romain Rolland's work was a cry against fascism, and the passivity of the Vichy government. Out of such passivity, however, was the resistance in France born.

On 14 August 1922, Romain Rolland wrote to his friend Kalidas Nag, that he had been requested by Ganesan, the publisher in Madras, to write an introduction to Gandhi's essays. He declined because he feared that this might affect his chance to visit India. In his diary (17–20 August 1922) he communicates that Gandhi is not an internationalist (like Romain is) but is a nationalist of the 'loftiest' kind from whom all the criminal, petty and base nationalisms emerging at that time in Europe were very distinct (Rolland 1976: 5). He thought Gandhi was more like Francis of Assisi, rather than Tolstoy, or himself. While he could not write the introduction to Young India, his imagination was fired by Gandhi's ideas.

On 21 December 1922, Rolland wrote again to Kalidas Nag that his sister and he had read 700 or 800 published pages of Gandhi's writing. They had noticed Gandhi's mistrust of science and technology. However, Rolland believed that scientists may be faulted, but not science, and believed (unlike Tolstoy and Gandhi) that 'it's the living spirit of God' (ibid.: 7).

In April 1923, he records in his diary that he was visited by C.F. Andrews, the friend of Tagore and Gandhi:

> Gandhi is small, insignificant-looking, except when he begins to speak, and of unruffled patience. There is nothing severe in his manners; he laughs like a child and adores children. His asceticism is extreme. Although it is visible at first glance that Andrews does not quail at privation and physical ordeals, he smilingly admits that when he was Gandhi's companion in Africa, life was hard. Gandhi's principle is that life is a preparation for suffering martyrdom and death, and the results he has obtained in Bengal are surprising. Andrews approves of my comparison of Gandhi with St Paul and Tagore with Plato. He says smilingly that Gandhi is very much St Paul. (ibid.: 13)

In the diary extract for September 1923, he records that he is visited by W.W. Pearson, who like C.F. Andrews, also describes Gandhi to Rolland, but this time through an event.

Pearson relates Gandhi's first visit to Santiniketan. On the evening of his arrival, everything was topsy-turvy. Tagore was not here. Pearson and the other teachers wanted to discuss the courses and teaching:

> Gandhi first wanted to find out about hygiene and material conditions. He visited the whole establishment and came out of the kitchen in a rage, saying, 'The cooks are dirty. Send them away!' and they had to be sent away then and there. Afterwards, since the service was disorganized, he set the pupils to the housework and the cooking (and

> of course, the masters with them). And the strange thing is that from the start everyone obeyed him. We were no longer the masters, says Pearson. All the pupils enthusiastically obeyed all of Gandhi's orders. I asked 'What sort of voice has he?' Pearson replies, 'He has no voice. He speaks no louder in public than we are speaking here (we are on two sides of a table). Then no one hears him. Yet the whole crowd hangs on his lips and follows him blindly. He has a magnetic power'. (Rolland 1976: 16)

Romain Rolland also records that his book on Gandhi had created a stir and that the Orientalists were fuming that someone outside their exalted circle should have anything to say (ibid.: 17). However Gandhi liked Romain Rolland's reading of his life and work, and Mahadev Desai records on 25 January 1924, quoting Gandhi, 'Romain Rolland is at this point not only a poet he is a seer with the vision of the truth' (ibid.: 18).

Romain Rolland was soon visited by Miss Madeleine Slade (diary, October 1923). Interestingly, Andrews, Pearson and Slade all visit him in the same year. He describes Madeleine as the daughter of an English admiral who has broken away from her familiar circles to devote herself to artists, and had organised classical music concerts in London, 'and a strange thing among impresarios, managed to get herself into debt while making a profit for her artists' (ibid.).

Tragically, Willie Pearson died in a train crash two days after his meeting with Romain Rolland in September 1923. In a letter to Ganesan, Rolland wrote:

> In this last evening, his thoughts were constantly about the Mahatma with a religious tenderness. Before his departure as if moved by a presentiment, he left with me the photographs which represents him with Andrews by the side of Gandhi in the Transvaal in 1913 or 1914. (ibid.: 21)

On 22 March, Gandhi wrote to Romain Rolland from Andheri:

> Dear Friend,
> I appreciate your loving card. What does it matter that you have in places made mistakes in your essay? The wonder to me is that you have made so few and that you have succeeded though living in a

> different and distant atmosphere, in so truly interpreting my message. It demonstrates once more, the essential oneness of human nature though flourishing under different skies.
> Yours truly,
> M.K. Gandhi
>
> P.S Pray excuse the pencil hand. My hand is yet too shaky to manage the ink pen.
> M.K.G. (Rolland 1976: 29)

The entry for Rolland's diary on Sunday, 1 June 1924 further records:

> I am receiving piles of volumes and albums to sign. The striking thing is that among those who own copies of my books there are hotel staff, chauffeurs, etc. On the way from Zurich to Vienna, didn't I see a copy of my Gandhi in French in the hands of a young sleeping-car attendant? (ibid.: 32)

On 14 September 1925, he records that he is again visited by Madeleine Slade. She has decided to convert to the faith of Mahatma Gandhi and has decided to enter his ashram. He writes:

> I was the unintentional instrument of her destiny. When she first knew me, two years ago in England, her mind was prey to a violent and passionate disturbance, and she could find no way out. She suffered from it for a long time. I guided her a little and introduced her to Gandhi. She directed her passion towards this figure whom she at once saw as a new Christ, she read all his works, but did not think of following his doctrine. It was the last autumn, during the Mahatma's great twenty-one day fast, that the illumination came to her. She determined to devote herself to him, she wrote to him, and he replied. She learned Urdu, learned to spin the *khaddar* and adopted the strictly vegetarian Hindu diet. She cashed her small personal fortune, and said goodbye to her parents. The fine thing is that, despite the total intellectual disagreement between her parents and herself, they accepted it—even the admiral—regretting it, unable to understand, but recognising the moral nobility of her action. No French parent, I fear would have been capable of this self-abnegation and respect for her liberty. Now she is setting off with the joy of a young novice about to become a Carmelite. Gandhi is sending an Indian from the Ashram to meet her in Bombay, where she is to

> land, and take her by rail that night to Ahmedabad. He has warned her that life in the Ashram is hard, that they eat what they earn each day by their labour and that the climate is difficult for a European, but nothing can stop her. Besides, she knows India, having been there at the age of fifteen on her father's flagship. At that date she saw only the English society there, her life was an eternal round of parties, and it exasperated her. Now she says, 'Everyone is sorry for me, people say to me, "How lonely you'll be, lost among those Indians". I say that it will be the first time in my life when I shall not be. (Rolland 1976: 45)

Romain Rolland records in his diary in September 1925, that he writes to Gandhi to recommend his

> daughter, Madeleine Slade, who is leaving for Bombay on 24 October. She is writing us letters full of mystical joy—which still find room for common sense and humour. She said her example has carried along her parents, her mother is spinning, and her father, the admiral is weaving (cursing Gandhi all the while). (ibid.:48)

The letter Romain Rolland wrote to Gandhi is dated 1 October 1925 and describes Ms Slade, 'Europe cannot offer a nobler or more disinterested heart to your cause. May she bear with her the love of thousands of Europeans, and my veneration' (ibid.).

Gandhi wrote on 13 November 1925:

> Dear Friend,
>
> I have your very kind letter .... What a treasure you have sent me! I shall try to be worthy of that great trust. I shall leave no stone unturned to assist her to become a bridge between East and West. I am too imperfect to have disciples. She shall be a fellow seeker with me and as I am older in years and therefore presumably in spiritual experience, I propose to share the honour of fatherhood with you. Ms Slade is showing wonderful adaptability and has already put us at ease about herself. (ibid.: 50, 51)

Rolland writes to Madeleine Slade and communicates how important a life of service is. He sees her to be some kind of Mary Magdalene. 'I can see you out there in the morning before dawn on the nocturnal roads around Sabarmati, by the side of the Mahatma singing to yourself the divine melody of the Hymn of Joy. There it would not be out of its element' (Rolland 1976: 53). He is overjoyed for her, but feels deeply the tragedy of Europe:

> I rejoice to know of his being near to you, and your being near to him. In this old Europe, so full of genius, but at the moment covered as it were with a cloud in my beloved land of France, where still there blossom as many souls, simple and pure, courageous and charming, but who live apart leaving the government of the world and the guidance of opinion to the worst—I fight, alone, without the hope of saving those who do not wish to be saved. But I saw for the future the corn that will (open) when we shall be no more. The grain does not come from me: I have searched it out all through the world. The most beautiful is that which my bird Spirit has brought back from the Orient—the grain of the Great Soul, which itself has gathered grain from the Sacred Books of Asia and we have recognized there, mixed with Hinduism, the savour of the Gospel. All the seeds of life come from the same divine granary. (ibid.: 54)

He calls her by her new name Mira, and asks for her blessing:

> Will you ask once of your great friend and Master to offer up with you a brief and silent prayer for us, for our peace, for the salvation of ours, so that we may know to the last how to be vanquished without bending.
>
> Mira, I embrace you. A happy Christmas and New Year from the lands of sorrow and the cradle of the Epiphany. (ibid.)

On the diary page for 25 December 1925, he says that Madeleine's series of letters to his sister

> will in due course constitute an amazing document for the religious historian. Her conversations with the Mahatma and the spirit of adoration in which she listens and retains them are just like a new gospel. Certainly, Gandhi is not inferior to Christ in goodness and sanctity, and he surpasses him in touching humility. As to Madeleine Slade, as I foresaw, she is a Holy Woman to the new Saviour. (ibid.)

There are certain allusions to the difficulties that Mahatma Gandhi is going through during this period. There is an entry 21–24 June 1926 that pertains to Hindu–Muslim conflicts and the differences between Tagore and Gandhi. According to Tagore, Gandhi was a modern-day Hamlet. Tagore sees the present and the future of his people in a most discouraging light. According to Romain Rolland, Gandhi wanted to solve the political problem without solving the social problem. Tagore felt that this was like building one's house upon the sand (Rolland 1976: 62, 63).

Let us now turn to another text to see what kind of information we can glean about the 1920s, the period of the Khilafat movement. Ian Henderson Douglas summarises Abul Kalam Azad's perspective on Khilafat, obedience to the Caliph, rebellion not permitted, the caliph heads all Muslims, Muslims when attacked must unite, and 'In the present circumstances, the first duty of every Muslim is giving up whatever helps the British, and the second taking up whatever will repel them' (Douglas 1988: 178). While the question of non-violence was always problematic, the Khilafat movement persuaded Muslims not to join the army. J.M. Shelat (1965) in his introduction to the *Trial of Gandhi of 1922* writes that Gandhi described civil disobedience as disobedience, which was a state of peaceful rebellion, more effective than an armed result and consists in a refusal to obey every single state-made law (Shelat 1965: xvi). After the *Moplah*s revolted in Kerala, Gandhiji decided to go to Malabar accompanied by Mohammad Ali, who was arrested by the British at Waltair Station. On 21 September 1921, Gandhiji gave up his attire and wore the loincloth. He knew that the burning of foreign cloth would be possible only if he accepted the poverty of the poorest in the country. In answer to Tagore, Gandhiji asked that the poet see spinning the wheel as a sacrament:

> When all about me are dying for want of food the only occupation permissible to me is to feed the hungry. To a people famishing and idle, the only acceptable form in which god can appear is work and promise of food as wages. God created man to work for his food and said that those who ate without work were thieves. Eighty percent of India are compulsorily thieves half the year. Hunger is the experiment that is driving India to the spinning wheel. The call of the spinning wheel is the noblest of all. Because it is the call of love. And love is Swaraj. The attainment of this Swaraj is possible within

> a short time, and it is so possible only by the revival of the spinning wheel. (Shelat 1965: xviii)

It was a meditative practice that was enjoined on the common people. At the time of the suicide of cotton farmers, the symbol of the charkha needs to be revitalised in popular debate. Food and weaving are the central symbols underlying the correspondence of Mirabehn and Gandhiji. Let us now turn to the trial itself, since the British arrested Gandhi for his political tracts and his friendship with the Ali brothers.

His deposition is in Session Case Number 45, 1922. He accepts the guilt that is imposed on him by the Advocate General for the Bombay, Madras and the Chauri Chaura occurrences, which he called diabolical crimes (ibid.: 207):

> Non-violence is the first article of my faith, it is also the last article of my faith, but I had to make my choice. I had either to submit to a system which I consider has done an irreparable harm to my country or incur the risk of the mad fury of my people bursting forth when they understood the truth from my lips. I am deeply sorry for it. I am therefore, here to submit not to a light penalty, but the highest penalty. I do not ask for mercy. I do not ask for any extenuating act of clemency. I am here to invite and submit to the highest penalty that can be inflicted upon me for what in law is a deliberate crime and what appears to me to be the highest duty of a citizen.

Much of the work of the French theorist Rene Girard is to analyse the appearance of the scapegoat. The judge R.S. Broomfield said in response to Gandhi's plea that:

> The law is no respecter of persons. Nevertheless it would be impossible to ignore the fact that you are in a different category from any person I have ever tried or am likely to have to try. It would be impossible to ignore the fact that in the eyes of millions of your countrymen you are a great patriot and a great leader. Even those who differ from you in politics look upon you as a man of high ideals and of noble and even saintly life. (ibid.: 194)

Yet, the judge said, he would pass judgement only on the breaking of the law:

> I do not forget that you have constantly preached against violence and that you have on many occasions, as I am willing to believe, done much to prevent violence, but having regard to the nature of your political teaching, and the nature of many of those to whom it is addressed, how you could have continued to believe that violence and anarchy would not be the inevitable consequence, it passes my capacity to understand. (Shelat 1965: 194)

The judge compares the case to that which was decided against Mr Bal Gangadhar Tilak and sentences Gandhi for six years. Gandhi's plea dated 18 March 1922, for Case no. 45 says that he will try to explain why he had changed from a staunch loyalist who had aided the British. This was at the time of the Boer War (1899) and the Zulu revolt (1906). For his work in South Africa he received the Kaiser-e-Hind from Lord Hardinge, Gandhi says, 'I raised a volunteer ambulance corps in London, consisting of the then resident Indians in London, chiefly students. Its work was acknowledged by the authorities to be valuable.'

In Kheda, too in 1918, he attempted 'to raise a corps and the response was being made when the hostilities ceased and orders were received that no more recruits were wanted' (Shelat 1965: 172). This was in spite of the treatment which he had received in the hands of the British in South Africa:

> My public life began in 1893 in South Africa in troubled weather. My first contact with the British authority in that country was not happy. I discovered that as a man and an Indian I had no rights—more correctly I discovered that I had no rights as a man because I was an Indian. (ibid.: 169)

He had continued to hope he said because he believed by good conduct ('by such services') full equality with the empire could be achieved (ibid.: 173). He understood his folly in optimism, for India had been reduced to such poverty, had been ravaged by such famines:

> Before the British advent, India spun and wove in her millions of cottages just the supplement she needed, for adding to her meager agricultural resources. This cottage industry so vital for India's existence has been ruined by incredibly heartless and inhuman processes as described by

> English witnesses. Little do town dwellers know how the semi-starved masses of India are slowly sinking to lifelessness. Little do they know that their miserable comfort represents the brokerage they set for the work they do for the foreign exploiter, that the profits and the brokerage are sucked from the masses. No sophistry, no jugglery in figures can explain away the evidence the skeletons in many villages present to the naked eye. I have no doubt whatsoever that both England and the town dwellers of India will have to answer, if there is a God above for this crime against humanity which is perhaps unequalled in history. (Shelat 1965: 179, 180)

He strongly believed that 'the administration of the law was prostituted consciously or unconsciously for the benefit of the exploiter' (ibid.: 183). He said:

> The greatest misfortune is that Englishmen and their Indian associates in the administration of the country do not know, that they are engaged in the crime I have attempted to describe. I am satisfied that many English and Indian officials honestly believe that they are administering one of the best systems devised in the world and that India is making steady though slow progress. They do know that a subtle but effective system of terrorism and an organized display of force on the one hand and the deprivation of all powers of retaliation or self-defence on the other have emasculated the people and induced in them the habit of simulation. This awful habit has added to the ignorance and the self-deception of the administrators. (ibid.: 185)

Gandhi was imprisoned for 'disaffection' under Section 124, which was aimed at suppressing the liberty of Indians. He said:

> Affection cannot be manufactured or regulated by law. If one has no affection for a person or thing, one should be free to give the fullest expression to his disaffection so long as he does not contemplate, promote or incite to violence. But the section under which Mr Banker and I are charged is one under which mere promotion of disaffection is a crime. (ibid.: 186)

Gandhi said that he considered it a privilege to be charged thus because some of the best-loved Indians had been charged under it. He said he had no disaffection against any single administrator, or the person of the king, but towards the government he did feel disaffection for it had caused more harm than any other previous system (Shelat 1965: 188). Disassociating from evil was what non-cooperation was about (ibid.: 190). He said: '... inflict me the severest penalty if you believe that the system and the law you are assisting to administer are good for people of this country and that my activity is therefore injurious to the public weal' (ibid.: 192).

In the preceding discussion, I have shown that the Khilafat movement, the desire for autonomy from the colonial government, the promotion of solidarity between Hindus and Muslims led Gandhi to the adoption of the loincloth as his customary attire, which became a symbol of his identification with the large masses of the poor. In the next section, I will deal with the question of *khaddar*, as an integrative symbol of the National Movement. In an earlier paper, on the friendship between Gandhi, C.F. Andrews and Principal Rudra of St Stephen's College I have discussed how Gandhi's support of the Khilafat movement took place in meetings held at St Stephens's College (Visvanathan 2001, 2007).

The Economics of *Khaddar*

In this section, I will move to the question of *khaddar*, which Gandhi believed was central to freeing the people from servitude and the claims of imperialism. Today, in the face of the rising statistics of the suicide of farmers to which there seems no solution (for while the nation-state looks towards its technocratic elite as compatible players in the race for world supremacy, locating the debates on agriculture as 'commerce' rather than as 'livelihood' and as a result, a stoic Farmers' Movement rises), our reading of Gandhi in postmodern contexts helps us to understand how similar the structure of enslavement is regardless of who is the purveyor of power. I am indebted to the collection of materials on khadi which Bharatan Kumarappa has edited for us since this makes the task of reading the *Collected Works* easier. Using 'representative' texts is a time-honoured method in cultural studies. When we separate activism from theory, we are presuming that writing is not a specific task for activists. Both Marx and Gandhi communicated very sharply that polemic is a strand embedded in social science because transformative visions are the definitive space of the encounter between the varieties of tradition and the multiple forms of the industrial which beckon to us. While the methods of praxis are substantially different, we know from the work of C.F. Andrews, that questions of socialism, religious experience and Gandhism could well enter into dialogue.

Gandhi, towards the end of his life, in 1944, at a seminar organised on spinning at Sevagram on 1, 2 and 3 September, said that, 'Charkha as an emblem of non-violence stands for self-sufficiency, the ability to get rid of exploitation and domination' (Kumarappa 1959: 146). Gandhi believed that society had to be responsible for the villages of India, and that:

> We have to strike a new departure. We have ignored the proletariat for centuries, and while we have arrogated to ourselves the right of commanding their labor, the thought has never crossed us that they have a right to dictate their wage, that labour is as much their capital as money is ours. It is time we began to think in terms of their needs, their hours of work and leisure, and their standard of living. (ibid.: 118)

At this conference, which was held after he had been imprisoned for two years (he described it as two years of penitential thought), he said, 'India will be known by her villages, not by her cities' (ibid.: 150). Further, he argued, 'Lectures are not enough—research is necessary' (ibid.: 151).

He said when they had begun the *khaddar* movement as part of the struggle for freedom, there were present Maganlal Gandhi with a few friends (ibid.: 154). 'Even with our limited funds we were able to distribute among our village brethren more than four and a half crore of rupees up to date (1944)' (ibid.: 144). Training institutions were to be developed (ibid.: 151) and what he had learnt was that specialisation would be a minimalist and degrading business—everyone should acquire all-round knowledge (ibid.: 163).

If we were to look at *Young India* for 1925, as Kumarappa does, we would see that Gandhi saw the replacement of men by machines as problematic. He says that our people will be killed off by excessive industrialisation. By 1925, he is exhorting everyone to use the spinning wheel. Some wanted women to spin and to allow men to continue the battle with methods more manly (Kumarappa 1959: 270). He goes on to show that men and women have been adept at various kinds of work through the ages, and men have excelled at women's work where it is professionalised and more paying (cooking, spinning, stitching). If people were to clothe themselves, everyone would have to spin—politician, poet, potentate, pandit, pauper, male, female, Hindu, Mussalman, Christian, Parsi or Jew—each will have to give half an hour to spinning for the sake of the country. Gandhi wrote of the importance of a religion of humanity, which was not the exclusive prerogative of any sex or class (ibid.: 28; *Young India* 11 June 1925).

Gandhi did not expect anyone to give up gainful employment for the charkha. It was an activity for the unemployed and as a sacrifice by those who were cerebrally engaged in the task of reconstruction, and that would be by way of example and in order to cheapen *khaddar* for everyday use (Kumarappa 1959: 30).

Durability was not the question, mill cloth was cheaper and perhaps more long-lasting, though there was evidence to the contrary, spinning employed the peasantry. Agriculture and spinning were symbols of the labour required for supplying their primary wants. He wrote:

> Around the charkha, that is amidst the people who have shed their idleness and who have understood the value of co-operation, a national servant would build up a programme of anti-malaria campaign, improved sanitation, settlement of village disputes, conservation and breeding of cattle, and hundreds of other beneficial activities. Wherever charkha work is fairly established all such ameliorative activity is going on according to the capacity of the villagers and the workers concerned. (ibid.: 31)

The immediate task, Gandhi wrote in *Young India* (19 January 1921), was how to feed and clothe ourselves. There would be a transition period where khadi would be coarse, but in a couple of months, Indians would be weaving the fine cotton that was the envy of the world (ibid.: 37). A spinner wrote that with the coming of foreign yarn, the weavers would not buy from her, whereas earlier, she had earned enough to live in dignity, including conducting the rituals such as the marriage of her daughters, and *shraddha* ceremony of a parent. She moaned that the foreign yarn was such it rotted in two months and that the women of Bilayat must be poorer than she was if they could not sell their yarn in their own country. Gandhi commented, 'She could have stood her own even against the foreign yarn, if behind it there had been no policy of determination to capture the Indian trade and kill the national village industry' (Kumarappa 1959: 39; *Young India* 21 May 1931).

The three concerns of Gandhi were spinning for self, hire and sacrifice (Kumarappa 1959: 49).

Gandhi knew that townspeople longed for *khaddar*, that there was a sound market in khadi. He wrote:

> A continued quantity of khadi can be maintained without the slightest difficulty inside of one month. Skilled weavers are to be found all over India. Spinning and the antecedent processes can be learnt inside of one week by those who have the will and the industry. India produces more than enough cotton for all her requirements. (ibid.)

The khadi method stood for non-violence, a new method in politics (ibid.: 50); *khaddar* economics put people back within the frame (ibid.: 66). There will have to be a better and more real bond between ginners, carders, spinners and weavers on the one hand, and the khadi workers on the other (ibid.: 68).

Gandhi says:

> cotton cultivators must become spinners and weavers.
>
> This will free them from the clutches of the speculator. This means that the All India Spinners' Association will have to educate the cultivators in the economics of khadi. There is no doubt that in order to overtake all the branches of khadi work it is necessary for khadi workers to come in close touch with the cotton growers, because even for buying cotton for the manufacture of khadi for town consumption, it would be necessary to come in touch with the cotton growers, and buy from them directly instead of buying in the market as is being done at present.

> If we could be independent of the speculator and the fluctuations of the cotton market and stabilize the price of khadi, we shall have to come in touch with the cultivator and induce him to deal with us directly. The greater the progress of khadi, the more shall we find that our methods have to be far different from those hitherto adopted by the commercial world, which believes in selling at the highest price obtainable and buying at the cheapest rate possible. The world commerce at the present moment is not based upon equitable consideration. Its maxim is 'Buyers beware'. The maxim of khadi economics is 'Equity for all'. It therefore rules out the present soul-killing competitive method. Khadi economics are designed in the interest of the poorest and the helpless, and khadi will be successful only to the extent that the workers permeate the masses and command their confidence. And the only way of commanding their confidence is doing selfless work among them. (Kumarappa 1959: 68, 69)

Gandhi quoted Rajagopalachari to say that a spinner's life was woven in the khadi, that standardisation of thread was not possible, but he would fix in time a standard for quality when selecting yarn. Gandhi believed that khadi was the way in which villages are made starvation proof (ibid.: 72). Gandhi asked for higher wages for the spinners and weavers. 'Then why not dignify the spinner by a wage which will be equal to any other wage?' (ibid.: 113; *Harijan* 10 August 1935). We know by 1944, he is asking the proletariat to state its own wage for labour was the only capital that they had.

How would this interlacing between growing cotton and selling khadi begin? The following are the basic points of Gandhi's manifesto on the survival of cotton workers, so integral to Indians as a people. He argued that:

1. The workers should master all the processes from cotton picking to weaving, so as to be able to teach others.
2. Organisers should make a register of all the carders, spinners, weavers, etc., within their circle of jurisdiction.
3. They should know the variety of cotton used by their spinners and see that they do not attempt to spin a higher count than it is capable of.
4. Spinners and other artisans should be warned that unless they use khadi in their own household, they may not get any work.

5. Artisans should have support by way of facilities.
6. There should be a check on yarn, so that uneven and weak yarn is set aside.
7. Yarn should be accumulated enough for a piece—this will ensure the durability of khadi and improvement in texture and appearance.
8. All pieces thus prepared should have labels attached to them giving the names of ginners, carders, spinners and weavers where these are different.
9. There should be interlinkages between members.

   The lowest-paid worker, the lowest-paid labourer is daridranarayanan (Kumarappa 1959: 16).

Gandhi well understood that cotton was at the heart of commerce and that the townspeople longed for good cotton. What he wished for was the integration of town and country in such a way that the peasants would not starve, that development included them, and that the profits made from their labour would benefit them. I quote him again, for the heart of the problem of neglect, which results in suicide and degradation, is posed by him in such a way that it is the finest form of practical wisdom. To free his people from the 'clutches of the speculator' … this was Gandhi's ultimate dream:

> This means that the All India Spinners' Association will have to educate the cultivators in the economics of khadi. There is no doubt that in order to overtake all the branches of khadi work, it is necessary for khadi workers to come in close touch with the cotton growers, because even for buying cotton for the manufacture of khadi for town consumption, it would be necessary to come in touch with the cotton growers, and buy from them directly instead of buying in the market as is being done at present. (ibid.: 69)

I sincerely believe that young people are taking on the responsibilities of Young India. The dialogue between political parties, which is what democratic unions are about, must engage in catalytic ways with the crises of our people through education, writing and activist work. The tasks of the Freedom Movement still lie with us as we read history in order to understand the poignancy of debt, misery and hunger. While young people concern themselves with the task of building India in the 21st century, the question of its visible poverty must be reread in new and optimistic and pragmatic ways. In the next section, which was written at the invitation of Rathi Vinay Jha and the Fashion Council of India in 2007, I put forward some of the axioms of how to think about handicraft, technologies and adaptative processes by which weavers can think of self-survival of their families and communities.

Weavers and the Fashion Industry

My attempt here is to link the various strands of the design and consumption patterns of the fashion industry to locate the motifs of the worker as a central category. The 5,000-year civilisational history of India has often been focused on the survival of the arts for purposes of popular consumption. However, as Jyotindra Jain has often argued, from the School of Arts and Aesthetics in JNU, artisanal culture, which often incorporates the postmodern dimension of kitsch, must be allowed to survive despite over-exploitation of cultural resources without providing adequate means of livelihood to those communities which have brought these ancient traditions this far. Vijaya Ramaswamy in her book, *Textiles and Weavers of South India* (1985) has argued that the history of South Indian textiles goes as far back as the ancient sites of archaeological interest in Coimbatore and Puducherry. Spindles made from pierced areca nuts and beads or pot shards have been found. She cites Sangam classics to describe ports from where weavers were sent out and describe the streets of weavers which were often built near the towns. Spinning and weaving is part of the mythic vocabulary. Vishnu is *tantuvardan* or a weaver because he has woven the rays of the sun into a garment for himself. According to Ramaswamy, the cotton-carder's bow is in evidence from between 2nd and 6th-century CE. Indigo was often used, as were other dyes made from vegetables and barks. Huge vats from the 1st and 2nd centuries have been found in Arkamedu. Tailors were known in ancient India, for they catered to the lower classes from the hub of the markets near the temples. There are references to the cloth merchants in the second century of the Common Era, for the Romans purchased cotton substantially. In medieval India, the Vijayanagar kings supported textile production, but the colonialism of the British led to the vanquishing of cotton and the weaver. Gandhi's preoccupation with cloth and the producers in the economics of cotton is very well documented.

I am also concerned with how we look at certain elements within the larger framework of the Design and Fashion Industry. It presumes that we would be concerned theoretically and empirically with (a) circulation of wealth in society through the provision of human rights amenities to workers; (b) community support to workers; and (c) the focus on philanthropy and welfare for workers, not reducible to charity. I use certain success strategies in the Handloom Industry, which is a staple of design and fashion. The Andhra Dastkar report of 2007 states that successful collaborative activity between states, producers, designers and workers have focused on:

1. organising collective procurement of raw materials;
2. enabling production by interlinking between institutions; and
3. marketing the product.

What remains central is negotiating with the industry for the well-being of the weaver. The marginalisation of the weaver (and we could substitute it with craftspersons in general) had been contested by voluntary organisations supported by the state and cooperatives.

Implicit in this understanding is that it is not the individual but the broader collective that is focused upon. Each collective is however made up of individuals in relation to each other, and the sociological imperative is to understand what goes on in the functioning of any institutional ensemble at any given time. The Fashion Council of India by drawing sociologists, economists, the media and those directly interested in the marketing of clothes has shown the imperative need to link different personnel as a symbol of their concern to be part of a modernising sector, where human rights and work ethics is part of management procedures and initiatives.

In this context, business and the survival of weavers are supportive categories. Research and institutional support are integral. Government support has gone a long way in furthering the cause of handlooms. Some syncretism has been integral, through the mixture of policies of design schools, district cooperative banks, weavers' service centres and the National Handloom Development Corporation (Dastkar report of 2007). Non-governmental organisations have noted that sometimes this negotiation between the interstices of structures communicates that master weavers as entrepreneurs often failed to share profits with the weavers. This marginalisation was contested by cooperatives. Research and Institutional support are integral. Malfunction in any one of the chains will set off a series of distress in others.

The number of weavers is in some states decreasing. Data shows in the aforementioned reports that even where there are corporations, the weavers are sometimes not paid, and in Karnataka, there had been a sharp decrease, from 2,500 to 700–800 weavers with the Karnataka Handloom Development. The cause has once more been the non-payment of the weavers. Credit and marketing have been key distress areas. Rural crises such as pests, droughts and famines have been rampant. Institutional credit to the co-operatives is low yarns and dyes produced by them, and debit situations arise very easily. Capital may also be required for investment in looms and their repair, and also for domestic and social expenses. The indebtedness of the weavers is legendary.

Dastkar Andhra's central question is how to translate market information for the producers. Sometimes as they note, standardisation itself becomes a problem for when working with cooperatives the worker is in a situation, where he/she loses skills for uniqueness or working with different yarns. Further, the purism that might be associated with handlooms gives way to greater levels of compromise. Power looms and handlooms are not seen in dichotomy, for they are seen within the same organisation to provide different functions. Even the mix of natural and synthetic yarn is not an ideological obstacle. Aesthetics is a primary concern—when this is missing, however cheap or resilient the fabric, such as the case with Janata saris, the pile of unsold materials is hard to dispose of. When pleasing in texture and visual design, the hostels and hospitals become target buyers. In 2006 June, according to the Dastkar report, the departmental purchase had increased from

20 to 50 crores of rupees. The looms had increased from 2,500 to 2,600 in number. However, since the middle class is now the new patron, it is crucial to participate in the larger market, and with designer-increased interest in fabric, for not just clothes but also furnishing, the weaver must be taught how to contribute to the needs and demands of consumers. By adapting to the market, they can use their skills towards the resilience and survival of themselves, their craft and their families and community. Rathi Vinay Jha of the Fashion Council of India, and a former IAS officer who spearheaded much of the publicity programmes of Co-Optex (Tamil Nadu Weavers Co-operative), suggests an entire shift in the vision of designers to playing a nurturing role, rather than a stridently exploitative role. State patronage has to be supported by those groups who see the survival of the arts as central to big business. A lot of the questions of capitalism and worker benefits has been in the hands of the buffer class. This mediating class, whether in capitalism or socialism, consists of the intelligentsia, which includes academics, media, non-governmental organisations, social workers, lawyers and politicians. The central problem they must address is weaver indebtedness.

B. Puneetha, a JNU research scholar argues in an unpublished M. Phil dissertation, following the findings of the Council of Scientific and Industrial Research of 1957, that 'The handloom industry although traditional in nature, involves technical aspects like winding, warping, sizing and bleaching. So, the industry also needs adequate finance to carry out the process.' She draws from the work of Raghubir Shahai, Seemanthini Niranjana and Uzramma to draw attention to why Agriculture Ministry does not focus on Handloom. My fieldwork in the decade of the 1990s showed that fisher people face the same sort of neglect from agricultural ministries (1994, 2000). B. Puneetha focuses also on the physical ailments of the handloom weavers, such as failing sight, swollen feet and tuberculosis. Like fisher people, weavers are often looked down upon. They come to the city as masons, rickshaw pullers and hawkers.

Uzramma of Dastkar Andhra argues that many new people from other occupations now become weavers, so caste-based activity is breaking down to include learning of new skills, by fisher people, toddy tappers, Muslim weavers as well as cosmopolitan design students from metropolitan cities. Puneetha's data for Salem shows that there is a joyful integration of new weavers into community and work. Another JNU scholar, Orjit Kshetriym, has argued for traditional weaving practice in Manipur, that friendship ties in traditional community integrate weavers to the new associations and unions. Co-operative interaction is the solution to pauperisation.

In the *Seminar* issue of 2003 and the public lectures in Canada and India in 2006 and 2007, Uzramma has argued for adaptation and relearning as the new skills of survival. Locating cotton as the fibre that was the traditional wealth of India from days of export to Rome in ancient times, she says that we now only, sadly, contribute 2.5 per cent of the world textile trade, and that too is grey sheeting! She says millions are involved in handloom production, which is still the largest employer in the country after agriculture, 12 million families and more are involved, not including loom and reed makers, dyers, winders, sizers and other specialists. While handlooms are expensive, they do contribute to a fast-growing design industry, with some dialogue in place about chemical dyes and IIT scholars coming in to design non-intrusive and ecologically sustainable power looms for traditional weavers.

The desire to accommodate and educate craftspeople is the preoccupation and life work of Laila Tyebji of Dastkar. In the *Seminar* issue of 2007, focusing on design and handicrafts including fabric, she asks for craft skills to be placed with other vocational training, for schooling for children which integrates these various levels. She argues here that in a handloom-weaving area, the course skills to be taught are product design, bookkeeping, display, merchandising and entrepreneurial skills; also, money management, communication, textile design, draughtsmanship, scale drawing and history of the craft are technical skills. This includes exposure to other weaving skills and styles, different yarns, counts, looms, interaction with designers and artists and craftspeople from different parts of the world.

Laila Tyebji has suggested that craftspeople should themselves be trainers and that state and design centres should collaborate in drawing them into pedagogic structures. Business houses must be able to interact with these professionals on equal terms. Traditional artists when exposed to research centres are able to come away with degrees and new skills and can impart traditional knowledge to others.

In this regard, Jaya Jaitly in the same issue of *Seminar* 2007 says that the success stories of traditional *haat*s or markets in cosmopolitan markets and trade centres have proved the viability of this project. She also describes the case of Niranjan, a kalamkari specialist, who learned from his father Guruppa Chetty and researched old textiles at the Victoria and Albert Museum and then added to his skills.

We have the wonderful archival work of N.H. Nolte in the Edinburgh Botanical Museum, who suggests the link between chintz designers and artists for medical and botanical illustrations.

It is suggested, therefore, by Jaya Jaitly, that schools should encourage the learning of traditional crafts like *chikan*, *kantha* or mirror work. The National Institutes of Design should encourage opening up a 'composite package prepared by master craftspersons where history, local culture, techniques, motifs and meaning of a particular craft are taught' (*Seminar* 2007). This is a theme, well drawn out by Rta Kapur Chishti who looks at innovations in khadi, and like other educationists concerned with community welfare of peasants, tribals and pastoralists often living in urban clusters, argues for 'the linking of hand and heart and head'.

This is well captured by Poonam Bir Kasturi in the issue of *Yojana* July 2007, a NID graduate in her reading of DESI (Developing Ecological Sustainable Industry) begun in 1994 by Prasanna, the founder of the Kavi Kavya Trust. Prasanna integrated Dalits and Backward caste women and taught them how to weave, dye, embroider and paint. He chose the kurta as the focus of his industry, selling these at village fairs, Sunday markets, seminars, schools and colleges, at places where performances were happening; in short, at any public fora.

The other riveting example is of Kurukshetra Kendra in Dehradun, where former lepers produce the most brilliant hued rugs and bags and fabrics, which have found successful markets in Italy and France. Fabindia is another successful organisation that has been able, according to its analysts, to formalise induction, training, account keeping, and has a manual of rules and regulations. In short, the handloom sector must maintain visibility of its human rights concerns. The aim of all organisations must be exactly this, its transparency and bureaucratic functioning. Where there is a lapse, each of us becomes implicated in the whole working of the organisation by our participation in it, as here neither ignorance nor inefficiency will stand the scrutiny of the court of law.

One of the problems which arise when weavers and designers interact is the inbuilt syndrome that weavers and artisans in general face. It is believed that handicraft and rural-based workers need to be paid less because their needs are fewer. This is merely another form of internal colonialism. The business perspective that, 'How do you work out a responsible wage, and still manage to keep prices down?' is problematic. From piece work, ghettoisation, slums and starvation contexts, to collaboration, cooperation and dignity is the bridge that we need to start putting together.

References

Bapu's letters to Mira. 1924–1948. 1949. Ahmedabad: Navajivan Publishing House.

Douglas, Ian Henderson. 1988. *Abul Kalam Azad*. Delhi: Oxford University Press.

Gandhi, Rajmohan, 2006. *Mohandas: A True Story of a Man, His People and an Empire*. Delhi: Penguin, Viking.

Jaitly, Jaya. 2007. 'Crafting an Education for the Educated in Crafting Education'. *Seminar* Issue 570, February.

———. 2007. *Friendship, Interiority and Mysticism*. Orient Blackswan.

Jordens, J.T.F. 1988. *Gandhi's Religion: A Homespun Shawl*. London: Macmillan.

Kumarappa, Bharathan, ed. *Ahmedabad: Khadi*. Navajivan Publishing House, 1959.

Markovits, Claude. 2003. *The Un-Gandhian Gandhi*. Delhi and Ranikhet: Permanent Black.

Ramaswamy, Vijaya. 1985. *Textiles and Weavers of Medieval South India*. Delhi: Oxford University Press.

Romain Rolland and Gandhi Correspondence; Letters, Diary. Extract, Articles. 1976. Delhi: Publication Division, Ministry of Information and Broadcasting.

The Trial of Gandhi (of 1922). 1965. Text with introduction, edited by J.M. Shelat. High Court of Gujarat, Government of India.

Visvanathan, Susan. 2002. 'S.K. Rudra, C.F. Andrews, M.K. Gandhi: Friendship, Dialogue and Interiority in the Question of Indian Nationalism'. *Economic and Political Weekly* xxxviii (34), 24 August.

———. 2007. *Friendship, Interiority and Mysticism*. Orient Blackswan.

Young India, 1919–1922 Mahatma Gandhi. 1924. Triplicane: S. Ganesan.

8

Fishers, Farmers and Industrial Workers in India: An Analysis of Narendra Dev's Contributions

When Prime Minister Lal Bahadur Shastri coined the term 'Jai Jawan, Jai Kisan', he was referring to India's spine, since both farmer and soldier were the pivots of our rural economy. The freedom movement, which we call the Indian National Movement, was the force that allowed us to retrieve our sense of integrity. One thing has remained constant: the masses have remained poor, tied to custom (of which there are diverse forms), and their love for the country as citizens has been proved over and over again.

I shall first record my journey to Kerala, speaking with farmers and fishers in three different locales in November 2008. The second part consists of the close reading of fragments of Narendra Dev, one of the greatest socialists India has produced; his writing in the 1930s in support of the peasant movements is the finest symbol of the lasting value of ideas in our turbulent times. The conclusion draws again from the previous essay (Chapter 7) on Gandhi's preoccupation with farming and weaving as the symbols of hope.

Travelling through Kuttanad and Pallakad by bus and train, I see how much climate change has affected the peasant and fisher people in Kerala. Many of them will be drawn into contract labour, in Kerala itself or the Gulf. It is interesting that rice—a staple for Malayalis—is, like fish, thought to be under tremendous strain. Since it is a fish-and-rice economy, after all, that drives the native people, I decided to find out their status, by interviewing people in Pallakad, Allapuzha and the hinterland of Chenganoor in the summer of 2007.

John Kurian of CDS, Thiruvanthapuram, in an essay 'Traditional Ecological Knowledge and Ecosystem Sustainability' writes that the proverb, 'There is rice in the fields and fish in the waters' is a statement of fact and faith. It is according to him, 'a cruel paradox that farmers and fishers are among the millions who are deprived of even two square meals a day'.

Allapuzha: Fishers and the New Collaborative Ventures

In Allapuzha, at the Fishermen's Development Forum, I met the Director, who is a Catholic priest. He has one primary motive, and that is to create one professional in every fisherman's family. In 2007, 10 students cleared the entrance for the medical exam. Nursing is another viable option for students. He is confident that an emancipated group of individuals is emerging who are capable of dealing on a one-to-one basis with politicians and bureaucrats. They are able to say what they want. The greatest problem they are now facing is with Kerala's tourism project. According to him, there are 700 pleasure boats, now, on the Allapuzha backwaters. They are causing water pollution, and further, because of tourism, prostitution is on the rise among the fisher people and activists have to deal with an HIV-positive vulnerable population. The fisher people are being displaced from the seashore, but the land is being bought by hoteliers, who are building on the beach. This means that the fisher people cannot access the beaches where they traditionally fished. Right to livelihood, right to life is the primary concern of activist-priests like him. The Fishermen's Development Forum in Allapuzha is now crucially concerned with diverting occupations. In 1994, activists had told me that artisanal fishing, which is ecologically sensitive, was heading towards extinction, because of a lack of support from the state. The tsunami made that spectre of extinction a truism. However, this year, activists seemed much more optimistic than in the last two years. There are self-help societies in every fishing village which are concerned with this aspect of surviving the odds. Fish-pickle making, coir-yarn production and entry into artisanal trades and of course professional services in education and health are the career lines now being developed. For Peter Thayil, who has been one of the creative agents of change and coordination among his fellow fish workers, that his son goes to college is a great achievement, just as is for his daughter to have completed a nursing-degree course. In 2021, Thayil's daughter and family live in Ireland where she works as a nurse and his son is a chef in Dubai. Upward mobility has been one of the aims of education and access to education has always been much sought after in Kerala.

In September 2007, there was a Tsunami Agitation, which demanded that the tsunami rehabilitation fund of approximately 1,500 crores should be used appropriately. Allapuzha, which witnessed the tsunami should receive 100 crores for infrastructure development such as electricity, roads, sanitation and water. Women demonstrated when the roads were not tarred and corruption had stalled its completion. They accused the contractor of using a substandard amalgam of materials in making the road, and broke it up, demanding good materials and tarring. Their dharna had good results. In September 2008 there was again another agitation for proper use of tsunami funds, asking that there should be proper allocation to tsunami-hit villages.

Activist organisations working with fisher people have provided rafts made of thermacol, which have made a difference, and lifted them from the poverty line, where, they had remained after the tsunami for almost two years. Now they are able to earn at least 50 rupees a day from fishing, and this is supplemented by the earnings of women in the household.

Another success story has been two cases in Ponnapra and Omnapurra fishing villages, where 20 fishermen in each case had bought five cents of land together by pooling resources, and have set up an association. This meant that they are able to unite and work together as a team. Kerala cannot have unregulated tourism because it would alienate the local people. Sex tourism as it appears in the Philippines would be disastrous for the local economy. The government, while being interested in revenues and foreign exchange, must orient itself to the life chances of the people.

Palakkad: The Rice Belt of Kerala

Kuttanad being low-lying has had a disaster with unseasonal rains, and the rice farmers here, as in villages around Chenganoor, have been badly affected. Palakkad, on the other hand, has better drainage, so rainwater does not cause waterlogging as it does in the central part of Kerala. With climate change, things have changed since the 2018 floods. Flood water generally drains off, leaving the soil insufficiently irrigated. Further, farmers here receive irrigation water from the Mallampura Dam, which traps water at the foot of the Ghats. There is a construction boom in Palakkad, and this includes a 1,000-bed speciality Ahalya Eye Hospital, which has an ayurvedic spa as well. With construction increasing, 20,000 people are expected to benefit from professional employment, contract labour and allied services. A four-lane highway is also in the offing. Generally, now, Palakkad is going to be a boomtown. This has been confirmed with the establishment of the Indian Institute of Technology there.

However, farm labourers in the hinterland Palakkad villages of Thenukurishy and Kannady are concerned by the fact that they are the last generation, and that the work of cultivation is not acceptable by a new generation that is educated and prefers clerical work, masonry or construction.

There is no agricultural labour available, so even farmers with smaller landholdings are dependent on threshers who come from Tamil Nadu. These cost 1,500 rupees per hour. There has been a lot of debt among Palakkad farmers, and some unable to pay back their loans to banks have committed suicide. But rice is their staple, and that is what they wish to grow. The losses, however, are more than they can handle. Farmers in Chenganoor and Allapuzha feel the same—without any profit, they feel the loss terribly.

Appukutty Masha, a retired schoolteacher near Kannadi village, explained to me the process of what cultivation means to him. Love for agriculture is his legacy. The Mallapuram dam that came in 1956 made the farmers independent, to some extent, from the rain. But the dam lacks water regularly in the summer because of insufficient rains; the water is sent every fifteen days with regular breaks in between. For three days now, the canals have been dry and everything, consequently, shrivels. Masha loves farming and since he has a pension, he can manage even in the years when there is loss from drought or unseasonal rain. But what about the others? He says that by putting the fertilizers himself without hiring farm labourers, he had saved 500 rupees a day. He is sixty-five, but despite his age, he enjoyed paddy cultivation.

Interestingly, the women who were weeding a nearby acreage said they too liked their work. The mud is warm and soft and squelchy, and as they are bent double, they do not speak. 'Do you like your work?' I ask them hesitantly. 'Of course!' one old woman said. 'It's for food, it's sacred.' There are others, though, who are old now, who remember nothing but decades of drudgery.

The labourers have already cooked their food in the morning. They will work from 8 AM to 4 PM with an hour's break for lunch. The children will return from school when they reach home. One old woman makes me promise that I will communicate how poor they are: the 80 rupees a day they receive will be finished at the grocers' on the same day itself.

The men in the teashop explain the debt cycle to me. Farmers borrow 25,000 rupees a season (in 2008) to cover the costs of buying *vith* or seed and fertilizers, wages for labourers for clearing and planting, hiring of threshers, and transport for the markets and depots. If the rains fail, or there is an unseasonal flood (both happened last year), then the entire crop is lost. There is endless risk and once the crop is gone, there is no way of returning the money, and the interest on the loan increases. Where is the farmer to go?

The only good thing about being a farmer, according to one man, was that one could eat good food which one grew: rice and fruit and vegetables. The chemical fertilizers were the only option because the seeds were such. They were ostensibly high-yielding seeds that had to be bought every season but crushed the farmer in a debt cycle he could never evade. With organic farming so much in the limelight, I ask them whether this will not help their cause. They say what a former agricultural officer told me in Allapuzha, that it is cost-prohibitive. The reason is also as everyone knows: the seeds farmers buy are hybrid, and not the ones which they traditionally used, which are regenerative. There is an organic farm, they tell me, near Erimayur village; they have heard of it, but the concept has not percolated. In 2009, at a conference on ecology at Nehru Memorial Museum and Library, I met an agricultural officer from Palakkad, who told me they have had great success with organic farming and would wish to see that the rice reached the poor at the lowest cost.

The 'tradition' is chemical fertilizers. In Allapuzha, Shylaja, a woman farmer of Thuttikad Nedumbedi, tells me that the flooding last year and the paucity of rain when it ought to have rained, had made her plant her second crop in late November, she is, therefore, two months late. Seasonal practices are being disrupted by climate change. Abraham Verghese has a fertilizer-and-pesticide shop in the heart of town. He does not believe that organic farming is viable because it is too costly. He keeps organic manure for the farmer with small landholdings, who grows food for his family—a mixture of bone meal and ash is used as fertilizer. To most who come to him for advice (for he has an ability to keep customers at ease and answers their queries), he sells chemical fertilizers as they specifically ask for them. Each of these people who visit him has a problem with pests, flies, weeds and rodents: the list is endless. Since one-crop farming has rampant dangers, most farmers grow a variety of things. Multi-cropping or intensive farming has been the tradition in Kerala. In Palakkad, wherever the paddy has not been planted this year, for instance, plantains are grown. The Kerala proverb '*vazzaeku vellam koddukuumbam cheerae ku kittum*' means when you water the plantain, the spinach also gets water. Biodiversity has been the ethic.

Both men and women in Kerala, regardless of religion, caste or class, are conversant with agricultural practice as well as with marketing. While waiting at the teashop where labourers come to get themselves a cup of tea, a bevvy of women were heading for the panchayat office. It is an official trip combined with the sense of an exhilarating social outing. They board the bus and assure me that they would answer my questions on their return!

How difficult is it to cultivate rice? Mathai Sam, who grows rice for his family and not the market, explains the process to me in the hinterland village of Chenganoor.

Chenganoor: The Everyday Grammar of Growing Food Crops

Ideally, there are two *krishi*s or harvests, but this year, because of climate change, Sam cannot sow his second crop since the monsoon season brought no water. He planted 35 kg of seed which he bought from the Agriculture Department at 10 rupees a kilogram. (Because of unseasonal rain, he lost half his crop and will have to buy rice for his family in March 2009.) In order to plant, he hired a tractor from the Agriculture Department for three days, for two hours each, incurring a total cost of 1,400 rupees. Describing the process, he said:

> We first soak the seeds in water after the land is cultivated. Then we gather the seeds and put them in sacks. Then we throw it on the ground. We throw water on the seeds by hand to make them damp, otherwise, they will fly about. Then we throw compost, urea, potash, bone meal and neem powder on the earth. After three days, the seeds start to sprout. Then we put neem and lime to save them from pests. After 30 days, the sprouted plants are transplanted. Three days following this, we treat it with fertilizer, throwing it by hand into the field.

After 60 days, pesticides are usually sprayed, but he does not since it is for his family's use. After 90 days, harvesting takes place. Workers spend four days threshing with their feet. Then the grain is dried and placed in the store or *arra*.

That is a lot of work, and so it is said, in Kerala, that every grain of rice bears the name of he or she who eats it. Its preciousness never allows for waste, and it goes by the name of *anna* in the scriptures (Panikkar 1977).

The survival of the peasantry is the leitmotif of India's success despite global recession. The crops have always been bountiful though there are innumerable critics of modern industrialised agriculture which takes away the daily livelihood of the common farmer, known in general as the small farmer. However, we must accept that the resilience of the Indian economy is entirely due to this section of our population, which is also the stable element of our modern banking system, the keeper of the savings account.

I now turn to two great thinkers Acharya Narendra Dev and Mahatma Gandhi, who were both leaders of peasant struggles, where the everyday struggle of the national movement was anchored. As in Chapter 7, where I had used the lives of Romain Rolland, Madeleine Slade and Mahatma Gandhi as leitmotifs, here I will abstract from the writing of Narendra Dev, to employ concepts useful for postmodern India and its mosaics of tradition and modernity.

Acharya Narendra Dev: Interpreting His Contribution to the Socialist Movement in the 1930s

Acharya Narendra Dev had historic links with Banaras Hindu University and Lucknow University, where he served as both an academic and vice-chancellor. He was an authority on Sanskrit and Buddhist matters, conversant in many languages (knowing Sanskrit, Pali, Prakrit, French, German, Urdu, Hindi and English), interested in philosophy and the arts, trained in inscriptions and archaeology and a lawyer as well. The freedom movement saw many people like him, who were able to serve the people without repudiating them, as well as having an ability to be loyal in serving ideas. His dream was that of freedom, citizenship and what he called a democratic intelligentsia, by which he meant that socialism could serve as a conveyor of ideas, without shackling individuals. Justice V.K. Krishna Aiyyer in his lead essay in *The Hindu* of 24 December 2008, writes of similar issues, asking for the constitutional imperative towards freedom of thought, socialism (to be read as concern for the poor), liberty, equality and solidarity.

Narendra Dev writes, that the ultimate goal is 'to every man according to his needs' and quotes Marx to the effect that 'the real content of the proletarian demand for equality is the demand for the abolition of classes. Any demand for equality which goes beyond that of necessity passes into absurdity' (Dev 1998: 26).

It is this reading, which approximates a mosaic, which allows ways of life to coexist, which lets a Jamshedji Tata or a Birla stand side by side with Gandhi. Patronage implied human rights and justice.

Industrial workers, as Chitra Joshi has argued so brilliantly in her book *Lost Worlds* (2003), implied peasantry coming into the workplace with myriad castes, class, village or religious backgrounds. Patronage, however, was never a viable concept for the peasantry which always communicated that the world order was centred around its quest for survival. Socialism is a representation of that interactive space where the redistributive ethic is a constant. We find it in traditional societies where the chief receives only in order to give away.

Narendra Dev's journey was one of reinventing traditions and mobilising the peasants. He had gone with his father when he was a young boy to the Lucknow session of the Congress in 1899. He was soon influenced by Tilak.

He took a vow of swadeshi, having been influenced by extremist politics. The Congress was seen to be elitist and moderates preserve, representing the upper-middle-class and landed gentry.

Hari Dev Sharma, former director of Nehru Memorial Museum and Library, who had edited Acharyaji's writings gives us a background history of Narendra Dev's work (1998). He says that after 1916, there were two key figures in Congress: Annie Besant and Tilak. In 1916, two Home Rule leagues were formed—one headed by Besant the other by Tilak. To popularise the programme of Besant's Home Rule League, Nehru, the Secretary of its UP branch, visited Faizabad, where he met Narendra Dev. After the meeting, the Faizabad branch of Besant's Home Rule League was established with Narendra Dev as its secretary (Dev 1998: xx).

A group within the Congress comprising Nehru, S. Srinivas Iyengar, Subhas Chandra Bose, Dr Zakir Husain and others was unhappy with the traditional Congress line. They formed the Independence for India League to press Congress to adopt Independence as its goal (ibid.: xxii).

The Congress, at Calcutta in December 1928, passed a resolution that if within a year the British government did not grant Dominion status, it would pass a resolution demanding complete independence at its next session. This it did at Lahore in 1929. It also passed a resolution for launching a struggle to achieve it. This, Hari Dev Sharma, the editor of the *Collected Works of Acharya Narendra Dev*, sees as a result of the influence of the League (Sharma 1998: xxiii).

In pursuance of the Lahore Resolution, the country observed 'Independence Day' on 26 January 1930. The 'Independence Pledge' severely indicted British rule. It held it responsible for all the ills—economic, political, cultural and spiritual—India suffered from.

India was in revolt. Acharyaji played a leading role in organising the people for the coming struggle. He moved from place to place, explaining the meaning of complete independence and propagating the use of the spinning wheel as a symbol of swadeshi. This is the link that I wish to make in this paper that Narendra Dev's socialism persistently accepted Gandhism as a viable method for understanding the survival of the peasantry.

On 5 March 1931, the Gandhi–Irwin Pact was signed. The salt satyagraha came to an end. Acharyaji was appointed member of the Congress Working Committee in April 1936. Thus, the Congress Socialist Party (henceforth CSP), represented a genealogy: Besant, Nehru, Gandhi, Acharya Narendra Dev, Jayaprakash. Today, however, Narendra Dev's contribution remains well-known only to socialists and historians of the Freedom Movement. Like Gandhi, he gave us a lasting legacy in terms of understanding grassroots movements.

The Congress Socialist Party was not interested in power politics, it did not want to capture power and position in the Congress organisation through political alliances. The CSP did not want to disrupt the unity of the congress because it represented Indian unity and democracy (Sharma 1998: xxiv).

The Congress Socialists were egging on the Congress to launch a mass struggle against the British government. In October 1940, Gandhiji decided to launch the individual satyagraha. Although he was not well, Acharyaji participated in the satyagraha and was imprisoned in the Gorakhpur and Agra jails (ibid.).

In September 1941, when Acharyaji came out of jail, he had lost 18 pounds in weight. Gandhiji invited him to stay with him at Sevagram. He was hesitant. However, when he went to Wardha for the All India Congress Committee (AICC) meeting in January 1942, Gandhi persuaded him to stay at Sevagram. He took great care of Acharyaji; they became closer to each other. It was the time when Gandhiji was thinking of launching another struggle against the British. Soon after, the AICC met at Bombay on 7 and 8 August 1942 to consider the Quit India resolution. Gandhiji made a marathon speech. The resolution was passed by an overwhelming majority. However, 12 Communist members of the AICC and Dr P. Subbarayan, the father of Mohan Kumaramangalam, voted against it. Acharyaji was one of the speakers at the historic session. Opposing the Communists, he said that it was a pity that at the time of the final struggle, there were still people who were not prepared to make the sacrifices required of them. The session concluded in the small hours of 9 August 1942. Gandhiji and the members of the Congress Working Committee were arrested the same day and kept in detention—Gandhiji and his entourage in the Aga Khan Palace at Poona and the members of the Congress Working Committee in the Ahmednagar Fort. Acharyaji, while at Ahmadnagar Fort, completed the Hindi translation of Poussin's French version of the *Abhidaharmakosha*, an important work on *Sarvastivada*, which he had done in Banaras District Jail in 1933. He summarised many other works on Buddhist philosophy. He also helped Jawaharlal Nehru with *Glimpses of World History*.

Acharya Narendra Dev worked very closely with the peasants. First, in Faizabad. In 1930, he visited various districts to study their desperate condition. In 1931, a committee was appointed by the Congress and Acharya Narendra Dev was its member. He submitted a report on the problems of the *kisan*s of Basti, Gorakhpur and Sampuranand.

After 1934, Acharya Narendra Dev enlisted the peasants to the Congress: this changed the class character of the Congress in the fight against British Imperialism. Peasant organisations were already in existence, and these came together in Meerut on 15 January in 1936 to form the All India Kisan Organisation, where the CSP was holding its conference.

On 11 April 1936, the representatives of the *kisan* organisation again met in Lucknow. Thus was founded the All India Kisan Sabha. Initially, it was called the All India Kisan Congress. Some called it All India Kisan Sangh. Later the name was changed to All India Kisan Sabha. In founding the Sabha, CSP leaders played a major role. Acharya Narendra Dev wanted them linked to the Congress. In a letter to Nehru, dated 1 December 1928, he wrote:

> I have received copies of the constitution and membership forms. Hindi forms are ready. The Hindi translation of the Constitution is also ready

> and will soon be printed. At present I am concentrating on big towns because it is only in such places that we can get suitable organizers and can expect a fair enrolment. I am experiencing some difficulty in the matter of selection. I know I have to proceed cautiously. I have to avoid communalists. Even the Congress circle is tainted with the poison of communalism. (Sharma 1998: 1)

One of the interesting problems of reading this particular fragment is the continuum that the Acharya requires between town and country, and the marked exclusion of the communalists. Ideologies are always marked by such clear-cut orientations. They provide in social science, the meeting point between thought and action, which is called praxis.

Narendra Dev's voice is very clear here, and as Roland Barthes argued in the *Rustle of Language* (1984), scholarship consists of science, literature and pleasure. The last often comes from ideology, philosophy, social science or theology, if not from pure invention. When it comes to Narendra Dev, the ability to integrate thought and action is what makes his life so pre-eminently a source of strength for those looking for criticisms of exploitative or genocidal ideologies. N.C. Goray writes in B.V. Keskar and Menon's anthology of commemorative essays, that Narendra Dev created a solid ideological base. He remained a Marxist while having differences with the official Marxist party. The Congress Socialist Party remained at the forefront of the 1942 struggle. While Nehru's socialism was vague, Acharya Narendra Dev was consistent and articulate. He was concerned directly with the implication of political work for the role of the peasantry, the decentralisation of power (Keskar and Menon 1971: 90). Ashok Mehta, in the same volume, draws our attention to Acharya's emphasis on *kisan* sabhas, cooperatives and trade unions. Goray is also emphatic of the role played by Narendra Dev with regard to the question of language and linguistic states, and his concern and analysis of individualism (ibid.: 91). Perhaps the latter point is pivotal in understanding Narendra Dev's trajectory.

Yusuf Meherally writes that Acharya Narendra Dev began his studies as an archaeologist at Queen's College, Benares. He took his master's degree in 1913 in epigraphy, palaeography and numismatics. He decided to leave the quiet life of academia and took up law. When he completed his degree, he returned to Faizabad in 1915 and took up the secretaryship of the local Home Rule League. Mehrally also says that Narendra Dev was influenced by Tilak and by A.K. Coomaraswamy (Keskar and Menon 1971: 99).

In another letter to Nehru on 9 February 1929, Acharya writes in H.D. Sharma's edited *Selected Works of Acharya Narendra Dev* (1998)

> I think the apathy that we see around us is, more or less, due to want of any intellectual convictions. I therefore think that the primary work lies before us is to stimulate thought by providing intellectual food for our people. For this the League should run a weekly paper, if necessary funds are forthcoming, and have a bookshop of its own where such literature can be forthcoming. (3)

In a more specific directive, he writes a letter to the Secretary, Independence of India League, dated 20 March 1929:

1. Wherever possible, branches of the League shall be organised;
2. Suitable literature shall be published in the languages of the province for popularising the objects of the league;
3. Labour and peasant unions shall be formed; and
4. The League shall cooperate with the Congress in strengthening its organisation and furthering its programme.

While speaking at the Presidential Address at the Patna Congress Socialist Conference on 17 May 1934, Narendra Dev argued that a true Marxist was not dogmatic or sectarian. The dialectical method allowed for the unity of opposites and was thus a method of great elasticity (Sharma 1998: 10).

Such a person, he believed, would emphasise collective action based on the organisation of the masses and their inclusion in the national struggle. This would be more constructive than hoping for unity in terms of a basis that does not exist.

Towards this direction, Acharyaji believed that the two methods to be used are propaganda and organisation. This was the direct opposite of unorganised protest called spontaneous peasant risings or riots and without leadership, ideology or charismatic heroes, these were immediately quelled, for 'it is only the revolutionary intelligentsia that can organise them for disciplined action' (Sharma 1998: 12). He went on to say that 'we are being irresistibly driven to the widening of the social basis of our national movement by formulating economic policies for the welfare of the masses. Socialism is in the air' (ibid.).

In a manifesto that is still valid today, Acharya Narendra Dev asked for 'a platform of unity,' where the peasants would be at the centre of attention. The labour movement saw the peasants as a valuable ally for the All India Working Class Party (ibid.: 13).

Acharya Narendra Dev was extremely clear that industrial work and peasant identity could go hand in hand. This was the tacit assumption of the freedom movement, where so many of Gandhi's ideas were drawn from peasant politics. Narendra Dev writes:

> One more advantage would have accrued to us as a result of such a policy. In India, where the labour force is drawn from villages and where the industrial worker remains a villager at heart the worker can act as a standard bearer of revolution in villages. (ibid.: 15)

He believed that overproduction, when accompanied by maldistribution, resulted in a terrible crisis. His voice is still very valid for us today:

> The tragedy of the situation is that though productive powers of society have grown excessively, the purchasing power of the people has somehow vanished and millions of workers and peasants have been ruined. Millions of workers have been thrown out of employment and those who still work have their wages reduced and the other social benefits taken away from them. This is the inevitable consequence of an economic system whose basis is exploitation. (ibid.: 16)

Much of what he writes is a good description of present-day labour crises, where the resolutions have been either shootings or lay-offs:

> The rights of free speech and public assembly are being everywhere attacked and the right of strike is being narrowed down. What do these facts indicate? That capitalism has entered into a blind alley and does not know how to get out; that it is seeking a solution of the difficulty by having recourse to palliatives and temporary expedients, by controlled capitalism or by fascism. As the danger increases the possibilities are that it will tend more and more towards fascism. (ibid.: 19)

In many of the works of writers like Romain Rolland and Simone Weil writing in the 1930s, we find a similar preoccupation with human rights and justice, and the preoccupation with peasants and working-class lives, for the bulk of the movement against fascism had its roots among the de-classed.

Today, however, we see that capitalists hope to monopolise farms everywhere, edging out the small shops and the small farmers. The farmers' movement takes on the large corporate houses, which hope to appropriate the commons and the small farms with the help of the state.

Acharya Narendra Dev believed as industrialisation became productive, redistribution would be the socialist answer to bridging the gap between labour as producer and bourgeoisie as a consumer. So also with Marx, in the valuable axiom, 'to each according to his need'.

Narendra Dev quotes him:

> One man will excel another physically or intellectually and so contribute at the same time more labour, or can labour for a longer time .... Further, one worker is married, another single, one has more children than another, and so on. Given an equal capacity for labour and thence an equal share in the funds for social consumption, the one will in practice and receive more than the other, the one will be richer than the other and so on. (Sharma 1998: 26)

In the 20th century, feminist arguments for the right to work and receive equal wages received substantial attention.

I will close the argument for reading fragments as cultural anthropologists do by returning to Gandhi's ideas on cotton and the close inter-relation between farmer and weaver. It is a motif well worth repeating since the omnipresent consumer culture is dependent on the weaver for fabric. The desperation of peasants is augmented or buttressed by the hunger of the globalised world for fabric. The testimony of the charkha as the most desired object for clothes and furnishings in the globalised world brings us back to the key debates of the 1930s and 1940s—food, fabric and freedom.

Today I sincerely believe that young people are taking on the responsibilities of Young India. The dialogue between political parties, which is what democratic unions are about, must engage in catalytic ways with the crises of our people through education, writing and activist work. The tasks of the Freedom Movement still lie with us as we read history in order to understand the poignancy of debt, misery and hunger. In the next essay, I will read some of the texts which help us to understand the new locations of tourism, pilgrimage and urbanism, where, like fishers, the forest people merge with peasantry and traders, in the new contexts of globalisation and changed forms of community and communication.

References

Bapu's letters to Mira, 1924–1948. 1949. Ahmedabad: Navajivan Publishing House.

Dev, Acharya Narendra. 1998. *Selected Works,* Vol. 1, edited by Hari Dev Sharma. Delhi: Radiant Publishers.

Jordens, J.T.F. 1998. *Gandhi's Religion: A Homespun Shawl.* London: Macmillan.

Joshi, Chitra. 2003. *Lost Worlds: Indian Labour and its Forgotten Histories.* Delhi: Permanent Black.

Keskar, B.V. and V.K.N. Menon, eds. 1971. *Acharya Narendra Dev: A Commemoration Volume.* Delhi: National Book Trust.

Kumarappa, Bharathan, ed. 1959. *Khadi.* Ahmedabad: Navajivan Publishing House.

Kurien, John. 1998. 'Traditional Ecological Knowledge and Ecosystem Sustainability'. Available at www.researchgate.net/publication/240777625_Traditional_Ecological_Knowledge_and_Ecosystem_Sustainability_New_Meaning_to_Asian_Coastal_Proverbs (accessed on 18 September 2021).

Markovits, Claude. 2003. *The Un-Gandhian Gandhi.* Delhi: Permanent Black.

Gandhi, Mahatma. 1924. *Mohandas: Young India, 1919–1922.* Madras: S. Ganesan.

Gandhi, Rajmohan. 2006. *Mohandas: A True Story of a Man, His People and an Empire.* New Delhi: Penguin, Viking.

Panikkar, Raimundo. 1977. *The Vedic Experience: Mantramanjari.* Delhi: Motilal Banarsidas Publishers.

Romain Rolland and Gandhi Correspondence; Letters, Diary. Extract, Articles. 1976. Delhi: Publication Division, Ministry of Information and Broadcasting.

Shils, Edward. 1958. 'The Intellectuals and the Powers; Some Perspectives for Comparative Analyses'. *Comparative Studies in Society and History,* 1 October.

The Trial of Gandhi of 1922. 1965. Text with introduction, edited by J.M. Shelat. High Court of Gujarat, Government of India.

9

Foresters and New Orientations to Survival

Grass for cows, and the variegated forest grown in the last forty years by the cooperation of housewives, college students and local farmers; November 2019.

400-year-old tree in the courtyard of Sri Ramanasramam; November 2019.

Kathleen Morrison, in her essay on pepper in the hills, considers the role of tribal communities in the Western Ghats in the production of pepper valuable for purposes of trade with the West, right up to the early 20th century. She describes these uplands people as being hunters, farmers, pastoralists, even bandits as repudiating the idea of 'simple aborigines'. She writes:

> I will be concerned here to trace some of the changes and possible changes in the organization of foraging/trading groups in southwestern India coincident with the expansion of the coastal spice trade and the increasing integration of this region into a world economy in the immediate precolonial and early colonial periods; that is between about AD 1400 and 1700. (Morrison in Cederlof and Sivaramakrishnan 2005: 45)

Even today, there is great interest in pepper as a spice sought after by many outside Kerala. So far all the pepper I did bring home had been from Syrian Christian gardens. Tamarind for fish and pepper for everyday use is produced in the small kitchen gardens of relatives. How then shall we think about foresters and farmers and their present location in globalised contexts?

Tourism is one aspect, the other is survival in their habitat in the manner in which they are accustomed without being exposed to predators, who are culturally, politically or ideologically vested with powers to displace forest peoples. I wish to use the term forester since this takes into account all those who make biodiversity their concern. It might be relevant here to look at the website of the Australian and Kerala aboriginals where the similarity between them as a racial type has been communicated and endorsed. Colonial photography, as well as tourist photography, has raised many issues regarding the presentation of the self vis-à-vis the photographer and his or her subjects. The same questions are raised with regard to arts and artists in a globalising world, where the ethnic and the cosmopolitan museum are juxtaposed.

Ramchandra Guha refers to the contemporisation of tribal studies by writing about the painter J. Swaminathan who was the curator of the Bhopal Museum. He was a man who had admired Verrier Elwin, so he sent out thirty students to recover and learn from the natural archives of the tribals, namely their homes. 'The students fanned out into the forests and uplands while Swaminathan himself headed for Patangarh. Here he found one house decorated with the most vivid portraits of birds in flight and tribal deities in a zestful mood' (Guha 1999: 323). Bharat Bhavan built its collection around this artist Jangarh who was a Pardhan from Elwin's village and related to the latter's wife Lila. In contrast, perhaps is the story of the same tribal artist trapped in a modern Japanese art gallery, far from home, commissioned to produce 'tribal art' but destined to die homesick, alone, desperate, and by his own hand.

Much of the questions of tribal culture in the 21st century centred around the problems of nation-state politics, arguments for integration and assimilation, quests for nation and sovereignty, commercialisation of their territories and products through tourism, and the forces of globalisation, including accessibility to territories by police, administrators, hoteliers and political parties.

When it comes to the question of the forests, tribe and caste communities may be severally divided or interlaced with shared interests. Many of the new problems regarding the reading of caste, in the case of village communities and peasantry, draw from political scientists and historians as much as sociologists. Sociologists have tended to stay with the categorisations of caste within fieldwork studies. The enhancement of the varna model in terms of the continuous reading of jati as the established practice for the 1980s and 1990s of the 20th century has been valuable. Village studies have been substituted by a variety of area studies where caste and class have been analysed in terms of livelihood patterns. The best example of this kind of work is that of M.S.S. Pandian, whose *Brahmin and Non-Brahmin* (2007), has given us new indexes for reading caste politics in terms of the grammar of mobility. Similarly, the corpus of work associated with Satish Saberwal has defined the varied locations of power in the last 100 years. How can we understand domination, particularly when it appears through bureaucracy and law? What happens to caste and class and religious identity when tradition is re-read through the map of colonial interventions? In this context, we may benefit from Ananthamurthy's reading of the 'co-existence of time', where in a public lecture given at Nehru Memorial Museum and Library in the early 1990s, he spoke of each sentimentalising their experience and identity. Orthodoxies and the right to free choice with regard to marriage, food practices, occupation or companionship alternatives intermesh in contradictory but not problematic ways.

Kumari Jayawardena in *Erasure of the Euro-Asian* (2007) refers to poly-vocal voices, the blurring, highlighting, amnesias or stridency in the choices people make about recalling their past and intentions for the future, which are varied. Many sociologists now use narrative analyses to explain processes such as racial mixing or varieties of hybridities to understand globalisation. These methodologies steeped in self-proclaimed bias such as feminism or Marxism, Dalit or right-wing sociologies, all require some alertness to the matter of objectivity in social science.

Consider, for instance, Paul Gilroy's classic reading of race relations in the modern world, where questions of being what he calls 'between camps' is a routine aspect of existence. He returns to Fanon's preoccupation with 'epidermalised' embodiment, going on to argue that it is the reciprocity between environment and the body that we must be concerned with. Here, internal cannot be identified with genetic, but reciprocity is the key ensemble of relations between nature and culture (Gilroy 2004: 40). These are very old debates, where the 'curse of racial domination is the condition, of being black, but of being black in relation to the white' (ibid.). The ghettos of tribal peoples in reservations often resemble concentration camps as a 'novel form of political administration, population management, warfare, and coerced labour' (ibid.: 61).

If there is a mutuality between human beings and culture, how do we understand this relationship in modernism? We know that Max Weber's methodological call to stating one's bias before proceeding to explain a social phenomenon or the directive to keep politics outside the classroom has been of great significance. Similarly, Clifford Geertz's call to believe in the task of an objective social science is despite the calling to art, creativity, spontaneity and expressivity is well taken. Feminism has liberated many spaces of social documentation once rendered invisible or silent. Genealogical maps, questions of land-ownership, ghettos having a majority of women as heads of households because of issues or work or displacement, all draw our attention to the problem of gender and identity.

New questions regarding urban space are generated through media analyses, which include film, photography, advertising the world wide web and new forms of bureaucracy and domination. Analyses of citizenship rights and new forms of democratic judicial enquiry are pertinent to the questions of reading urban space. One of the most interesting debates is around the problem of the peasantry as it appears on the map of urban life and factory production. Sociologists and historians have proved over and over again how the factory worker is drawn from peasant or tribal background. Who is the immigrant to the industrial belt? The Special Economic Zones (SEZs) and the issue of confrontation between displaced peasantry, political parties, mafia bosses, provide many sociological issues that the 21st-century Indian cultural anthropologists have to encounter. Exclusion refers to large masses of people being out of the privileges of development, while their labour may be used to manufacture the means of production. Human Rights Watch groups have always been concerned with the problem of the servitude of the Indian masses to the state, and yet we know that the poverty of the large mass of the Indian people is matched by their resilience and their ability to shake up the government in power through the electoral process.

Many of these questions are raised in Paul Graves-Brown's collection of essays where the authors consider material culture as a problem not just of ideas and relationships but with regard to objects and things, where the human body may also be seen as an artefact. Things according to him have life histories—technologies, phases of invention, commercialisation and adoption. Artefacts are manufactured, used, discarded, preserved or reused. In this collation of essays, Bruno Latour, who uses the function of the key, to understand what it means to be locked in, locked out, be in a state of being controlled or innovating ways to escape control writes that when it comes to material culture we must look at 'circulations, sequences, transfers, translations, displacements, crystallization'. He says, 'Consider things and you will have humans consider humans, and you are by that very act interested in things. Bring your attention to humans, and see them become electronic circuits, automatic gears or softwares' (Latour in Graves-Brown 2000: 20).

This depersonalisation of knowledge through the customs of war zones and postmodern worlds help us understand how individuals become mere atoms to be observed on television or computer surveillance screens, having little identity other than their visibility. Mediation for Latour is a process of how networks are created.

In a seminar held at the Nehru Memorial Museum and Library, Delhi, the 'Kalpavriksha', a well-known Delhi-based non-governmental organisation, having its origin in the early 1980s at Hindu College, Delhi University, interacted with government officials, journalists, activists and university scholars. It is this intermeshing between various bodies of society that promotes a healthy and optimistic view of the world. Checks and balances, support and questions of criticism and free speech, disciplined in their motive while being completely judgemental, are the signs of a free society.

Kalpavriksh and Grain brought out a publication for public discussion 'Six Years of the Biological Diversity Act in India' at Nehru Memorial Museum and Library on 3 February 2009. They write in this text, that

> Human interactions with biological resources are determined by cultural contexts, religious beliefs and economic considerations. The diversities of local practices through which people spiritually revere, carefully select and collectively nurture diversity, comprise the means of managing these natural life forms. These practices aim at achieving a delicate balance between the need to use nature's resources to meet absolute needs and allowing for the regeneration of natural systems. There are, however, different worldviews, which seek to harness natural systems often resulting in its over-exploitation. The term 'diversity' then becomes a 'resource' which can be accessed marketed and controlled. This is where conflicts develop, between users of natural resources, precipitating at both ideological realms and practical instances. (Kalpvriksh and Grain Report 2009: 1)

Implicit in this Act of 2002 and the Biological Diversity Rules 2004, are certain key dimensions: the ban on transfer of genetic materials outside the country without permission; prohibition on claiming patents on Indian materials without permission; control of the collection and use of materials by Indians; but greater freedom for those communities traditionally engaged with these tasks' measures for research use; joint research with consequences for monetary benefits (national vs local interests); provisions for conservation and protection, and local communities to be involved in the manner of disposal of resources; protection of indigenous traditional knowledge; regulation of the use of genetically modified organisms; setting up of national, state and local biodiversity funds to support conservation and benefit-sharing; setting up of biodiversity management committees (BMCs) at local, village and urban levels, biodiversity boards at the state level, a national biodiversity board at the larger integrative level of the Indian state. Kanchi Koli, presenting the report, asked for the collaborative interaction of local peoples, non-governmental organisations, government and the intelligentsia.

I now come to regenerative forest policy and its success in the case of Tiruvannamalai. The materials are drawn from a larger work *The Children of Nature* written by me from my notes made during fieldwork in Tiruvannamalai, while based at Sri Ramanasramam, the hermitage of Sri Ramana Maharshi.

In Tiruvannamalai, a pilgrim town which I have been visiting since 1995 (Visvanathan 2008, 2010) the case of peasantry and afforestation has several dimensions, for, at one level, it is landless labour which is employed by the greenings association to plant saplings. Their wages are low, and they are local grasscutters who are in the pay of the association. Annamalai Reforestation Society has a board consisting of several members who appear annually for meetings. Yet the volume of work done despite this low-profile attitude is substantial. It is dependent on donations from visitors to Ramanasramam and the guiding light of the association is an old couple, Mahalakshmi and Suryanandan, who concern themselves with the day-to-day arrangements of the nursery and sapling transplantation. J. Jayaraman, the librarian at Sri Ramanasramam, has also been centrally involved since the gift of the land for the nursery was made by a friend of the *asramam*, who inherited some money from her father, and told J J, that she had never owned land. Once the land was bought, she transferred it to the Society. In some senses, it is like a miracle.

However, the real spirit behind the afforestation programme has been Abhitha Arunagiri, who has, according to V.S. Mani (one of the trustees of the Ramanasramam and a grand nephew of Maharshi Ramana), been the single person for thirty years most involved with reforestation. It is her story that is central to this tale, so I shall be using some of her letters and documentation on the web to communicate how efficacious her work has been. Presently, she works with school children and housewives, mobilising support from visitors, cafe owners, caregivers of various kinds and philanthropists of various degrees.

It is important to note how variegated the term 'peasant' can mean in globalised contexts. Those who stand for commerce and overbuild in Tiruvannamalai have stakes in saleable land as farmers or merchants, those who plant trees for ecological sustenance, also are tillers of the soil. Resulting from the problems of commercial overbuilding, there is tension in the town because the contestants will be set up against one another. Out of this division, arose a court case, which is also the subject of this paper.

The Arunachala Mountainscape Tiruvannamalai, South India: An Oral History Inscribed in Memoirs, Newsletters and Court Records

One of the most interesting problems in the study of the Ramanasramam in Tiruvannamalai, Tamil Nadu, is the understanding of the substantial work that has been done by its residents. This has included everything from clearing land and constructing to the more routine tasks of cooking, cleaning and keeping accounts. Work and worship have been the key idiom of life at Ramanasramam, the logos being 'activism and detachment' (Visvanathan 2007). The superiority of the rational method can only be an aid to the institutionalisation of the cult, and the family of the Maharshi, who has inherited the mantle of responsibility, has sustained its sense of virtue and integrity, by providing to the community which it serves, the tradition of hospitality and transparency. This works in two ways: firstly, by providing hospitality to those who come as seekers or visitors or are in abject need; secondly, by outrightly clarifying that donations are not the significant index of the *asramam*'s success.

Hundreds of people mill around in the ashram every day. They are visitors, who live in Tiruvannamalai or outside and come every day for a couple of hours. The most famous of these is perhaps David Godman whom everyone admires. However, since he is reclusive and reticent, and a famous writer of books on mysticism, not many people engage him in conversation. Many of the white visitors form cliques, spend time together at the teashop outside the ashram where they sit smoking cigarettes with the sadhus and watching the traffic, the beggars, and the grand and silent mountain. Some wear dreadlocks and communicate visually the idea that Saivism is the idea of excess. Visitors to the ashram however are encouraged to be circumspect and properly clad. One glance from one of the trustees is enough to communicate that someone is disorderly, and even children are disciplined regularly if they should chase the peacocks, pluck flowers and fruit or play too loudly in the hall. Yet, the everyday relationship between natural things and the order of the society is what much of the published narratives around

Ramanamaharshi consist of. Since much of what Ramanamaharshi said was recorded by loving scribes, we can only say that the visual evidence of the past is substantial. Ramana's family was also traditionally village or small-town notaries and lawyers, so the tradition of record-keeping was implicit in the family legacy.

What is interesting for the oral historian and the anthropologist is the act of inscription. Everything that is recorded is a verbatim text, which, when it stands the test of time (an index of publishing history), must also be cross-checked or verified.

A lot of the conventional questions raised in the theology of inter-religious dialogue are surpassed in non-dualism with the eternal resolution of boundarylessness. This might raise existential problems for those of us who are situated in mundane worlds but to those who enter the realm of the boundless sacred, it is a given. To believe or not to believe is not the question, for, in India, we are free to do either.

It is understood in the light of Ramanamaharshi's teaching that the contemplative path is chosen by seekers because they need to, whether they be householders or others. It is a path that is voluntary and does not offer riches or physical apparatus of any particular convenience. What it does offer is a stillness of the mind, which we call tranquillity and the ceasing of the apparent struggle that goes into the fulfilment of duties. Maharshi's teaching was immensely practical in the carrying out of duties so that they no longer felt burdensome but filled the doer with a sense of that happiness, which Ramana called *sahaja*. There were devotees who looked for visions and palapable evidence of their years of meditation, bur Maharshi believed that these were not necessary to the path of spiritual fulfilment.

In this essay, I attempt to do two things. One is to record the work of an Australian ecologist called Abhitha Arunagiri, who has laboured for thirty years to provide green cover to Arunachala, the holy hill which is the embodiment of Siva and Shakti, in divine embrace. When myths provide a mnemonic, which is a natural landscape, then the orientation of the sociologist is to how this may affect the actions of individuals. The second problem is to consider the time-bound case of a court ruling on Arunachala, the holy mountain, and the negotiations between various parties, such as ecologists and development agents, and government bureaucracy. Since court cases keep circulating in various stages of appeal and counter appeal, my data is only a representation of social relations which have a historical location. It does not attempt to keep up with the events, which constantly change.

Individuals as Catalysts: Biography and Social Action

In 2005, on my tenth visit to Sri Ramanasramam in as many years, a woman called Abhitha Arunagiri stops me on my way. We are near the gardens where the peacocks gather, where there is elephant grass cut every day as fodder for *asramam* cattle. The garden overlooks a water tank and these flamboyant but tame birds can hide from the monkeys under the lemon trees. Aruna's interests over the last thirty years have ranged from forest cover, engendering protection from forest fires, community participation, informal and formal education for children and adults alike, water harvesting and puppet theatre. The Arunachal Kadu Siva Plantation is her creation with help from an Australian NGO and resource base. Abhitha Arunagiri writes in one of her newsletters 'The AKSP Report' (my newsletterbuilder.com):

> We have not had an appreciable fire for two summers, thanks to the community participation fostered very largely by our two District Forest Officers, who have recently been transferred. These gentlemen were tremendously encouraging and helpful to all of us engaged in the Greening of Arunachala, in fact, we of the AKSP owe our very existence to them and have only recently realized the auspiciousness of their term.
>
> The AKSP has permission to plant on the hill within the area designated Reserve Forest, this area is off-limits to other than Forestry Department personnel unless special permission is given. Very good reasons promote this structure. Within this special permission which we have been given, we, in turn, honour the original, cognitively competent considerations behind it. AKSP is very happy to be planting on Reserve Forest because in this way we are enabled to work without disturbance.

In another report (saranam.com), Abhitha writes:

> The past two monsoons have given sinking rain and a new lease of life to the parched landscape of the denuded mountain, Arunachala, the embodiment of Lord Siva. Luxurious waterfalls have resulted in overflowing tanks for two consecutive years so we have enormous optimism for our task of the greening of Arunachal.
>
> During this 2006 season, members of the Village Forest Committee of Arunachal Kattu Siva Plantation realized that eleven streams flow down from the slopes within the areas allocated for our responsibility. After nearly twenty-five years engaged in fostering the return of a forested natural lingam, I feel confident that the Greening process will surmount all difficulties, it is too strong for defeats now.
>
> A sure sign of awakening within the community to the value of the forest is in progress presently near to our site; the renovation of three previously neglected Vediyappan shrines, carried out by the Panchayats of two adjacent villages and by ourselves.
>
> This indicates that the wilderness is being recognized as valuable once again, as it was in antiquity. Vediyappan is the god of wilderness.
>
> This means it is much more likely that the plantation on the mountain will be respected, now it will be protected by the psychological involvement of the community at large. Moreover, our Forest Department Conservator in Vellore and the Principal Chief Conservator in Chennai are determined to put a stop to the illegal grazing wood cutting and burning which have so far thwarted our efforts until recently. We have not had a fire for two seasons now.

Abhitha writes in detail from Sri Ramanasramam, where the greening programme has had its greatest support,

> The town of Tiruvannamalai on the east side of the mountain became District Headquarters some twenty years ago, causing an unprecedented increase in population, now around two hundred thousand. Over-exploitation of water is endemic. During these years a growing awareness of environmental mismanagement has contributed towards the present-day upsurge in intention to reforest the potentially resourceful monolith.

Arunachal Kadu Siva Plantation is linked to Rainforest Information Centre in Lismore, Australia and has taken responsibility for six hundred hectares of denuded Reserve Forest Lands on the lower slopes of the mountain. The thrust of this project is social ecology. Twelve rural people, mostly illiterate, are engaged in water conservation strategies, seed collection and nursery work, and the plantation, maintenance and protection of saplings on the slopes. Day to day decisions are made on the basis of dialogue reaching consensus.

The primary objective of the Greening of Arunachala is the rejuvenation of our artesan system. However the Arunachal Kadu Siva Plantation has a wider social-ecological import.

(a) to undertake responsibility for solutions to civic needs
(b) to participate in making decisions about these responsibilities.
(c) to utilize and regenerate indigenous knowledge
(d) to follow through the work beyond the call of duty
(e) to communicate about its meaning on every opportunity with members of their own villages and in the wider community.

The reforestation of Arunachala will furnish Tamil Nadu with a perfect environmental precedent site because a mountain in the centre of a plain is such a conspicuous advantage in water management.

Because the terrain has been so obviously ravaged in recent centuries that a return to health will be spectacularly dramatic.

The transformation will be witnessed regularly by a vast number of persons from all over India since Arunachala has become an extremely popular pilgrimage place with an estimated six to eight million visitors every year.

The upsurge to reforest the mountain manifests in the educated culture. The Tiruvannamalai Greening Society, formed a few years ago by community members and administrative officers, has still not been formally recognized by the State Government. A recent move on the part of Devotees of the mountain to seek legal protection for the sacred mountain has recently failed entirely in the Supreme Court, paving the way for the building of hotels and tourist facilities on private lands adjacent to the Mountain.

Abhitha's work is formidable in terms of its consistent 'local base' stability.

Captain Narayanan and the Arunchala Case for Greening of the Holy Mountain

Abhitha and I have spent some time talking with Captain Narayanan, a long-time resident of Ramanasramam, about the greening of the holy mountain. He tells us that he has spent many years fighting for the ecological survival of the hill and has been a participant and witness to the court cases which have centred around its environmental protection. They were successful in some things, like making sure that the construction of the administrative officer and the commissioner's bungalow did not take place on the *pradeekshana* (circumambulation route) but the residents of Tiruvannamalai are hostile to any suggestion that no building of commercial buildings take place on this route. Over time, the *asramam* has lost its ability to hold out and has taken a more submissive position. It is well known that the town has attracted millions of people over millennia. Its magnetism is both mythic and therapeutic. I believe this is one of the great sites of Indian religious and cultural heritage and should have the status of a World Heritage site. As Captain Narayan, a retired ship's commander, hopes their plea that Arunachala will receive this status will in time be heard, so do I.

Commerce and tourism are the catchwords of the 21st century. We cannot deny the impulse to prosperity that the people of a small-town feel. How to safeguard the interests of the people is the task of oral historians and sociologists and policymakers. My suggestions are that all small towns which have benefited from commerce and tourism have merged with the ecological patterns of the terrain. Hotels and shops should be concentrated in a new quarter away from the site of antiquity and conservation. The temple and the mountain itself can allow for the cohabitation of the Archaeological Survey of India and local merchants (as in the case of Rome and Delhi). The 14 km walk around the sacred hill may be kept free as a trusted site for present-day ritual purposes as well as for travellers and tourists of future generations. The percolation of the benefit from tourism should be made visible to the people by way of jobs, schools, medical facilities and small-town necessities for recreation and learning. Garbage collection is now better organised, but workers still do not have gloves to scoop up the muck from open drains.

Banking is perhaps easier now; I do not hear complaints from foreigners. The search for the mysteriousness of god goes side by side with the mundane aspects of survival. The class and comfort interests of foreigners seem palpably the new aspect of trade in Tiruvannamalai. From being a small town, quiet and almost rural, in 1995, when I first visited it, it is now a bustling tourist town. Nameless, as devotees wish to be in their service of Bhagavan, for the cultural anthropologist, personal biographies and official histories are interesting juxtapositions to the telling of a story.

At the *asramam*, it is understood that Ramana's teaching participated in the sense of the experience of the godhead, that ignorance is removed because the mountain Arunachala liberates, that one would not be there but that one is a seeker. Because it is a congregation of seekers, the experience of bliss is commonly understood among those who gather here. Those who know of this describe it as a calmness of the heart and mind, the tranquillity that forces them to return or hope to return. K. Swaminathan, a biographer of Ramana, and the editor of Gandhi's collected writings in 100 volumes described wanting to return to the *asramam* to see Bhagavan, as so strong a desire that he wished he could be tied down by elephants.

When I first visited 'Thiru', as it is called by frequent visitors to the town, it was a 'small' town. Now it has burgeoned by the influx of pilgrims (5,000 visit the temple every day, according to the local chemist who has a shop next to the Arunachala Temple) and the numbers multiply as the years pass. It seems to have become the hub of priestly and commercial activities. Television has contributed much to the missionising appeal of Saivism. The descriptions of market, temple and pilgrims remain fairly constant in the anthropological literature whether it be Christian, Muslim or Hindu. Religion and commerce, with the possible yeast of politics, make a town what it is. In Tiruvannamalai, there is faith, but fortunately no communalism.

To me, as a theoretician of dialogue, between religions, non-dualism is the answer to varieties of discord that we see as everyday occurrences in a globalised world. Non-dualism is the space in which everyday pluralism surfaces. It is an existential quality, which allows the myriad nature of the world to be ever present. As individuals, we enter a space of communitas and, this involves both respect and sharing.

On the other hand, technological imperatives (such as the megaphone) can be very rude interruptions in the quiet and sacred spaces that nature allots us, and which is confirmed by cultural or theological formulae. Tiruvannamalai, eleven years after my first visit in 1995, provides such a sense of shock and rupture. Trucks bringing agricultural produce and other merchandise, buses bringing pilgrims by the hundreds veer through a traditional street with enormous noise in its wake. The gods during carnival time are taken around in tractors that spew the most horrible smoke. The pollution levels, because of diesel and firecrackers during festival occasions must be seen to be believed.

And every day is a festival in this ancient town because every day is a holy day. Every day brings to pilgrims, according to legend and faith, honours and rewards, both material and spiritual. And who can be excluded? The numbers only increase. As a result, there are problems with discipline and order. Residents of the Ramanasramam are forced to become aggressive bouncers who keep the crowds at bay, using only their eyes, linked arms or speech to keep the crowds from hurting each other or damaging the shrines. Women who visit Ramanasramam to meditate say that young men in the crowds swirling outside at *deepam*, the annual core festival of Tiruvannamalai are lascivious and eager, and hands reach out to touch women's bodies. The swirling river of people is charged with very mortal emotions.

A great deal of Durkheimian sociology is about the size density and violence of the city, and how this affects social interaction. At the Ramanasramam, residents are able to cope with the greatness of numbers by coping with their needs pragmatically. Five thousand guests a year stay in the *asramam* rooms, according to Dr Murthy who is the keeper of ledgers and keys: he shows me by adding serial numbers in the heavy visitor's book. During festivals and Sundays, day-trippers constantly float in and out, for a brief view of the maharshi's *samadhi* and garden. The bookshop remains open all night, and the monks and householders looking after it never sleep, it seems, for the throngs of people are so continuous. The cooks are kept busy without a day's break, and seemingly without any holidays, in the service of Bhagavan. Pilgrims have now started celebrating their functions and commemorations of their birthdays and anniversaries by coming to the *asramam* and asking for special foods to be cooked. It has the appurtenances now of an industrial kitchen, and to cope with the crowds, sometimes the priests help the regular staff. They have to run with heavy buckets of rice, sambhar (spicy pulses cooked in tamarind), vegetables, *rasam* (the savoury soup known in the West as mulligatawny), buttermilk, *payasam* (sweet milk and vermicelli) among an entire convoy of pilgrims. Three to five hundred people are fed on festival days and weekends, in 20 minutes, before the 'second batch' is called in. The 'second batch' consists of Ramana office staff and workers, and the atmosphere is easier and colloquial. There is a general camaraderie, food is sometimes short and buttermilk watery, but the workers eat heartily with conversation and laughter and an unselfconscious joy in the everyday-ness of their routine obligations and duties. While *asramam* guests are fed on washed banana leaves, workers and residents have stainless steel plates ('ever silver' is the local name for these plates) and only if they are not entirely integrated as wage workers are they given banana leaf or stitched leaf plates. Service versus wage work is a very sharp divider. Those who serve in the *asramam* often come from wealthy households, bringing their capital with them as donations to the *asramam*. They are known as *sadhaka*s who attempt to attain the light, which is beyond all thought, all events.

When there is doubt about achieving the light, the answer always, in Ramanasramam, is to follow the 8-fold path, which includes celibacy, vegetarianism and yoga, and the goal will be achieved. These are people permitted to renounce the world and so become its ornaments. Some find it as karma-yogis transcending therefore the dualism of thought and action.

For a cultural anthropologist, what is not difficult to imagine are the routines, and the symmetry arising from these. The ethnographic present, which decades later may be read as a historical record, achieves a certain symmetry when it draws from tradition. The everyday tasks are set out and are immediately comprehensible. Times of meditation, community prayer, chanting, meals, work, social interaction and silence, all of these are exact. Yet the clock time of the factory does not approximate the rhythm of ashram life. As numbers increase, there is a strain to conform to the ethos of service and the velocity of demands. Each visitor feels he or she is unique and looks forward to comfort, quiet and aesthetic pleasure. Learning the roots of detachment is linked to various other tasks which include conformity to the values of the *aśramam*—the penultimate rules are silence, meditation and work. Ramana Maharshi never believed that idleness was the path to spiritual experience. Meditation was a part of everyday life, and while some were set apart for this, the risks were always elaborated. 'Discount all visions as distractions' was Maharshi's primary advice to novitiates to continue meditation. These were seen to be 'disturbances'. There is no reason for those of us who have particularly stressful lives in war-torn cities to believe that meditation will not lead to calm lives, and the ability to carry out our duties whatever these are.

Maharshi always said of nature, that manifested or unmanifested, we as human beings shared in the essence of the largeness of its existence. Much of how we read nature is in the animistic terms of poetry and love. Durkheim read this in the metaphors of power magnetism, current, force, all of which he saw as common to religion, magic and science. In the postmodern world, the boundaries between these are again blurred.

To understand nature in terms of mystery is part of the quest for solitude, whether it is in religion or science. Love is part of this quest. Thomas Merton writes that 'identification by love leads to knowledge, recognition, intimate and obscure but vested with an inexpressible certainty known only in contemplation' (Merton 1975: 68).

This search for solitude is represented in the unity of the self.

> To love solitude and to seek it does not mean constantly travelling from one geographical possibility to another. A man becomes solitary at the moment when, no matter what may be his external surrounding, he is suddenly aware of his own inalienable solitude, and sees that he will never be anything but solitary. From that moment, solitude is not potential—it is actual. (ibid.: 79)

He goes on to say that the spiritual aspirants' mystical experiences were in order to be peaceful in order to seek God (ibid.: 83).

This is we know, very often the reason and the site of abstract and mystical poetry. But Merton recognises that the true solitary seeks, and would presume any attempt to distract him or her from this path as futile. And yet, when we create the material conditions of that solitude, we stand the chance of losing it.

One of the problems of populism is the ability of people to believe that the space they occupy belongs to them. Much of the questions raised by social anthropology is about how we look at trusteeship. The definitive nature of the organisation of space is a legal question, which is in the purview of the Forest Department, the Archaeological Survey, municipal offices and so on. Having delineated the path of silence as integral to the location of Arunachala as a historical site that communicates that mysticism is a social fact, how can this silence be protected?

How increased numbers of pilgrims affects the town has already been mentioned. In the ashram, monastic life is continually under threat. Dr Murthy, the keeper of the keys, tells me that he keeps out people with money who want to use the ashram as a holiday resort, people who are eager to meet friends and relatives for festive occasions like New Year. This is complicated by the fact that each language group has a new year quite different from others complicating festive and ritual life … 30 per cent of *asramam* visitors are, for instance, Telugus, who have now built their own imposing guest house, just across the road, facing Arunachala, since the *asramam* cannot accommodate their number and the frequency of their visits and their desire for stays of rather long duration.

There is the excerpt in Merton's work from the writing of Barry McLaughlin in *Nature, Grace and Religious Development*:

> Yet one of the surest signs of the resolution of the identity crisis is an increased capacity for being alive, for being responsible for oneself. The gradual process that will end in perfect identity involves an awareness of the fact that there are decisions in life and aspects of life's struggle that a person must face alone …. And as a person in this formative isolation becomes more able to appreciate the moods and feelings of others, he also becomes more able to have meaningful relationships with them. (cited in Merton 1980: 42)

'Togetherness' and 'herdism' according to Merton is not what community is about. To love, one must respect the other; one must comprehend the need for solitude. To incorporate, to merge, to present the ideas of 'family', 'brethren' or 'community' as ways to integrate the solitary who has his/her own path is a common method.

Yet Merton has a fear of those who take to monasteries the 'emptiness and angst' of depersonalisation. There can be politics, tension, marginalisation. Merton contrasts what he calls normal life with the life of solitude. 'Normal' life is about comfort, reassurance and diversion:

> If we fulfil the role imposed on us by others, we will be rewarded by approval. These roles impose definite limitations, but in return for accepting the limitations we enjoy the consolations of companionship, of understanding support and so on. We are made to feel that 'we belong' and are therefore 'all right'. What the seeker of solitude does is to renounce these, the monk is some one who wanted to 'look into something else'. (100)

The world is a complex web of loves, hates, joys, greed and hope and we traverse it in our different ways, always hoping for that reconciliation that will allow the earth to prosper. It is in this context that I raise the problem of the court case which pertains to the greening of Arunachala. I place it here, for purpose of record, for the battle to protect the holy hill has been at the forefront of many devotees' lives.

The Court Case Regarding the Greening of the Holy Mountain

> It was alleged that the public in general and the followers of Lord Arunachala and innumerable persons who go around the hill found there are encroachments, unauthorized constructions, deviations, illegal felling of trees, destruction and devastation of water tanks. Caves, temples, ashrams and other religious places in the Hill Arunachala, and in the Holy town of Thiruvannamalai, and the monuments have to be protected, by removing the encroachment,

> by restricting and regulating the constructions. It is submitted that the entire Holy Pathway and Holy Hill be protected, and requests various reliefs/directions against the petitioner and various public authorities.[1]

In March 1999, the Municipal Commissioner argued that there was a bias in the manner of description. 'It was submitted that the first respondent has invented the Holy Pathway and the Holy Hill Arunachal afresh without any basis or record. It was submitted that the petitioner as a Civic Body is taking action to control development'.

The petitioner argued that there were no temple encroachments at Arunachaleswara temple, except the shops which were permitted by the temple authorities. The other petitioners against the Arunachala Giri Pradikshina Society and others were the Aathaiandal Village Panchayat, Adi Anamalai Panchayat and Adaiyur Village Panchayat; the Hindu Religious and Charitable Endowment also filed its opposition against the respondent.

In May 1999, the High Court appointed an expert body to provide a report to the court with suggestions regarding maintenance and preservation of the heritage town of Tiruvannamalai and the pathway around the hill. Mr T.S. Arunachalam, Acting Chief Justice of the High Court Judicature at Madras, was appointed as Chairman of the Body. Justice Arunachalam was to be assisted by the District Collector, who was to be the Secretary of the Expert Body and also assisted by an architect; an IAS officer; an archaeologist; the Conservator of Forests; the Secretary to the Government; the Municipal Administration;

1 The case is known in the Supreme Court of India as the Civil Appellate Jurisdiction, nos 12443–47; it arose out of the final judgement and order dated 11 May 2001, passed by the High Court of Judicature at Madras in writ petition no 17109/97, 7396, 7397, 7398 and 7400 of 1998. The petitioner was the Commissioner, Tiruvannamalai Municipality and the respondents were Arunachala Giri Pradaksina Samithi and others.

The case in the Madras High Court centres around the fact that the Government of Tamil Nadu had provided guidelines for the preservation, maintenance and development of thirty-eight temple towns by G.O.Ms no. 163, Rural development and Local Administration dated 6 July 1993. In 1997, writ petitions under Article 226 of the Constitution of India were filed before the High Court of Judicature at Madras, by the respondents as a Public Interest Litigation.

the water supply department; the PA to the District Collector; the Director of Town and Country Planning; the Director of Municipal Administration; the Executive Officer and Joint Commissioner of Annamalaiyar Temple; the Municipal Commissioner; the executive officers; the presidents of the village panchayats of Anapuandan, Athiuandal, Adi Annamalai, Vengikul and Adaiyur; the Executive Engineer, Tiruvannamalai, Annamalai Reforestation Society; the Executive Engineer, State Agricultural Engineering Department; the District Revenue officer; the Revenue Divisional officer; the Deputy Commissioner, HR and CE; the engineers with the Highways and Rural works having jurisdiction along the Srepradakshina Salai; and the surrounding regional transport officer.

There were in the expert committee representatives of important *asramams* such as one representative each of Yogi Ramsurat Kumar, Ramana Maharshi, Seshadri Swamigal and Gowthana Ashrams. Three prominent public persons who had an interest in conservation and maintenance were to be nominated by the expert body.

The records of the care provided to me by Sriram Panchu and Dayan Krishnan describe the consequence of setting up the expert body thus:

> 8th December 1999. The expert body exceeded its scope and gave its report to the High Court and suggested that a single authority should be created, which should have power to implement the plan not only in Thiruvannamalai town, but in all other Panchayats falling within the limits of the master plan on the lines of the Chennai Metropolitan Development Authority. A District Heritage Conservation Act (Bill) to ensure protection and restoration of all heritage buildings, precincts and areas, until the Bill becomes an Act. The Town Planning Authority will act on the basis of recommendations of the District Heritage Conservation Committee, in all matters relating to heritage. A Heritage Conservation Fund for financing projects identified by the District Heritage Conservation Committee has to be set up and the Committee can decide what will be the sources of this inflow for this fund. The Expert Body suggested in all 29 suggestions. In all it suggested changes in existing building rules, provision of some basic infrastructure.
>
> 29th February 2000. The Report of the Expert Body was placed before the petitioner Council pursuant to the order passed by the Hon'ble High Court.

> 2nd May 2001. The Government of Tamil Nadu filed its objection to the draft scheme stating that the present scheme is against the Constitution of India. It tries to set up an executive authority endowed with enormous powers and which encroaches into the powers and responsibilities of the Constitutional Body. On the whole, the scheme appears to allocate all land use, water and sanitation functions to the committee. As per the XII schedule of the Constitution of India, these are functions of Municipalities and they cannot be transferred to a Committee, which has nominated members only. The scheme is both impractical and unnecessary to expect all Departments of Government to function under the directions of this Committee. The Committee cannot be allowed to function as an organization that is beyond existing legislation and deemed to function like a superpower.[2]

There is a substantial shift in this note, from a position reached in the Madras High Court, where respondents and petitioners accepted that they had interests in common, which was the protection and maintenance of a holy town. Here, questions of authority and hierarchy are being raised, and while the Expert Body consisted of members who were specialists in their field, belonging to the government, both state and central, along with townspeople, and ashram delegates, the actual praxis of power is the problem now. Can the offices of government be supervised and directed by a committee proposed by the judiciary? The opposition to the committee is put forward very sharply in the court record:

> 30.3.2001. The petitioner Municipality filed an affidavit stating that the proposed scheme authorizing so much powers to such committees will make serious inroads into the powers of the Municipal Council and the local authorities. The Committees proposed are contrary to the provisions of the Tamil Nadu District Municipalities Act, 1920 and these Committees will run parallel to the Municipal Council and the same is against the provision of Article 243 of the Constitution of India. (*Commissioner Tiruvannamalai vs Giri Pradikshina Samithi and ORS.*)

2 Supreme Court of India, Civil Appellate Jurisdiction, Nos 12443–47, *Commissioner Tiruvannamalai vs Arunachal Giri Pradikshina Samithi and ORS.*

The assumption that the municipality makes as petitioner is that the High Court has exceeded its jurisdictions and taken on a privilege that is associated with the executive, legislature and judiciary.

Interestingly, the court proceedings in the High Court of Judicature at Madras on Friday, 11 May 2001 has a preface. The order passed by Justice Jagadeesan, Honourable Justice E. Padmanabhan states: 'The Law in the past was directed unconsciously and it should now be directed consciously, to the same end as custom, manners, religion and other types of social control, namely with the preservation, furtherance and transmission of civilization.'

It is this conflict between governance by judiciary and governance by a state institution that sets up a dialectic. Public Interest Litigation according to one of the lawyers who fought the case for Arunachala Pradakshina Samiti is always vulnerable at a time when individuals may have honourable intentions but not the staying power to keep with a case till the end.

Since it was a matter of encroachment and over-build, all those who had a commercial interest in construction became offensive, and Ramanasramam was visited by a large number of individuals, saying they were townspeople, and if asramam did not withdraw its case, there would be trouble. According to Abhitha Arunagiri, an Australian ecologist who has lived in Tiruvannamalai for 30 years, it was very frightening for residents. I quote from her letters to me (personal communication):

> A recent move on the part of Devotees to the mountain to seek legal protection for the sacred mountain has recently failed entirely in the Supreme Court, paving the way for the building of hotels and tourist facilities on private lands adjacent to the mountains. Someone said the opposition of the town was so tremendous, that the ASI did a deal with them: they would stand back if the Municipal Council started to keep the town clean.

The real question was of livelihood, and if the pristine quality of conservation was to be put into institutional space and its guardianship assured, then a great deal of how people made a living from the merchandise of objects by sale to pilgrims would decline.

Curiously, the petitioner in the Supreme Court, the Municipal Commissioner, argues that pilgrimage cannot be confused with tourism and that Tiruvannamalai is a sacred town, where the livelihood of people is at stake. He describes archaeological survey operatives or tourism development 'intrusion' as having to do with visitors who are not pilgrims. That is not his concern. He also provides the Supreme Court with photographs of Tiruvannamalai at the time of day in the morning when there are few people on the street, and the roads cleared of garbage, to show how well the municipality deals with crowds and refuse!

In the Madras High Court, the municipality had stated that

> It was bound to grant permission for the construction under the provisions of the Tamil Nadu District Municipalities Act, 1920 and the rules framed thereunder. There is no authority whatsoever to prevent the construction on private lands adjoining the Giripradikshina pathway and beyond the 50 metres of Giripradikshina pathway and also there is no authority to limit the height of construction not exceeding 6 metres either adjoining the Giripradikshina pathway or in the remaining portion of the path and up to 50 metres beyond the Giripradakshina pathway against the principles contained in the Heritage Act and the guidelines issued thereunder in G.O.Ms no 22. MAWS Department dated 30.1.1997. (*Commissioner Tiruvannamalai vs Giri Pradikshina Samithi and ORS*)

The municipality argued that the shops are permitted by temple authorities and that it is discharging its duties. The Honourable Judges wrote:

> Admitted Facts and stand of petitoners and respondents.
>
> On the facts of the case it is clear that there is no controversy, besides it is almost admitted by everyone, including the respondents about the existence of the Holy Hill Arunachala which has been personified as Lord Shiva and the existence of Giripradikshana Path over which millions go around the Holy Hill, commencing from the sixteen pillar mandapam of the eastern entrance of the temple, and ending with the very same sixteen pillar mandapam. Everyone concerned wholeheartedly supported and expressed that either the State or Central Authorities should step in to regulate the entire area, remove the

> encroachments, regulate the construction of buildings so that visibility of the Holy Hill is not affected when it is viewed from any corner of the Giripradikshina path, besides the requirement of the necessary basic amenities or facilities to pilgrims and the villages and the residents who reside on either side of the Giripradikshina path as well as the Tiruvannamalai Municipal limits. Everyone anxiously expressed that the entire pathway should be maintained free from all encroachments whatsoever, and all the obstructions and encroachments between the pathway and the Holy Hill have to be removed and regulations have to be brought in concerning the height of the building or location of the buildings and as to the using of the space and leaving of vacant place abutting the Giripradikshina path on both sides and with respect to various measures to be taken in this respect to preserve the Holiness and sanctity of the Holy Hill Arunachala.

The Honourable Judges asked the state government to follow up the consensus reached by both parties that the Holy Hill needed protection:

> During the entire hearing everyone has supported the move, but only had different views as to the steps to be taken or the extent to which restrictions are to be imposed and with respect to the details of restriction to be imposed and the regulations to be followed. In fact we called upon the learned Additional Advocate General to get instructions as to whether the State Government is in a position to take up immediate legislation for the area in question which would give quietus to all the issues. But the learned Additional Advocate General on instructions expressed the State government's inability to bring forth comprehensive legislation and the response of the State government so to say is not only lukewarm but it has failed to comprehend the problem and it had failed to respond. (*Commissioner Tiruvannamalai vs Giri Pradikshina Samithi and ORS*)

The judgement continues:

> However in principle though the state govt. agrees they are not willing to take up the appropriate legislation, and time granted in this respect also had not elicited any response. In the light of the said background this Court on 4th May 1999 passed a detailed order

> with the consent of the petitioners as well as all the respondents and everyone concerned. The said direction is a consent direct as everyone agreed that Giripradikshina running to the length of 16 km or thereabout from Anmanalaiyur Temple proceeding along with Tiruvoodal Street, Sangam Road, Pei Gopura Street, and Soma Vara Kula Street etc., and ending at the same starting point of Annamalayar Temple has to be cleared from all encroachments and unauthorized constructions and a comprehensive scheme have to be framed for the area and Giripradakshina Salai in the larger interest of the public as well as in the interest of residents of Tiruvannamalai Town as well as Villages in and around the Hill. (*Commissioner Tiruvannamalai vs Giri Pradikshina Samithi and ORS*: 42)

The judges reiterated that both parties are agreed on the sanctity of the hill. This very sanctity will be disrupted by unregulated construction, haphazard in nature, and a health risk to all. They note that:

> Mr Sriram Panchu, Senior Counsel appearing for one of the writ petitioners persuaded this Court to frame a scheme so that the entire locality could be protected not only from encroachment, unauthorized construction, deviations, but also the cleanness of the town and environment could be saved from further deterioration. (ibid.)
>
> In furtherance of the objectives resolved in consensus, the Honorable Judges, requested a study of Tiruvannamalai which would be presented by an Expert Body. One of the recommendations was certainly forbidding megaphones in public places! The judges did see that the townspeople would have to make sacrifices for the greater good. (ibid.: 78)

The Arunachalam Committee gave an extremely detailed and constructive report, and as a memento to town planning, it is a valuable record for urban historians and sociologists. The Tiruvannamalai Municipality reacted sharply. The court records state:

> In fact, the counsel on record for Tiruvannamalai Municipality attended all the hearings but did not object to the proposal to frame a scheme. The counsel for Municipality, the State, the Centre

> were called upon to get instruction from the respective authorities, whether they are willing to take comprehensive measures, but all of them despite opportunity failed to avail the opportunity, which would exhibit their failure to discharge the public and statutory functions. Further, all of them also represented that this court may frame appropriate schemes. In the light of the above, we are unable to appreciate or sustain the belated objection raised on behalf of their municipality as if their power or jurisdiction is being reduced. Factually, it is not so as none of the powers of the Municipality as conferred by the District Municipalities Act or the Constitutional provision are being interfered with since the provisions of the Scheme is in addition to the statutory provisions. We overrule the objections and herby frame the Scheme appended herewith which shall be implemented by everyone. (*Commissioner Tiruvannamalai vs Giri Pradikshina Samithi and ORS*: 79)

When it went to the Supreme Court, the Municipal Commissioner basically communicated that it was not his place to take orders from a parallel body, the Expert Committee, which presented itself as a superpower. The municipality's jurisdiction had been replaced. With the suggestion that the central government believed that heritage and tourism were important issues, the Commissioner made a distinction between tourists and devotees, saying that their needs were different. The violence of the agitators (who wished to build guest houses and adjuncts for commercial reasons) when they appeared as an unruly crowd, according to informants at Ramanasramam, was such that the public interest litigation was withdrawn. In October 2007, an informant at the *asramam* said jubilantly, that the ecological struggle was still on!

One resident of Ramana Ashram, Captain Narayanan, told Abhitha and me that:

> At least the Municipality did not get to build their offices on the Chengam road, as they wished, (the circular road outside Asramam), otherwise imagine the bottleneck that would have been created, with people from all over the hinterland appearing with their papers for an audience with the Commissioner, and jostling with pilgrims on this narrow road!

What is interesting for me as a reader of these court records is how much faith is captured even within the secular jurisdiction of the courts. The litigants, lawyers and judges accept the sacred manifestation of the divine, and the right of the people to worship and live in a territory that is infused by the heady sense of myth which communicates both love and maya as central theological concepts.

In the following essay, I shall look at another mythologised frame, which is Shakespeare's Sonnets, the latter word etymologically being linked to music, but since the sonnets were seen to be poems, a lot of the debates centre around questions of audience and the social contexts of their authorship. As I tread the familiar arena, I am drawn to the questions of work and livelihood patterns, from which we may receive some insights for globalised modernity that tussles with similar questions of livelihood and gender.

References

Arunagiri, Abhitha. AKSP mynewsletterbuilder.com (Personal communication by email).

Case, Supreme Court of India. 2001. Civil Appellate Jurisdiction, Nos 12443–47.

Cederlof, Gunnel and K. Sivaramakrishnan. 2005. *Ecological Nationalisms*. Ranikhet and Delhi: Permanent Black.

Gilroy, Paul. 2004. *Between Camps: Nations, Cultures and the Allure of Race*. London: Routledge Taylor and Frances.

Godman, David. 2000. *The Power of the Presence*. Pondicherry: Avadhuta Foundation.

Graves-Brown, P.M. 2000. *Matter, Materiality and Modern Culture*. London and New York: Routledge.

Guha, Ramachandra. 1999. *Savaging the Civilised: Verrier Elwin, His Tribals and India*. Delhi: Oxford University Press.

Jayawardene, Kumari. 2007. *The Erasure of the Euro-Asian, Recovering Early Radicalism and Feminism in South Asia*. Colombo: Social Scientists Association.

Koli, Kanchi and Kalpavriksh. 2009. Report of the National Dialogue on Six years of the Implementation of the Biological Diversity Act at the Conference Organized by Kalpavriksha, Grain and the National Forum for Policy Dialogue at NMML. 3 February, Delhi.

Latour, Bruno. 2000. 'The Berlin Key or How to Do Things'. In *Matter, Materiality and Modern Culture,* edited by P.M. Graves-Brown. London and New York: Routledge.

Merton, Thomas. 1975. *Thoughts in Solitude*. Trowbridge: Redwood Burn Ltd.

———. 1980. *Contemplation in a World of Action*. London: Mandala Unwin.

Morrison, Kathleen. 2005. 'Environmental Histories, the Spice Trade, and the State in South India'. In *Ecological Nationalisms*, edited by Gunnel Cederlof and K. Sivaramakrishnan. Ranikhet and Delhi: Permanent Black.

Mudaliar, Devaraja. 2002. *Day by Day with Bhagavan*. Tiruvannamalai: Sriramanasramam.

Pandian, M.S.S. 2007. *Brahmin and Non-Brahmin, Genealogies of the Tamil Political Present*. Ranikhet and Delhi: Permanent Black.

Saberwal, Satish.1995. *Wages of Segmentation*. Delhi: Orient Longman.

Sadhu, Om. 1997. *The Path of Sri Ramana*. Pondicherry: Sri Ramana Kshetra, Kanvasha Trust.

Visvanathan, Susan. 2006. Travellers and Pilgrims. *Think India Quarterly* 9 (4), October–December: 10–27.

———. 2007. *Friendship, Interiority and Mysticism*. Delhi: Orient Blackswan.

———. 2008. 'Dreams and Death'. *Indian Anthropologist* 38 (1): 1–16.

———. 2008. 'Tsunami New Year'. *Samyukta: A Journal of Women's Studies* 7 (2) (2007–2008).

———. 2010. *The Children of Nature: The Life and Legacy of Ramana Maharshi*. Delhi.

10

Medieval Music and Shakespeare's Sonnets

H.G. Koenigsberger asked why do we not see the substitution of the attendance at jazz concerts as a substitutable form of sacred venues for the playing of music? Is there not a homology between the great churches of medievalism and the presence of the oratorical and musical forms of contemporary musicians, who have a hold over the young? (Ed Ostrem Eyolf et al. 2005: 9).

A new forum of shared music that has appeared is that of music available on the world wide web for sale or free download. Jon Sayles' website which plays recorded music from the 14th to 17th century is an example of this oeuvre. He is particularly interested in the work of John Dowland, a contemporary of Shakespeare (jsguitargeek@yahoo.com.) The mp3 downloads are free of charge and Sayles' only request is that there should be communion and interaction between fellow enthusiasts and musicians. Prof. Susan Iadone, a reputed teacher of Renaissance music combines the philosophy of sharing as well as inscribing this music for her students and creating archives of published music. It is interesting that in her note to Jon Sayles, forwarded to me by Sayles in answer to a request, she says that Shakespeare's sonnets have not been set to music, because it was possibly not a genre that was meant to be sung.

However, pop musicians like Rufus Wainwright, Gavin Bryars and David Gilmour have adapted the sonnets to music. Shakespeare's sonnet 18 was adapted by David Gilmour of Pink Floyd fame. *When Love Speaks* is the recording by Rufus Wainwright, Annie Lennox and Bryan Ferry. The website of London's Royal Academy of Dramatic

Art has further information as does Shakespeare Geek and Creative Commons License, BBC Radio under Lyrichord, where lute music is highlighted. John Dowland's *First Book of Songs* or *Ayres* was published in 1597 and was the most reprinted music book of that time. It would not be surprising if the sonnets approximated a familiar-enough genre of Dowland and Wyatt and others whose music is still of great interest to the film and theatre world, and within the contexts of information-sharing in the family, music and words could be well adapted. Prof Robin Hemley, expressing the sense of the common ground of academia as a world community (university, universe, universalis) at a Writers' Workshop which we attended in Shimla and Delhi, in October 2008 (Australia Pacific Writers' Workshop) sang 'Full Fathoms' Five' to fellow participants after work hours. He said his sister, who had been a stage actress before her death taught him this song when he was a young child. It is these motifs of family life, which draw our attention to the great role of autobiography in the dissemination of information, and the nature of social constructions of the relevance of this information.

Since the late 1980s, Shakespearean studies had been anathematised in Delhi as being a consequence of Macaulayism. This had an impact on the teaching of Shakespeare in the undergraduate departments, as more emphasis was being placed on functional grammar. However, the numerous Shakespeare productions in Indian languages continued to fire interest in the subject, the best known perhaps being the Kathakali Shakespeare plays which were presented on stage in Delhi by performers from the Kathakali Centre in the Qutub Institutional Area. They used medieval music from Kerala, employing the *chendakar* or drummers to good effect with wonderful cadences of language since Shakespeare translated very well into Malayalam.

Whether we think of Berlioz's *Romeo and Juliet*, which is thought to be one of the most powerful forms of intercultural construction with Kathakali accompaniments, we are dealing with the translatability of Shakespeare into what we may call the common plateau of the human condition, and that is what all great art or great techne tries to do. As Marcel Mauss and Henri Huber would argue, in 1902, there is a magic to this and the volatility of this magic is not just to transport us but to transform the very nature of the reality that we know. The great German writer of the 1930s, Norbert Elias, when describing what culture is, in *The Civilising Process* (1978) spoke of how Shakespeare was the equaliser of culture and hierarchy so that plebs and aristocrats shared the Shakespearian stage and the circle of the audience, where so much of the vitality of medieval dialogue was set up—to recognise oneself in the plays. However, in Germany, Shakespeare was essentially an aristocrat's domain. Shakespeare was a poet for whom a memorial was created at Poet's Corner in Westminster Abbey, so it is taken for granted by the world in general that the sonnets have a musical or lyrical quality to them. Prof. Susan Iadone writes to Jon Sayles that (in answer to a query which I had put to him on 19 February 2009)

> Shakespeare's sonnets have not been set to music, that I am aware of. Somebody may have made a contemporary setting, using their own music and his words, but there is nothing original, as they were not meant to be sung. There are many texts from his plays that scholars speculate had been sung, but the music has been lost. Do you remember that book, *Musique de la trope de Shakespeare*? That has what I think are all of the extant songs from the plays ... I think I might have an old xerox of it somewhere. Some composers also made arrangements of the better-known tunes for gamba solo, as well.
> Susan Iadone

The answer from Susan Iadone (24 February 2009) came in response to my earlier letter to Mr Sayles on 19 February 2009:

> Dear Mr Sayles,
>
> I chanced upon your website a couple of weeks ago, as I was researching a paper on Shakespeare and the Sonnets, and heard your absolutely wonderful renderings of Dowland. Thanks so much for making the music available to all of us. I will be presenting your work at a conference which is on internet and pedagogy ... the paper is on sonnets set to music ... do you know of anyone who works with free mp3 download as you do, specifically for Shakespeare's sonnets? That would help. Anyway, all research is about distractions, and Dowland turns out to be someone who is

> hugely popular (I had never heard of him) and so I am setting up a parallel space for him in my paper, using your website and the information and the music you play, so that others come to know of your work. The conference is the 4th annual carnival of e-creativity (2009), and its director is Shankar Barua.
>
> Susan Visvanathan

We may see these ideas about the relation between music and words at work in Frances Yates' well-known book on the theatre in the Renaissance called *The Theatre of the World* (1987). Robert Fludd was a contemporary of John Dee, archivist and astronomer at the court of Queen Elizabeth I but he was much younger than him. Both were influenced by Paracelsus. In Fludd's writing, the theme takes a musical form and is worked out in terms of musical proportions. The proportions of the microcosm and their relation to those of the macrocosm, of the *musica humana* to the *musica mundane*, are the foundation ideas of Fludd's voluminous work. The Renaissance philosopher to whom he was perhaps most indebted was Francesco Giorgi, whose *harmonia Mundi* is on similar lines to Fludd's work. Giorgi had related musically to architectural proportion by using 'vitruvian man' as a symbol of divine and human proportions. The image of the Vitruvian man was certainly also present in Fludd's mind (Yates 1987: 43). His treatise on music was written between 1592 and 1600. In the late 16th and 17th centuries, St John's College was a centre for the high church revival led by William Laud, who was a contemporary of Fludd at St John's. An important aspect of this revival was the introduction or rather reintroduction of music into the liturgy. Laud was keen on the use of organs and his friend Sir William Paddy, a great luminary of St John's and deeply interested in music presented an organ to the college. Church music, court music and love poems were all interlaced in what Joan Kelly describes as that interesting union during this period of divine love and court poetry, and the abstract and transcendent liaisons, which often had corporeal aspects as well.

Alan Sinfield in *Shakespeare, Authority, Sexuality: Unfinished Business in Cultural Materialism* (2006) argues that Shakespeare's sonnets are popularly believed to be directed to the Earl of Southampton. The sonnets have no addressee; 'the Boy' appears to be encouraged to marry and to procreate. Sonnets need not be saying anything about Shakespeare's sexual orientations. He certainly used the theatre and parts for boys to play with nuanced roles.

Does the boy encroach on the poet's woman love as a treacherous friend? Is there a liaison? The options, Sinfield engagingly writes, are 'Yes', 'No' or 'Transcended' as ideas or ideals. Art transcends and is passed down from generation to generation either through print or oral traditions or through mechanisms of access that may or may not be realised.

What is patronage? The poet must believe in the integrity of his art. Sexual passion however is more intense than transcendence. What is the place of the minion? It is delight and self-abnegation. A secret love cannot be dislodged by public pressure and that is the essence of the sonnets, which like any art form can be read free of biography and without the anchorage of the creator's sensibility.

John Dowland, whose first book of songs or *Ayres* was published in 1597 was a contemporary of Shakespeare (website Encarta). His music written for the lute and still sung by radio and stage artists approximates the idea that religious and love music approximated a common form. This idea, which is also apparent in the sonnets, deal with spiritual and material pleasures, seasons, activities and objects of desire drawing from a common root. The Reformation and the varieties of dialogue that are set up amongst intellectuals, of whom musicians and poets are the most celebrated, provided a backdrop to how we think of patronage in 16th- and 17th-century England. John Dowland's *Lachrymae* is available in a rendering on BBC Radio on the website of Lyrichord, where the performances of Russel Oberlin and Joseph Iadone are still remembered.

A reviewer on the website of *Sonnets Set to Music* called Tepi, writing on Stephen Boot's edition of The Sonnets, writes:

> One reason that Elizabethan lyrics are so powerful and memorable is that they were compressed in an age when poetry was still linked closely with music. Elizabethans were often competent musicians, and many of their poems were true lyrics or songs. Often their poems

> were set to music, and all were probably composed while the gentle plucking of a lute or some such instrument was running somewhere through the back of the poet's mind.

The website awaytoteach.net uses sonnets as teaching practice in schools, and theatre practice is employed to enact the sonnets.

Who was the dark lady of the sonnets? No one knows—she might have been a lute player in a tavern, where Shakespeare spent much of his time away from home. Germaine Greer in *Shakespeare's Wife* (2007) argues that given there were plagues and fires, it would need a competent woman to run the home and bring up three children past these catastrophes. Anne Hathaway would have to be someone who could cook, garden, weave and yes, maybe sell mead, to augment the income of a household where debt was not unknown. That Shakespeare was away for long years but came back whenever children were to be propagated or property bought, is a statement by itself.

Why Shakespeare was so popular is explained by Frank Kermode in *The Age of Shakespeare*:

> With Henry the 8th, there was a tremendous surge in the writing of plays. The commercial development of drama was one more sign that the world as regulated by liturgy was being supplanted by a world more concerned with capital and labour—a word in which time itself had a different quality. (2005: 12)

The churches were stripped, communion tables replacing them. Books replaced the old images—wall paintings, stained glass and decorated altars (ibid.: 13). Kermode writes:

> Shakespeare was then living a presumable bachelor life in Bishopsgate, not too far from the Theatre. Of his private life very little is known, though the Sonnets fuel a great variety of conjectures. We can harmlessly suppose that in these years, when so much of his time was devoted to the fortunes of the English monarchy, Shakespeare was as aware as any other intelligent person of the uneasy state of the kingdom—the Queen old and difficult, the succession still in question, Essex increasingly dangerous. (ibid.: 67)

Let us now look at Germaine Greer's reading of the biographical details of Shakespeare's life. The book is called *Shakespeare's Wife* and is published in 2007 by Penguin. She uses parish records, local histories and all the archives of Shakespeare museums to recover for us the sense of the everyday. Warwick and Henley Street both appear in the space of history and drama, of legends and oral accounts. For anyone who has wondered what Anne Hathaway did at home while Shakespeare was writing and producing plays, here is a probable history.

We see that work and housewifery were safe places for a woman bringing up children. Through the chronicle of plague and deaths, we see how family, neighbourhood, friendship ties and a peasant economy allow an independent woman to survive the greatest odds. Local economies depend on the work of women, and Greer gives us a lifetime's obsession, moving us in her sure-footed manner away from the idea that here was a woman 'unloved'. She uses the text of the rigour of work, property and prosperity to negotiate with the history of the petty bourgeoisie, where being the daughter-in-law of a glover and someone who was in politics would lead to spaces of pride, but in time, also of debt. The literary and erudite master is away but returns to enquire, and so Greer asks the profoundly feminist question, what dignity would labour provide in such circumstances? By looking at a variety of occupations, and concepts of upward and downward mobility, Greer is able to negotiate with the unpleasant fact as to how the life of the arts is often seen to be dependent on shadow economies, such as the tavern and the whore house (themes dealt significantly over and over again by men in Shakespeare studies and institutionalised by those using Baudelaire as their excuse). Here Greer looks at the house, the garden, the street, the shop, the church as viable loci of understanding town and country in medievalism. There is a great deal of poetry in the book, sonnets as well as plays, and Shakespeare's imagination goes hand in hand with a history of absconding from daily duties, recreated in memory and our practical understanding of a world long gone, but still so present.

Medieval Music: Questions of Looking at the Elizabethan Court in Terms of Power, Patronage and Hierarchy

'And greasy Joan doth keel the pot' is probably the most vivid description of women's lives as recorded in history. Yet when we look at Shakespeare's wife, sister or daughter as Virginia Woolf would have us do in her *Room of One's Own* (1945), we are set to ask a host of questions. The sonnets were written with both men and women in mind, the Earl of Southampton being the best known of patrons, and of course with Anne Hathaway and the 'dark woman'. The dark woman could well have been a lute player and we have a visual representation of her by Caravaggio (Wikipedia www.luteplayer). What we see in Shakespeare's time, and the time immediately preceding this, is the shadow of how the state could be oppressive, executing people at will. Around this, there would be a culture of poetry and protest, sometimes sublime and sometimes overt. Ratna Raman (personal conversation) suggests that George Herbert would articulate ideas of God and nature, as being central to his reading of the politics of court. However, Wyatt, also known as a silver poet, would use verse to castigate Anne Boleyn, who was once his lover, but now the vulnerable and yet powerful wearer of a crown. 'Off with her head!' as Lewis Carrol writes was probably a legend that the British were well used to, and auditorily the space of looking at how patronage was often replaced by exile or death an interesting abstract motif when one looks at freedom and art.

This essay seeks to read the poems of Shakespeare in terms of the texts of the time, loosely called Elizabethan but wrought in terms of the fact that Elizabeth would have grown up in the early court of her mother, where names such as Thomas More and Wyatt would have predominated public discourse. Can we then read the music that was published in her time as centred around the political questions of that time? And why did the publication of music cease? It was perhaps because Protestantism denied music since it profoundly affected the senses (Kermode 2005: 18). Books replaced (during the Protestant wave in Elizabeth's time) the stained glass, the decorated churches and altars, the wall paintings where the authority of the Roman church lay in its paraphernalia.

One of the presumptions of this essay is that the book was a central symbol of the power of ideas. Frank Kermode writes that,

> It was in this age that the book became a familiar object, with incalculable consequences. Since records are fairly thorough, it is known that between 1558 and 1579, 2760 books were published. Between 1580 and 1603 the number rose to 4370. John Guy calculates on the basis of an average print run of 1250 copies that this 'represents an average of just two books per head of a population of four and a half million over a generation and a half.
>
> Part of the endless bustle around St Paul's must have been caused by the bookstalls, for St Paul's, in a sense that social centre of the city, was also the centre of the book trade, and it was not far from where the newly arrived aspirant would find himself. The proportion of citizens who read may seem small, but there were enough of them to make bestsellers, one of which was Shakespeare's Venus and Adonis, an example of the Ovidian-erotic mode, which went into nine editions in the poet's lifetime. One could go to St Paul's and buy a sermon, or a six-penny quarto of a play, or almost any other sort of book, from devotional tracts to romances. (2005: 38)

School education was also very rigorous, and so the poet would have a fair grounding in rhetoric and in Latin. Theology was a subtext in all education and Kermode wrote that:

> The Geneva Bible, as one would expect, offered glosses animated by extreme Protestant conviction, and for the next fifty years it was the version most read in England. Interest in matters of theological interpretation, fostered by access to this primary source were of spiritual importance, since they concerned the fate of the individual sinner, but they also encouraged close reading and an understanding of linguistic subtleties. (ibid.: 39)

As an Indian writer comments, 'Before the seductiveness of Shakespeare's text, and the plaisir of even the jouissance of our experience of it, how can our attention fix on Elizabethan or Jacobean politics?' (Shankar 1999: 48).

The subtext of all art however are its protagonists, and in Shakespeare's sonnets which appear very much like religious songs in the Bible known as psalms, there is an aura of bi-sexuality, often attributed to his love for his patron, or his wife, or for the lute-player in a tavern. Whatever the nature of his fealty to these great loves, they are nevertheless testimonies to a great and fearless imagination.

Germaine Greer in her classic work *Shakespeare's Wife* argues that Anne was a good representation of the verse in the *Proverbs* by King Solomon, which says, 'She girdeth her loins with strength and strengthened her arms. She seeth that her merchandise is good, her candle is not put out by night. She putteth her hands to the wheel, and hands handle the spindle' (Greer 2007: 10).

The important problem that Greer is raising for us is how does a woman survive, and see three children past the plague, which in medieval times was hard to do. Anne was sixty-seven years old when she died in 1623 on 6 August. She was thought to have been born in 1556. The house she was born in was called Hewlands Farm. Her family was a prosperous farming family. The oldest part of the house is from the late 14th century. It has a large hall, where all the family members would have slept for warmth around a large oven, which still exists. It was a well-established family, and though Anne was eight years older than Shakespeare, the marriage between them was an alliance of two substantial families living in a close-knit community (ibid.: 21).

Greer argues that Shakespeare's mother was upwardly mobile, and that escape from the mother to an older woman's arms was not an unlikely event. She was the country girl, and Campion's *Book of Airs* describes just such a girl:

Joan can call by name her cows
And deck her windows with green boughs
She can wreaths and tuties make
And deck with plums a bridal cake
Is not Joan a housewife then?
Judge true-hearted honest men.
Joan is of a lovely brown
Nest as any in the town
Hair as black as any crow

And does nimbly trip and go
Happy is their hour and time
Who can give sweet Joan the wine?

Clearly, as this poem describes young lovers, never mind differences in age or temperament, as they attempted to seduce one another, and to the shock of the community when their temper and age did not match at all. Greer uses texts from the plays to prove the experiential quality of this differential love. 'He is very well-favoured and speaks very shrewishly. One would think his mother's milk were scarce out of him' (Greer 2007: 510).

The Reformation suggests that Anne might have been able to read. Women were encouraged to read and to teach children to read the Geneva Bible. Greer writes that girls were taught to read and sew, knit and spin, boys to read, write and work with accounts. She quotes Nicolas Browne who said in 1595:

> In the shops of Artificers and cottages of poor husbandmen … you shall sooner see one of these new ballads, which are made only to keep them occupied … than any of the psalms, and may perceive them to be cunninger in singing the one that the other. And indeed the singing of ballads is very lately renewed … so that in every faith and market almost you shall have one or two singing and selling of ballads. (2007)

Maybe Will taught Anne to write and certainly he wrote her poetry, the one skill he had manifested very early. One evidence is Sonnet 145:

Those lips that love's own hand did make
Breathed forth the sound that said, 'I hate'
To me that languished for her sake,
But when she saw my woeful state,
Straight in her heart did mercy come,
Chiding that tongue that ever sweet
Was used in giving gentle drone
And taught it thro' anew to greet:
'I hate', she altered with an end
that followed it as gentle day

Doth follow night who like a fiend
From heaven to hell is flown away.
I hate from hate away she threw
And saves my life, saying 'not you'. (Greer 2007: 58)

Anne was eight years older than Shakespeare. She was independent, her father was dead, and she was unmarried. Above the age of twenty-one, Greer argues that a woman was free and could marry whom she chose. Anne was twenty-six. She would have known how to milk and to make cheeses, and to bake bread. She would have cooked, cleaned, swept, gardened, washed clothes, grazed cows. And she would have sung. Their family name was Gardener because there were so many Hathaway's in Warwickshire. That there was no gossip about her, and that she was not hounded out because of the relationship she had with Will Shakespeare, is the location of Anne's identity that Shakespeare loved and wooed her. Greer also argues that Laslett's study shows that men and women married startlingly late in Elizabethan England, and the youthfulness of the husband in contrast to his wife's age was not unknown. In any case, he was dominated by his mother.

Shakespeare had to leave in search of work very early. John Shakespeare, William's father was greatly in debt. His mother was hugely influential in his life (ibid.: 26). She had been a favourite daughter, inheriting her father's valuable property over seven older sisters. The custom was to favour the younger child. Mary Shakespeare's father Robert Arden had a large estate. She opted to marry a glover, who became an alderman because the contrast between the artisan's and the farmer's life was the contrast between town and county. She was a wealthy farmer's daughter who persuaded her husband perhaps to engage in the wool trade rather than in the messy tanning trade of glove and animal hides (ibid.: 32). For a glover to deal in wool was illegal since each trade had its boundaries by custom and birth. Yet having been on many committees in 1576 while his fortunes were failing, John Shakespeare applied for a coat of arms. Mary Shakespeare's property was mortgaged for 40 pounds, and it was lost (ibid.: 39). There was an economic recession in the 1580s, and while they were in financial crises, William impregnated Anne and married her. So there too was a dowry lost!

Circumstances being what they were, it is not surprising that William needed a patron, and hence the bisexual nature of the sonnets, which in whole were dedicated to his master the Earl of Southampton.

Anthony Burgess in *Nothing Like the Sun* (1985) is convinced that Shakespeare's absorption in tavern life was the cause of his terrible death. According to this version, Anne Hathaway is nagging him:

> I know not what money you earn. I know that you are seen smiling in silk with your fine friends. And I know that –ah, 'tis no matter. Let me sleep. God knows I have had little enough sleep lately."
>
> "What is it that you know?"
>
> "Oh." She turned away from him with a deep sigh. "There are poems you have written. They were brought to Master Field for his printing."
>
> "That is old stuff, my poems. I brought home Lucrece, though none here would read it. Field himself told me that my father would read Venus but you said it was filthy or some such thing."
>
> "I said not that. But it is about naked goddesses."
>
> "Aye, a naked goddess tumbling a boy in the field."
>
> She did not see that. She said: "There are little poems, and some are to men, and some are of a black woman. She snivelled. "Thou didst never write such to me –
>
> "Sonnets? Is it sonnets? What is this about Field being given my sonnets?"
>
> There follows a terrible quarrel. She has one of his poems in her possession.
>
> WS, frowning, puzzled, took up the poor little bound volume of devotional chatter, weak warnings of the Spanish antichrist and the End of the World. He found a folded piece of good parchment and even before unfolding, at once remembered the May night, his trembling fingers (were they then now different fingers) pulling from his breast what had been defiled, turned sour and rancid, by the laughing defection of a black-haired girl and the jeers of her new lover. How many years ago had that been?
>
> My love being black, her beauty may not shine
> And light so foiled to heat alone may turn.

Heat is my heart, my hearth all earth is mine;
Heaven do I scorn when in such hell I burn. (Burgess 1985: 172)

Shakespeare's wife according to Anthony Burgess version is adulterous with his brother Mathew the lawyer and Shakespeare returns to the black whore of the taverns, solicitous and proud in her degradation. But then there is Sonnet 27:

Weary with toil, I haste me to my bed,
The dear repose of limbs with travel tired.
But then begins a journey in my head,
To work my mind, when body's work expired.
For then my thoughts, from far where I abide,
Intend a zealous pilgrimage to thee,
And keep my drooping eyelids wide,
Looking on darkness which the blind do see.
Save that my soul's imaginary sight
Presents thy shadow to my sightless view,
Which like a jewel hung in ghastly night,
Makes black night beauteous and her old face new.
Lo, thus, by day my limbs, by night my mind,
For thee, and for myself, no quiet find.

In Leslie A. Fiedler's *The Stranger in Shakespeare* (1974), the sonnets are read as the embodiment of the appearance of the stranger within oneself and amongst others. In the end, we don't know who we are, nor do we know who the other is, and each day begins new in mutual discovery or estrangement, love and death being the great puzzles of art and life.

Caraviaggo's lute player[1] (www.TheLuteplayer1596.photographinWikipedia), according to the text accompanying it, is one of the pictures available on the web—an androgynous figure rather like Shakespeare's Rosalind or Ganymede. The same theme has been picked up and elaborated in the film *Shakespeare in Love*. What should we believe but the intransigent nature of several stably fleeting loves and

1 The Lute Player (Caravaggio) - Wikipedia

the immortality of the verse that describes these? While this essay was concerned with why literate and oral forms may well be in consonance with each other in medievalism, my interest remains in the notion of labour. In the next essay, I will deal with this in a paradox of materials and styles, where both history and fiction will appear in juxtaposition so that readers will see that the term 'cunning' in earlier traditions referred to fine and careful work before the term became deleteriously defined as damagingly manipulative.

References

Burgess, Anthony. 1985. *Nothing Like the Sun*. Essex: Arrow Books.

Ed Ostrem Eyolf, Mette Birkedal Bruun, Jens Fleischer, Nils Holger et al. 2005. *The Cultural Heritage of Medieval Rituals, Genre and Ritual Museum*. Copenhagen: Tusculanum Press, University of Copenhagen.

Elias, Norbert. 1978. *The Civilizing Process: The History of Manners*. Oxford: Basil Blackwell; New York: Urizen Books.

Fiedler, Leslie. 1974. *The Stranger in Shakespeare*. St Albans: Paladin.

Greer, Germain. 2007. *Shakespeare's Wife*. London: Penguin.

Kelly, Joan. 1984. *Women, History and Theory*. London: University of Chicago Press.

Kermode, Frank. 2005. *The Age of Shakespeare*. London: Phoenix.

Mauss, Marcel. 2001. *A General Theory of Magic*. London: Routledge.

Shankar, D.A. 1999. *Shakespeare in Indian Languages*. Shimla: Indian Institute of Advanced Study.

Sinfield, Alan. 2006. *Shakespeare, Authority, Sexuality: Unfinished Business in Cultural Materialism*. London: Routledge, Taylor and Frances.

Woolf, Virginia. 1945. *A Room of One's Own*. London: Penguin.

Yates, Frances. 1987. *The Theatre of the World*. London: Routledge and Kegan Paul.

11

Time, Space and Memory: The Politics of Being at Home in Virginia Woolf's *Orlando*

Orlando (1928) by Virginia Woolf is a testament and fantasy. It represents the idea that by using motifs of reincarnation, timelessness, genetic continuity, dream time and memory, a story can be constructed. Each of these is a specific way of understanding the world, and of coming to terms with mortality and the losses incurred by disinheritance. Within this framework, Woolf asks the question, 'What is it to be a woman?'

Published in 1928 by Leonard and Virginia Woolf at the Hogarth Press, the work is part of a genre of colonial travel writing. It uses the idea of the female protagonist as an active principle, answerable only to herself, where she becomes the adventuress. Such a female escapes masculine regulation, though it may appear like a fantasy, which she voluntarily gives up at the end of the narrative. The civil servant is the epitome of the colonial imagination, and of course, marriage is a romantic idea, but then absence, too, is a valid plateau on which many marriages may function and singledom reappropriated.

Louis Green writes that,

> The need to see in history an unbroken continuity will tend to make him read the significance of a bridge period either forwards or backwards, seeing in it either a persistence of the past or a foretaste of the future. This will enable him to draw out connected strings of relationship from what at first seems a haphazard tangle of loose threads, but at the price partly of defeating his own ends in smoothing out into the appearance of natural extension what he initially sought to explore as decisive change. (Green 1972: 1)

He further argues that in the chronicles of early medievalism, these chronicles had a detachment as well as biographically 'an unconscious sense of the possible contradiction between the world of his experience and the overriding order within which he sought to place'. (It is the homology between chronology and the moral universe that is anticipated: morality as a changing sequence of events and motivations) (Green 1972: 6).

Green describes these early chronicles in Italy as authored by traders with a strict sense of accounts but they also have administrative responsibilities. The idea of microcosm and macrocosm is very intense, and they call upon the stars to chart their path.

Inherent is a morality but also an interest in detail. Green cites the historian Burkhardt to say that Giovanni Villani was among the earliest to display an interest in statistics of population, revenue, expenditure and food supply. His figures, though probably slightly exaggerated, have been found by modern students of the subject to be surprisingly reliable, suggesting that he had access to sources then available to the communal authorities but now lost. The chapters that contain these estimates are also a rich mine of information regarding aspects of Florentine life, and how many people it supported. The growth in population and changes in the character of manufacture over the previous thirty years are recorded; production, it appears, had fallen, as had the number of workshops, but with the improvement in the quality of the cloth made, the value of output had increased (ibid.: 42).

In contrast to this is the chronicle of a soul that will not die for Orlando travels across centuries; the only constancy in the narrative lies in the concept of the self, which does not change; it remains essentially the same. The imprint of events and actions are impressed upon the persona and is retrieved at essential moments, not as a memory, but as the subterfuge of the conscious self, working with the unconscious.

Virginia Woolf is working with several familiar tropes of the 1920s and 1930s: biographies of not just men and women, but also the history of the house as if the house itself had a persona.

Curzon, Viceroy of India, and Marquis of Kedleston writes:

> There are few subjects more interesting than the history of a great house. The circumstances of its building, the alterations made in it by

successive owners, the scenes which it has witnessed, the atmosphere which its exhales, combine to invest it in time with the almost human personality, that reacts forcibly upon its occupants, and may even affect the march of larger events. Sometimes a single individual will seem to have left an enduring imprint on the house. At others, it sets a similar stamp upon those who have dwelt within its walls. In the case of a great family mansion, which has passed for generations from one scion to another of ancient stock, the house becomes an epitome of the family history and is the outward and material symbol of its continuity. We may trace about its architecture and furnishing habits and tastes of successive generations. We may even, without being unduly fanciful, observe the influence that these features have exercised upon the characters of its inmates, imparting to them a sobriety or a liveliness of nature which in some cases at least appears to be the direct emanation of the dwelling itself. Great writers have not been slow to elaborate so promising a theme. Who can forget the House of Usher by Edgar Allen Po, the Gabled House of Nathaniel Hawthorne, or the grim and fated mansions which Sheriden Le Fanu loved to depict?

But a great Government House or official residence possesses an interest different from and in some respects superior to these. What it may lack in the continuity of occupation, or genealogical interest, or in mystery, it makes up for by the quick kaleidoscope of its story and diversity of incident of which it can boast. And when the tenants follow each other at the interval of a few years only, coming en masse and going en masse, the script for drama is immensely increased. The house has, so to speak, a new lease of life, and a fresh opportunity for adventure, with each recurrent wave every four or five years, and as one fugitive occupant after another disappears, it alone survives as a witness to their career or fortunes. They vanish in the generations of man almost as swiftly as a meteor in the sky. But their trail still lingers behind them in the places which they inhabited, and the walls are left to tell with silent eloquence the tale. (Curzon 1925: 1)

It is exactly this story that Virginia Woolf wishes to tell about Knole, the home of her closest of friends, Vita Sackville West. Woolf attempts to cross the borders of time in the telling of the story. The tone is so tender and persuasive, it reads like a dream or, as others have described it, the longest love letter in history. Androgyny becomes one of the keys to this biological and historical identity. The markers by themselves are potent because the frame of memory is indeed captive in the person. But who is this person?

Orlando is a mystery. The core theme of androgyny swerves into seamless bisexuality as the Shakespearian tale of Ganymede and Orlando. Individual history becomes transformed, sometimes even chronologically misplaced to produce archetypical history, the history of a persona rather than a person.

Woolf is completely in command as she translates the Catherine wheel of collective memory in the fluid vitality of the elixir, which we call fantasy fiction. Is the author concerned with reality or morality? The fleetness of prose lies in this juxtaposition where neither chronology nor truth valid frameworks for interrogation. The reality principle lies in its buoyancy and persuasiveness. *Orlando is* written in the guise of such a fantastic history. Woolf writes:

> It was clear that Rustum thought that descent of four or five hundred years only the meanest possible. Their own families went back at least two or three thousand years. To the gipsy whose ancestors had built the Pyramids centuries before Christ was born, the genealogy of Howards and Plantagenets was no better and no worse than that of the Smiths and the Joneses: both were negligible. Moreover, where the shepherd boy had a lineage of such antiquity, there was nothing especially memorable or desirable in ancient birth; vagabonds and beggars all shared it. And then, though he was too courteous to speak openly, it was clear that the gipsy thought that there was no more vulgar ambition than to possess bedrooms by the hundred (they were on top of a hill as they spoke; it was night; the mountains rose around them) when the whole earth is ours. Looked at from the gipsy point of view, a Duke, Orlando understood, was nothing, but a profiteer or robber who snatched land and money from people who rated these things of little worth and could think of nothing better to do than to build 365 bedrooms when one was enough, and none was even better than one. She could not deny that her ancestors had accumulated field after field; house after house, honour after honour; yet had none of them been saints or heroes, or great benefactors of the human race. Nor could she counter the argument (Rustum was too much of a gentleman to press it, but she understood) that any man who did now what her ancestors had done three or four hundred years ago would be denounced and

> by her own family most loudly—for a vulgar upstart, an adventurer, a nouveau riche. (2000: 104)

The specific orientation of the novel *Orlando* is to provide a cultural history of England using Queen Elizabeth I and Queen Victoria as its prologue and epilogue. It is to this purpose that Virginia Woolf seems to write a counter-history of morality. Implicit within this are very focused questions such as, What is the family in history? and How do we understand the social relations of production within the manor? Is there a concept of servitude when we understand the life of servants, or are they integrated into familiar and intimate spaces where varieties of relations of power develop? The central theme of the book is, then, What is love? Captured in cameo is the relationship not just of man and woman, whatever this may mean biologically and in terms of time, as the phantasmagoric allows physical changes to occur within the trembling of an eyelid, but it also captures the history of objects and the relationships of individuals to animals, field and forest, agriculture and commerce, and war. Orlando reads maps in a multiplicity of ways through the facility of the imagination and of the self, where the body becomes an interlocutor in a variety of ways. Surely Madame Blavatsky's experiments in consciousness were easily available to Virginia Woolf?

The traveller, like the novelist, is probably the greatest invention of the 19th century, and by the early 20th, the excitement of fiction captured the other common forms such as the notebook, the photograph and the diary as familiar forms of recording cultural and social transformation. *Orlando* works with the idea of mobility where the archetype of being locked in, either in terms of peasant consciousness or in the fixed obligations and roles of the aristocracy is debauched in a frisson of supernatural experience. There is no logic to this wandering. Time is stretched to its absolute limit, and then like a boomerang, releases the author, the reader and the wanderer, who become indistinguishable from one another.

Dennis R. Mills (1980) writes that the patronage principle was the most important aspect of the relation between lord and peasant. Orlando is continually concerned with the relations of his dependents to himself–herself and the objects and properties that he/she has. This establishes a close rapport with the map of his–her journeys, and the link with the town as opposed to his country seat. Virginia Woolf writes:

> Whether then, Orlando was most man or woman it is difficult to say and cannot now be decided. For her coach was not rattling on the cobbles. She had reached her home in the city. The steps were being let down; the iron gates were being opened. She was entering her father's house at Blackfriars, which, though fashion was fast deserting that end of the town, was still a pleasant, roomy mansion, with gardens running down to the river, and a pleasant grove of nut trees to walk in. (2000: 133)

Mills says this is characteristic of the landowners' interest in urban development:

> Although based in the countryside, the landed classes took a keen interest in the growth of towns especially when they reached a stage where large amounts of land were involved. In London this stage was reached by the eighteenth century, where building occurred, for example on land belonging to the Duke of Bedford in Bloomsbury, and to the Russell, Grosvenor and Cavendish and Henley families in the areas which still bear their names. In the nineteenth century as urbanisation intensified and lower housing densities were achieved, exploitation of the freehold of urban land by large and small owners alike became a commonplace. (Mills 1980: 31)

Why does Virginia Woolf use the photograph of Lady Curzon to represent the aggressive and emotionally aggrandising noble from Roumania, who pursues Orlando first as a woman smitten by Orlando when she/he is male, and as an oppressive male, when Orlando returns from her journeys as a woman? So, Orlando is caught between the concept of lover and husband, much as 'a fly on a sugar cube'. The symbiotic aspect of Lord and Lady Curzon are well known to colonial historians (Nicola Thomas, personal communication with the author). The portrait of one Lady Curzon, according to Virginia Woolf, hangs in the Knole gallery.

In the 1925 description of government houses in Calcutta, Lord Curzon has descriptions of portraits of Viceroys which hang there.

> The picture represents Hastings as a middle-aged, almost a prematurely aged man [he was 52 when he left India] bald and shrunken, very unlike

> the well to do cavalier who was painted in England by Stubbs, a few years later. In the background in the niche in the wall is depicted a marble bust of Clive. It should be added that the portraits of Hastings in middle life vary considerably according to whether they present him covered or uncovered. He became very bald at an early age; and accordingly when painted without hat, he looked prematurely old. (Curzon 1925: 114)

Colonial photography thus was an index of how mansions were ordered as a representative testament to power, and the intimacy and humour that the powerful displayed in relation to their peers is orchestrated in a completely new note by Virginia Woolf, when she displays family photographs of people she was close to in the book, reading this in a metalanguage of narratives of which she was the chatelaine. Why were the Curzons obfuscated in the dream time of the fantastic? Because they were close, intimately so, and therefore funny, sharing one persona, substitutable across time? The symbol of ornate clothes, for instance, so important to the Curzons as substitute Maharajahs in India is represented here in terms of a heavy-handed coquetry placed on the dual personality as plain bad taste. However, we have to remember that androgyny and clothes were a central theme in Vita Sackville West's writing, published as a biography of Joan of Arc. Clothes were essential to this task of delineating who the person was. Joan dressed in boys' clothes, and when she was arrested and put in the tower, she was forced to wear a red skirt, and Simone Weil used this motif in her own life when she was described as the 'Virgin in the Red Skirt' by her comrades. Reading the 1920s in this frame of a variety of metanarratives also means that androgyny was being posed as a framework within which Jung was establishing his reputation against Freud with the idea of anima and animus where the male and female principle would be integrated into both men and women in differential equations which were culturally emphasised.

What were people reading at that time? has been the basic motif in reading *Orlando* in this way. If we look at Rosalind Ormiston and Nicholas Michael Well's monumental and ornamental work (2010), we see that the preoccupation of a conglomerate of artists working together produced a local industry of handicraft production, which focused on the interiority of landscapes, flora and fauna. The preoccupation with medievalism and aestheticism then created the cocooning effect of using the past, legends and folktales, offering thereby a cushion against the rampaging effects of industrialisation. Bourgeoisie houses used to best affect the warmth of Morris' furniture and wallpaper and tapestries, bringing the traditions of the English aristocracy to these homes through the finesse of the craftsman, the perfections of a relearnt and reworked aestheticism. Needless to say, the jealous tensions arising between Morris and his friend Dante Gabriel Rossetti and the carnal love the latter had for Morris' wife Jane Burden became the reason for Morris to craft a path of his own, bringing about a tremendous shift to socialist ideas as the way to his emotional recuperation. Betrayal and sorrow were elevated to a space of craftsmanship that influenced Morris' contribution to poetry, calligraphy and coordination of aesthetic production. Just as Virginia Woolf and her husband Leonard Woolf were later wordsmiths in practical and intellectual terms, as writers and publishers, in the same way Morris engaged with the ensemble of art production, heralding the arts and crafts movement in its many aspects. Jane Burden had learned embroidery from her husband. Ormiston and Welles inform us about Jane's involvement:

> In notes written by her after his death, she explained that, 'He, (Morris) started experimenting before he knew me—he got frames made, had worsteds dyed to his taste by some old French people, and began a piece of work with his own hands.' Jane was referring to one of Morris's earliest embroideries, If I Can, 1855. Jane put her own skill down to Morris's perseverance and interest in the historical process of embroidery: He taught me the first principles of laying stitches closely together to cover the ground smoothly and radiating them properly. Afterwards we studied old pieces, and by unpicking them etc.; we learnt much. (Ormiston and Wells 2010: 111)

By integrating consumer and craftsperson, William Morris brought about the sense of an immediately tactile work in stark contrast to the tedium of factory production. The worldview was essentially that of a return to nature, not idealised or at a distance, but immediately perceivable through a process of representation. A collective of artists would share a common platform and emphasise the importance of tradition as an ongoing process.

Industrialisation and war were common motifs of the 19th and 20th centuries, and so were, simultaneously, love and reason. By fashioning their lives in assertion of emotion as the key to existence itself, the arts and crafts movement as much as the Bloomsbury group was relocating the common aspects of Victorian hypocrisy in a new dimension. The tragedies of these lives have been systematically chronicled as those who broke the conventions had to pay a price, the bleak currency of which was often depression, suicide or madness. By bringing together manual and mental labour, Morris attempted through experiential socialism to traverse what Marx had always communicated as essential to the cause, the abnegation of hierarchy. However, Jane Burden, the ostler's daughter whom Rosetti and he both craved, epitomised the legendary beauty of the legends and posed as Guinevere (for Rosetti) and as Iseult (for Morris). As an artist's model, she was exposed to the glittering world of 19th-century art and married Morris, bore him two daughters, but her love for Rosetti constantly pulled her back into a space of infidelity. Ormiston and Wells write:

> Jane Burden described Morris as 'short, burly, corpulent, very careless and unfinished in his dress … a delicate sensitive genius.' He was lightly unkempt and gauche but, after the charming Rossetti departed for the winter, Morris seemed to win her over by his dedicated sense of romance. They married in April 1859, Morris aged 25, and Jane aged 18. For Morris this marriage was a further declaration of rebellion against accepted Victorian values, marrying for love and out of his class; the wedding was a romantic notion made real, as though Arthur and Guinevere had stepped out of their medieval tales while Lancelot was away on some heroic mission. The poet Algernon Charles Swinburne (1837–1909) declared, 'having this wonderful and most perfect stunner of his–to look at or speak to. The idea of his marrying her is insane. To kiss her feet is the utmost men should dream of doing.' After a six-week honeymoon they started a five year period of contentment in the Red House, Bexleyheath. Rossetti meanwhile married his love of ten years, Lizzie Siddall, who in her time had been an early and vivacious Pre-Raphaelite inspiration. (Ormiston and Wells 2010: 34–36)

With Rossetti and Jane constantly returning to one another, Lizzie Siddall committed suicide and Jane entered the tunnel of depression as did Rossetti, while Morris remained within the warp and woof of artistic production, transcending the confusion of emotions with his discipline and hard work. The Bloomsbury group was equally crisscrossed by conflicting loves, and in its effort to promote emotional honesty, as opposed to Victorian hypocrisy, paid its taxes to state and judiciary. Yet, friendship and documentation through letters and diaries leave us a testimony of great worth. Virginia Woolf with her feminine solidarities and other associations that included Leonard and her friendship with Beatrice and Sidney Webb, anti-war polemic, and adult education, left us her fiction as a legacy of documentation, marriage and intellectualism, including the everyday stillness of events, simultaneously opaque and real and fragmental, as the death of a moth.

Living between the two world wars, Virginia Woolf cast her fate on the side of writing. Roger Poole (1978) believes that when she drowned in 1941 it was because she had no faith in life after the war. Fascism was the final enemy, and death by drowning an answer to her fate as a writer. Yet, in writing, she inscribed herself, and words became not just the point of prophecy, but also of recollection. The Bloomsbury School represented the transformation from Victorian mores to the new sexual revolution, which was typical of the early 20th century, where the occupational entry of women into the work world for First World War necessitated that they leave their homes and become workers. This meant that literature, too, was transformed. *Orlando* is that abandoned moment, when time becomes relative, as Einstein would wish to be practically explained; it is also when the mystical becomes immediately possible when nothing needs to be explained, and everything is. Existentialism was preordained in this lovely text because Virginia Woolf could negotiate past all the agonies of *Jacob's Room* (where women were as welcome as dogs in the Church or Cambridge) or the harrowing fate of women who have an intellectual life, besieged by illness and death as in *Voyage Out*, or living secretly and in camouflage with a passion for mathematics in *Night and Day*. In *Orlando*, the promise that the flame in the crocus will be lit, as dreamed of in *Mrs Dalloway*, comes to fruition. And of course, Leonard Woolf publishes the work immediately.

In writing this novel, Virginia Woolf works with the idea of a collective manuscript, which is immediately comprehensible to the readers of her time. As Jane Harrison, following Emile Durkheim writes:

> A high emotional tension is best caused and maintained by a thing felt socially. The individual in a tribe has but a thin and meagre personality. If he dances alone he will not dance long; but if his whole tribe dances together he will dance the live-long night and his emotion will mount to passion to ecstasy. Save for the chorus, the band, there would be drama and no dromenon. Emotion socialised, felt collectively, is emotion intensified and rendered permanent. Intellectually the group is weak, everyone knows this who has ever sat on a committee and arrived at a confused compromise. Emotionally the group is strong; everyone knows this who has felt the thrill of speaking to or acting with a great multitude.
>
> The next step or rather notion implied is all important. A dromenon is as we said not simply a thing done, not even a thing excitedly and socially done. What is it then? It is a thing redone or pre-done, a thing enacted or represented. It is sometimes re-done, commemorative, sometimes pre-done, anticipatory, and both elements seem to go to its religiousness. When a tribe comes back from war or hunting, or even from a journey, from any experience in the fact that from novelty or intensity causes strong emotion, the men will, if successful, recount and dance their experiences to the women and children at home .... The element of action re-done, imitated, the element of mimesis, is, I think, essential. In all religions as in all art, there is this element of make-believe. Not the attempt to deceive, but a desire to re-live, to re-present. (Harrison 1977: 43)

By using the biographical sense of 'I' to its fullest extent, Virginia Woolf makes the reader tread through centuries, using the folio of her great knowledge to make the historical personas of her culture come to life, and be comprehended in terms of the dance of humanity, where each can be understood by the flight of the imagination. Jane Harrison writes:

> Why do we 'represent' things at all, why do we not just do them and have done with it? This is a curious point. The occasion, though scarcely the cause of these representations is fairly clear. Psychologists

> tell us that representations, ideas, imaginations, all the intellectual, conceptual factors in our life are mainly due to deferred reactions. If an impulse finds instantly its appropriate satisfaction, there is no representation. It is out of the delay, just the space between the impulse and the reaction that all our mental life, our images, ideas, our consciousness, our will, most of all our religion arise. If we were utterly, instantly satisfied, if it were a mess of well-contrived instincts we should have no representations, no memory, no mimesis, no dromena, no drama. Art and religion alike spring from unsatisfied desire. (Harrison 1977: 44)

In contrast to Knole was the house built by Virginia's friend Roger Fry, which was in stark contrast to the house of 'gentlemen' which dotted the countryside, replete with the village church in its circumference of gabled windows. Fry contrasted the smugness of the English baronial villages with their morality and vapour-filled light. Woolf writes in her biography of Roger Fry:

> Of course, the English were incurably literary. They liked the associations of things, not things in themselves. They were wrapt in a cocoon of unreality. But again of course the young were all right - he had great hopes of the young. And the uneducated, whose taste had not been perverted by public schools and universities, had, he was convinced, an astonishing natural instinct—witness his housemaid, who had seen the point of Cezanne instantly. He was full of hope for the future, even for himself, late though it was, and much as he had groped and wandered and lost his way.
>
> And so, deriding the village churchyard, its owls, its epitaphs and its ivy, and all those associations which appealed to the impure taste of the incurably literary, he led his way back to the house that the neighbours thought an eyesore, with its large rooms, its great windows, and the bands of red brick across the front. There were many things to be seen there: old Italian pictures, children's drawings, carvings, pots and books—French books, in particular, tattered and coverless, which led to an attack upon English fiction. Why, he demanded, was there no English novelist, who took his art seriously? Why were they all engrossed in childish problems of photographic representation? And then, before he went to busy himself in the kitchen, out came the

> picture that he had been painting that morning. He held it out with a strange mixture of anxiety and humility for inspection. Could he possibly mind what was thought of it? It was plain that he did mind. He gazed at his own work, intently, in silence, and then said how at last he was getting at something - something that he had never been able to get at before. (Woolf 1976: 163–165)

In this new house, Virginia Woolf describes Roger Fry's commitment to a new art:

> He had designed the house himself, and he was proud of its proportions and its labour saving devices. His work-room upstairs was crowded with tools of various kinds, it was littered, yet orderly. Sheaves of photographs lay flat on shelves. There were paintings and carvings, Italian cabinets and Chippendale chairs, blue Persian plates, delicately glazed, and rough yellow peasant pottery bought for farthings at fairs. Every sort of style and object seemed to be mixed, but harmoniously. It was a stored, but not a congested, house, a place to live in, not a museum. (ibid.: 163)

To *Orlando,* she brought this very quality, believing that the new fiction must be tactile, must be contemplative and in every essence, using the re-incarnational guise, lived in.

The reception to the book was near ecstatic since Virginia Woolf sold 6,000 copies almost as soon as it was out, with enthusiastic first readings by Leonard Woolf and Rachel West. It had started as a 'lark', a relaxation exercise after writing *To the Lighthouse,* but the book's hedonism and finesse took the reading public by storm (Gilbert, in Woolf 2000: xxxiv).

What was truly interesting about Roger Fry was that the house was for him a metaphor. It was a space and more importantly, a site, from where his lifelong preoccupation with exhibiting art and a new school of art—the Bloomsbury School—would begin with Virginia's elder sister Vanessa as an absorbed neophyte. The commercial success of Impressionism in Paris could be used as a vantage point for changing the landscape of art itself in London. Schizophrenia and art became the bywords of the new school, which integrated the arts and humanities with a political perspective. They coped individually with breakdowns and deaths as best as they could, while forging the new spaces in which interior design would then stabilise. The watchwords could be Nijinsky and Diaghilev, or it could be Roger Fry's wife who had a tragic end, or Virginia herself, or the many others (the list is very long) who went into the mosaic of the Bloomsbury School. Its signalling systems were freedom for art, the morality that bohemianism always brought in its wake and, the joy and ebullience of rapid creativity without hindrance. Anscombe (1981), describes it thus:

> Vanessa's confidence grew not only from Roger's emotional support but also from his practical help. Apart from her Friday Club shows, she had rarely exhibited her work and until 1912 had shown only one canvas a year with either the Allied Artists' Association or the New English Art Club. Roger now included six of her paintings at the Gallerie Barbazanges exhibition in Paris and four in the Second Post-Impressionist Exhibition at the Grafton Galleries. In August 1912 she sold a painting for the first time, when the Contemporary Art Society bought The Spanish Model for five guineas; she was obviously delighted. (54–55)

The temporality of this art marked its luminescence, and a lot was also lost in the Second World War, which Virginia Woolf feared so much. It remained a testimony however to the right to be human that Woolf and her friends wanted so much because what they were collectively testing was not just Victorianism with its hypocrisy, but also fascism. As Michel De Certeau so masterfully wrote, there can be changes in the system, which need not be sought at the local level or the level of motivations, but we should focus 'on the level of an order of mental organisation' (De Certeau 1988: 140). Sometimes, there can be changes in the system without the system crumbling. They occur at the level of practice, without any manifest change in the system. It is this which typifies Virginia Woolf's ability to record political environments and to protest simultaneously, acts of literature as much as of feminist politics.

References

Anscombe, Isabelle. 1981. *Omega and After, Bloomsbury and the Decorative Arts* (photographs by Howard Grey). London: Thames and Hudson.

Bell, Quentin. 1982. *Virginia Woolf.* Suffolk: Triad Granada.

Curzon, George Nathaniel. 1925. *British Government in India: The Story of Viceroys and Government House*. London: Cassel.

Green, Louis. 1972. *Chronicles into History: An Interpretation of History in Florentine Fourteenth-Century Chronicles.* Cambridge: Cambridge University Press.

Harrison, Jane. 1977. *Themis.* Dublin: Merlin.

Mills, Dennis. 1980. *Lord and Peasant in 19th Century Britain.* London and Ottowa: Croom Helm.

Ormiston, P. and N.M. Wells. 2010. *William Morris: Artist, Craftman, Pioneer.* London: Flame Tree.

Poole, Roger. 1978. *The Unknown Virginia Woolf.* Cambridge: Cambridge University Press.

Waterton, Emma and Steve Watson. 2010. *Culture, Heritage and Representation, Perspectives in Visuality and the Past.* Surrey: Ashgate.

Woolf, Leonard. 2003. *The Village in the Jungle.* Delhi: Oxford University Press.

Woolf, Virginia. 1976. *Roger Fry: A Biography.* New York: Harcourt Brace Jovanovich.

———. 2000. *Orlando.* London: Penguin Classics.

12

Gandhi and the Indigo Workers

Indian indigo being qualitatively superior to the African variety was much desired by the West. Prakash Kumar writes that the French naturalists had travelled to the West Indies in the 17th and 18th centuries and translated local knowledge and brought back plant specimens in formally classified fashion, contributing to a new science benefitting European trade and colonialism (Kumar 2012: 32). The methods used by Indian, Caribbean and African farmers in processing indigo, too, were different. African indigo was dried in the sun after being processed, while the Indian farmers dried it in the shade, producing a much more vivid colour (ibid.: 38).

The importance of the method and technique of cultivating and processing indigo was imported to their colonies in America by the British, but by the end of the 19th century, they were insistent on the virtues of indigo exported to Britain from India. As a result, they forced indigo plantations on the farmers of Uttar Pradesh, Bihar and Bengal, and the result was prolonged agitations in Champaran in 1917 (Pouchepadass 1999) and the Gorakhpur region, known as the Chauri Chaura agitations (Amin 1995). Shahid Amin based his study of this people's movement on the data drawn from archives. Using Gorakhpur as his focal urban centre for oral-history data, Amin argues that the 'rioters' were intent on making their opposition felt as they had been forced to cultivate indigo. They burned a police station and a deputy commissioner of police died with his men. This was the key moment of the antagonism that surfaced and proliferated, where the crowd reacted and became violent. So, a peaceful agitation became a mob retaliation, and Gandhiji's name became associated with Chauri Chaura.

Chauri Chaura was the name of a railway station with no elements of township status, having only 2 textile shops in its vicinity. Nevertheless, it had the function of linking two small towns, where the mobilisation of peasantry occurred.

Dave St Aubyn Gosse (2012) writes that peasant insurrections such as these were frequent in Jamaica because the plantation owners were not willing to give up their slaves. Though there was a ban on the slave trade ending slavery in 1807, the Jamaican colonists attempted to use the previous century's slave owners' manuals to communicate that they were being fair to their workers. However, there were cases of summary executions of slaves by their owners and instances where they communicated that it was more expensive to work an adult slave, as the possibility of his death at work was fairly high since the master overworked him. More expenditure on prenatal and postnatal care would have to be incurred if slavery was to give way to hard labour (Gosse 2012: 18). Yet, Christian Cwik argues in his essay *The End of the British Atlantic Slave Trade or the Beginning of the Big Slave Robbery 1808–1850* (2019) that though slavery was abolished, the illegal slave trade continued in the Caribbean. The sugar industry was according to him, dependent on slaves from Africa he writes:

> During the Napoleonic war, the British Parliament, after more than a decade of debate, finally passed the 'Act for the Abolition of the Slave Trade' (but not slavery itself) on March 25th 1807, throughout its dominions and outlawed any further involvement in it by British citizens. Great Britain was preceded in this action by the United States Congress, which for different reasons passed a similar law on March 2nd of the same year, which would take effect on January 1, 1808. (Cwic 2019: 4)

Thus, indentured labour in the sugar plantations became of great consequence to the British government. Ships carrying goods (slaves) as well as equipment were confiscated by the navy. Under British rule, 600 slave vessels were captured and 1,60,000 slaves. The so-called liberated slaves lived in Sierra Leone, Jamaica, the Bahamas and Trinidad. The result was slave raiding and trade.

In India, tenant cultivators independently or under the supervision of British planters grew, harvested and produced indigo. Cultivating indigo in India was easy because the rains left behind swamps, which could not be utilised by the cultivation of rice, as the monsoon ceased much after the time for plantation of rice. These alluvial lands were the surplus that appeared in October after the rice had been planted in the eastern hill lands and Ganges-inundated plains in May (Prakash 2012: 87). A footnote provided by Prakash is extremely important: Fischer argues that the expression of discontent against indigo was spearheaded not so much by the peasants as by the traders, whose business interests were harmed by the displacement of cash crops by indigo (ibid.: 89, fn 18).

Over the next decades, the indigo contractors were beginning to wrest land away from the zamindar and his tenants. Leases were obtained from the landholder or tenant farmer to have tighter control over indigo cultivation by the British planters. Labour procurement was different from place to place as were the weather conditions (ibid.: 90, 91).

Jacques Pouchepadass, in his very dense and brilliant work (1999), suggests that till the aniline dyes arrived in the late 19th century, Indian indigo was a very carefully orchestrated product. The dealers were careful to examine each lot produced for its quality, and in fact, did not permit mixing of batches since the effect of seasons, fermentation or drying would create differences. It was a cash crop for export. While indigo had been sourced from India in the first century, with competition from the Americas and the West Indies, the export of indigo had ceased from 1729. Since sugar and coffee took precedence in the latter countries, the British became interested in reviving oriental indigo from the 1760s onwards (Pouchepadass 1999: 2). Indigo was mostly produced by indigenous entrepreneurs, inexpensively with the simplest equipment. By the 1830s, India provided indigo to Europe, America, Persia and Arabia (ibid.: 3). This intense commercial incentive to produce indigo meant that the planters often entered as 'unauthorised interlopers' forcing zamindars to agree to let their ryots cultivate indigo on the payment of an advance. Sometimes these luckless tenants could not produce the amount of indigo agreed upon and there would be violence. Pouchepadass tell us that:

> [s]uch conflicts could have been resolved peaceably if there had existed judicial and police administration capable of coping with them. Unfortunately, this was not the case. Each planter concluded contracts every year with thousands, sometimes tens of thousands of raiyats. He

> often had dozens of court cases on his hands. But civil courts were few, their jurisdictions immense, and court delays were normally a matter of years. These court cases obviously did not represent an appropriate recourse when disputes arose, as was frequently the case, about the year's indigo crop. (Pouchepadass 2012: 5)

Since they exercised the landlord or contractor's right to physical coercion on the tenants producing indigo, the Collector of Faridpur district in Bengal wrote, 'Not a chest of indigo reaches England without being stained by human blood' (ibid.: 8). Planters, who would not be so violent in their own country, imitated the zamindars who were known perpetrators of atrocities against ryots. Yet, for the most part, indigo cultivation continued without too much gap between contract and production statistics. By the mid-19th century, the law of the jungle had been replaced by Planters' Associations. The people who came in as planters were 'merchants, farmers, industrialists, lawyers, clergymen, doctors, civil servants and military officers' who were educated and part of a thriving middle class in their home country (ibid.: 9). The earlier contractors for indigo in the earlier phase were interlopers, younger sons and adventurers.

The production of indigo, as Pouchepadass describes it, was a very difficult process. First, the land had to be hoed, then cleared and ploughed. The seeds were planted, and when the plants came up, the plots had to be de weeded three times. Finally, when indigo plants flowered, they had to be cut and sheaves prepared and had to be taken by cart to the indigo factory. There it was beaten manually by workers, who were usually tribal or lower caste as the smell of the water was odorous and other labourers did not 'consent' to doing this work. It was only in 1841 that a planter invented a beating wheel, and in 1870, steam was used to move the wheel. Indigo needed a lot of water for the fermentation process, so only during or after the monsoons (June to September) or by collecting rainwater in dug out holes, could the process be completed (ibid.: 43).

The process of compressing the indigo into portable sheets involved pressing the pulp into wooden boxes which were imported from Sweden or Britain. These were very expensive but served to press down gradually the blocks of indigo, with the excess fluid percolating out. The blocks were cut down into bars and then into cakes and stamped with the plantation's brandmark (Pouchepadass 2012: 45). After that, they were left to dry. When desiccated, they were brushed down, removing the mould that had formed on them, and sent to Calcutta, via Patna, for export. Indigo plantations and factories were major employers of local people. Pouchepadass describes it thus:

> At the end of the 19th century, the 69 indigo factories (head factories and outworks) of Champaran district employed on an average 33,000 persons daily throughout the year and those of Muzaffarpur, 35,000 agricultural and factory workers combined. These annual averages, it is true conceal significant monthly variations. More than half the workdays were during the cool season (September to February), with the maximum in November, the slackest month was March. (ibid.: 52)

The manufacturing process was shorter, beginning from June to September.

If the riots of Chauri Chaura occurred, it was because of the forced cultivation of indigo. Yet, Gandhi's name was chanted while the mob proceeded to acts of violence. Gandhi said in the Trial Court where he was sentenced to six years of imprisonment:

> Thinking over them deeply and sleeping over them night after night, it is impossible for me to disassociate myself from the diabolical crimes of Chauri Chaura or the mad outrages of Bombay. He is quite right when he says, that as a man of responsibility, a man having received a fair share of experience of this world, I should have known of the consequences of every one of my acts. I knew that I was playing with fire. I ran the risk and if I was set free I would still do the same. I have felt in this morning that I would have failed in my duty, if I did not say what I have said here just now.
>
> I wanted to avoid violence. I want to avoid violence. Non-Violence is the first article of my faith. It is also the last article of my creed. But I had to make my choice. I had either to submit to a system which I considered had done an irreparable harm to my country or incur the risk of the mad fury of my people bursting forth, when they understood the truth from my lips. I know that my people have sometimes gone mad. I am deeply sorry for it and I am therefore here to submit not to a

> light penalty. I do not ask for mercy. I do not plead any exonerating act. I am here, therefore, to invite and cheerfully submit to the highest penalty that can be inflicted upon me, for what in law is a deliberate crime and what appear to me to be the highest duty of a citizen. (Shelat 1965: 166)

Gandhi explained how he had become a 'disaffectionist' towards the government established by law in India:

> My public life began in 1893 in South Africa in troubled weather. My first contact with British authority in that country was not of a happy character. I discovered that as a man and Indian I had no rights. More correctly I discovered that I had no rights as man because I was an Indian. (ibid.: 167)

Gandhi in his speech mentions his awards and services to the British Empire including the Kaiser-e-Hind, the gold medal received for his work in South Africa, by Lord Hardinge. He confirms his collaboration with the British during the Boer War (1898) and the Zulu Rebellion (1906). He went on to say that the Rowlatt Act, Khilafat Movement and Jalianwalan Bagh came as very rude shocks (ibid.).

> Little do town dwellers know how the semi-starved masses of India are slowly sinking to lifelessness. Little do they know that their miserable comfort represents the brokerage they get for the work they do for the foreign exploiter, that the profits and brokerage are sucked from the masses. Little do they realize that the Government established by law in British India is carried on for this exploitation of the masses. No sophistry, no jugglery in figures can explain away the evidence that the skeletons in many villages present to the naked eye. I have no doubt whatsoever that both England and the town dwellers will have to answer, if there is a God above, for this crime against humanity which is perhaps unequalled in history. The law itself in this country has been used to serve the foreign exploiter.

In Chapter XII of his autobiography *The Stain of Indigo*, Gandhi describes Champaran as the land of King Janaka: 'Just as it abounds in mango groves, so used it to be full of Indigo plantations until the year 1919. The Champaran tenant was bound by law to plant three out of every twenty parts of his land with indigo for his landlord' (Gandhi 1940: 304).

He writes that he had hardly any knowledge of the geographical position of Champaran or any idea of indigo plantations or that it was grown under conditions of great difficulty by the farmers of Champaran (Gandhi 1940: 304). 'Rajkumar Shukla was one of the agriculturists who had been under this harrow and he was filled with a passion to wash away the stain of indigo for the thousands who were suffering as he had suffered' (ibid.).

Rajkumar Shukla followed Gandhi everywhere because he wanted Gandhi to be in Champaran.

> I returned to the Ashram. The ubiquitous Rajkumar was there too. 'Pray fix the day now,' he said. 'Well,' said I, 'I have to be in Calcutta on such and such a date, come and meet me then, and take me from there.
>
> I did not know where I was to go, and what to do, and what things to see.'
>
> Before I reached Bhupen Babu's place in Calcutta, Rajkumar Shukla had gone and established himself there. Thus, the ignorant, unsophisticated but resolute agriculturist captured me.
>
> So early in 1917, we left Calcutta for Champaran looking just like fellow rustics. I did not even know the train. He took me to it, and we travelled together reaching Patna in the morning. (ibid.: 305)

However, Gandhi noticed that there was a huge gulf between Shukla and his lawyers, a gulf so huge that it could only be described thus: 'Between such agriculturist clients and their vakils there is a gulf as wide as the Ganges in flood' (ibid.: 306).

He also noticed caste differences and practices and was amused by them. He was soon in the public eye for campaigning on behalf of the ryots and received a huge amount of publicity and solidarity. Barely avoiding arrest, he travelled widely receiving complaints from ryots. On 15 May 1917, Gandhi sent his report on indigo plantations to the government. Pouchepadass comments:

> It was a criticism in due form of the indigo system, written on the basis of a voluminous preliminary statement compiled by his assistants after the raiyats' complaints. The government considered this report

> revealed nothing unknown to it concerning the situation on the plantations. (1999: 175)

Soon after this peasant insurrection followed with endemic violence across the indigo plantations. Indigo production fell because of the troubles, and the call to boycott, and the events following the First World War. Gandhi then believed that the only solution to the problems of the people of Bihar was education (Pouchpedass 1999: 185).

Between slavery and indentured labour, there was some difference, which was to do with the possibility of freedom after paying a tax to the British government for the right to work as free labour. Between the condition of the ryots and slavery, Gandhi saw no difference.

> Indentured labourers were those who had emigrated from India to labour under an indenture for five years or less. Under the Smuts Gandhi Settlement of 1914, the three-pound tax in respect of indentured emigrants to Natal had been abolished but the general emigration for India still need treatment. (Gandhi 1940: 301)

While Madan Mohan Malviya had put forward a resolution to abolish the indenture system in March 1916, Lord Hardinge responded with a vague assurance that in due course it would be attended to. Gandhi wrote in his autobiography:

> India had tolerated the system through sheer negligence, and I believed that the time had come when people could successfully agitate for this redress. I met some of the leaders, wrote to the press, and saw that public opinion was solidly in favour of immediate abolition. (ibid.: 302)

Gandhi began his tour for agitation in 1917 when Malviya's second petition for the abolition of indentured labour was refused by Lord Chelmsford. It was his long years in South Africa, as he said in the trial of the Chauri Chaura case, which had trained him for the long-drawn-out campaign against British colonialism.

J.N. Uppal writes that the British occupation of South Africa was accompanied by the establishment of plantations of cotton and coffee (1994). These were not successful so they turned to sugar cultivation. The local populations preferred to cultivate and work in their homesteads rather than engage in wage labour for the British colonialists. As a result, the colonists needed another source of wage labour (Uppal 1995: 44). Uppal states that:

> At first the indentured labour was sent to Natal largely from the Bengal presidency. South India was soon the leading source of supply. Whatever region they belonged to, the majority of emigrants were lower caste Hindus. Among the caste Hindus the largest group was that of Vaishyas. The Muslims and Christians were about twelve and five per cent respectively. All these people with their improvidence as one common factor were out to make South Africa their home. But from the very start, the majority of employers in the plantation did not deal with them in a manner that could have led to a smooth master- servant relation. The misery and despair because of which these migrants left their homeland could not have failed to make them exceedingly docile. The only problem that that should have bothered the planters was of occasional absence from duty by the workers for one reason or the other. The penalty prescribed for such default was rather harsh: forfeiture of two days wage for one day's work missed. (ibid.: 46)

Gandhi's work in South Africa was precipitated by the opposition of the colonists to the coming of the Indians, indentured labourers or a middle-class trading community to Natal. In November 1896, the Colonial Patriotic Union was launched in Durban with the intention of creating an obstacle to further immigration from India other than indentured labourers. Some wanted even indentured labourers to be denied entry. One of their leaders stated that while the whites made money out of the labourers, the traders made money out of the whites (ibid.: 117).

Another group, called The European Protection Association also formed itself as a rival camp to the Colonial Patriotic Union, and while they had similar motives, there were mutual hostilities, but together they represented the opposition to new immigrants to South Africa. The violence against immigrant Indians grew so intense that two ships carrying Indians were served hostile notices on 11 January 1897 (ibid.: 120). Uppal writes that:

> [t]he moment the word spread that the two ships were coming into the harbour, the mounted trumpeters, as had been planned, rode through the streets giving a call for the people to reach the berthing point. In no time, Alexandria Square had a crowd of over 3,000 including about 300 blacks armed with sticks. The ringleaders were determined to prevent the landing of the Indian passengers, by force if necessary. (Uppal 1995: 121)

When Gandhi left the ship, (his family having gone on ahead) at 4.30 PM, some white youth recognised him. He was surrounded by a mob and brutally thrashed and kicked. His life was saved by Mrs Alexander, the police superintendent's wife, who used her umbrella to clear the crowd (ibid.: 123). He could escape the crowd only by disguising himself: 'He donned the police constable's blue serge uniform, covered his head with a South Indian style red scarf tied around a helmet type metal plate and had face done up as necessary'. The crowd examined the house where he was thought to have hidden, could not find him there and dispersed (ibid.: 128).

From these experiences in South Africa began the long-term use of accepting imprisonment as a peaceful way of communicating dissent, which was a tool that Indians in South Africa, following Gandhi, used successfully to bring their problems to the attention of the world. In 1908, Albert West wrote to him, when he was in prison, from Phoenix saying that Kasturba was very ill. Gandhi wrote:

> Beloved Kastur, I have received Mr West's telegram about your illness. It cuts my heart. I am very much grieved but I am not in a position to reach there to nurse you. I have offered my all to the satyagraha struggle. My coming there is out of the question. I can come only if I pay the fine, which I must not. If you keep courage and take the necessary nutrition, you will recover. If however, my ill luck so has it, that you pass away, I should only say that there would be nothing wrong in your doing so in your separation from me while I am still alive. I love you so dearly if you are dead, you will be alive to me. Your soul is deathless. I repeat what I have frequently told you and assure you that if you do succumb to your illness, I will not marry again. Time and again I have told you that you may quietly breathe your last with faith in God. If you die, even that death of yours will be a sacrifice

> to the cause of satyagraha. My struggle is not merely political. It is religious and therefore quite pure. It does not matter whether one dies in it or lives. I hope and expect that you will also think likewise and not be unhappy.
>
> Mohandas. (cited in Uppal 1995: 273)

Kasturba steadfastly maintained solidarity with Gandhi. When he was arrested in 1922, she wrote in *Young India*:

> My dear Countrymen and Countrywomen, My dear husband has been sentenced today to six years of simple imprisonment. While I cannot deny that this heavy sentence has to some extent told upon me, I have consoled myself with the thought that it is not beyond our powers to reduce that sentence and release him by our exertions, long before his time of imprisonment is over. I have no doubt that if India wakes up and seriously undertakes to carry out the constructive programme of the Congress, we shall succeed not only in releasing him but also in solving to our satisfaction all the three issues for which we have been fighting and suffering for the last eighteen months or more.

She exhorted the people to give up foreign cloth, spin and weave, and all merchants to desist from trading in foreign cloth.

It is interesting then, that the judgement of Chauri Chaura became the catalyst for the prolonged struggle that led the Indian people to freedom from colonial oppression. It set the very metaphor for the prolonged practice of ahimsa. It was the mode by which time began to enter into a new vocabulary, where prison sentences became the currency for buying freedom. One can imagine what it would have meant in real time, or how freedom fighters willingly, following Gandhi, gave up so many privileges that they had taken for granted. Time in the prison without family, often in total seclusion, separated from loved ones and hobbies, was the prism in which ahimsa wove its steady hand.

References

Amin, Shahid. 1995. *Event, Metaphor, Memory: Chauri Chaura 1922–1992*. Delhi: Oxford University Press.

Cwik, Christian. 2019. *The End of the British Atlantic Slave Trade or the Beginning of the Big Slave Robbery 1808-1850.* Available at www. Academiaedu (accessed on 6 October 2019).

Dasgupta, Pannalal. 2011. *Revolutionary Gandhi,* translated by K.V. Subrahmonyan. Calcutta: Earthcare Books.

Gandhi, Mahatma. *Young India.* 1922. No. 2. Thursday, 23rd March, edited by Shoaib Qureshi. Ahmedabad: Navjeevan Trust.

Gandhi, M.K. 1940. *An Autobiography or the Story of My Experiment with Truth.* Ahmedabad: Navjeevan Press.

Gosse, Dave St Aubyn. 2012. *Abolition and Plantation Management in Jamaica 1807–1838.* Jamaica: University of the West Indies Press.

Kumar, Prakash. 2012. *Indigo Plantations and Science in Colonial India.* Delhi: Cambridge University Press.

Pouchepadass, Jacques. 1999. *Champaran and Gandhi: Planters, Peasants and Gandhian Politics.* Delhi: Oxford University Press.

Shelat, J.M., ed. 1965. *The Trial of Gandhi.* High Court of Gujarat, Government of India.

Uppal, J.N. 1995. *Gandhi: Ordained in South Africa.* Delhi: Director of Publications Division.

Index

Q

R

S

T

U

V

W

Y

Z

About the Author

Susan Visvanathan is the author of *Christians of Kerala* (1993), *Friendship, Interiority and Mysticism* (2007) and *The Children of Nature* (2010). She has published essays in various journals, the earliest of which was 'Reconstructions of the Past among the Syrian Christians of Kerala' in *Contributions to Indian Sociology* (1986). Prof. Visvanathan was Chairperson of Centre for the Study of Social Systems, Jawaharlal Nehru University (2009–2011) and Teacher-in-Charge of Department of Sociology, Hindu College (1992–1997). She has taught Sociology for thirty-eight years, of which twenty-five years were spent at Jawaharlal Nehru University, where she had the privilege of working with doctoral students. She retired from Jawaharlal Nehru University, on 9 March 2022. Susan Visvanathan has edited *Structure and Transformation* (2001), *Chronology and Event* (edited with Vineeta Menon) (2019), *Art, Politics, Symbols and Religion* (2019), *Structure, Innovation and Adaptation* (2019). She collaborated with the art historian, Geeti Sen, and edited two volumes of the India International Quarterly titled *Kerala* (1995) and *Women and the Family* (1997). Susan Visvanathan is a well-known writer of literary fiction who has been included in Bruce King's *Rewriting India: Eight Writers* (2014). Her first novella, a collection of integrated short stories, titled *Something Barely Remembere*d (2000) was published by Flamingo and India Ink, and was one of the 6 nominees for the Commonwealth Award, UK. It is now a text book for English Literature students in the 200 colleges of the Mahatma Gandhi University, Kottayam, Kerala. Prof. Visvanathan was Visiting Professor to the Maison des Sciences de l'homme, Paris (2004) and to Universite Paris 13 (2011). She was Charles Wallace Fellow at Ethnomusicology and Anthropology Department in Queen's University in Belfast, Northern Ireland in 1997. Prof. Visvanathan was Professional Excellence Award Fellow at Budapest, Central European University in 2018.